The Person You Mean to Be

The
Person
You Mean
to Be

How Good People
Fight Bias

DOLLY CHUGH

FOREWORD BY LASZLO BOCK

HARPER
BUSINESS

An Imprint of HarperCollins*Publishers*

HarperCollins books may be purchased for educational, business, or sales promotional use. For information, please email the Special Markets Department at SPsales@harpercollins.com.

FIRST EDITION

Designed by Bonni Leon-Berman

Library of Congress Cataloging-in-Publication Data has been applied for. ISBN 978-0-06-269214-6

18 19 20 21 22   LSC   10 9 8 7 6 5 4 3 2 1

For my family

Contents

Foreword

In 2014 I was eight years into what would become almost eleven years as senior vice president of People Operations and a member of Google's management team. I was in the midst of hosting our first re:Work conference, a convening of 175 leading thinkers and practitioners in behavioral science, economics, and human resources. There had been a series of superb talks, but then something exceptional happened.

Dolly Chugh took the stage. She delivered a talk entitled "Are We as Ethical as We Think We Are?" She bounded up, introduced herself, and then, paraphrasing Lin-Manuel Miranda's musical, announced: "I am thrilled to be in the room where it happens."

She had me at *Hamilton*.

And then she blew my mind.

Dolly asked: "How can it be true that some of the time all of us act in ways that aren't perfectly ethical, but amazingly every one of us believes him- or herself to be a good person?"

Let that sink in.

All of us sitting there agreed that we were good people. I certainly was!

But. But. But.

I could think of moments of which I was less than proud. Maybe something as trivial as jumping ahead of the car that pulled up to the stop sign just before I did? Or using my body language to edge out the person who had lined up next to me to board a flight? Or that moment when I'd read a homeless person's cardboard sign, but looked away before my eyes could rise to meet his face? Or when I saw something offensive online, wrote a bold comment in response, and then my finger hovered over the button—for so very long—as I debated whether or not to post it?

If we are honest with ourselves—and I mean deep inside with that voice that no one else in this world except you will ever hear—would a truly, completely good person behave the way we do?

Spoiler alert: no.

The person I want to be, the kinds of people we all aspire to be, are better than we actually are.

And then Dolly made it okay:

> The idea that we're capable as human beings of perfect ethicality, of being as perfectly ethical all the time as we imagine ourselves to be, is a unicorn-like idea. . . . The truth is all of us sometimes inflate the invoice, or stereotype the student, or favor the friend.

That anguish I felt in the first part of her talk is universal. We all have an idea of who we believe we are, which stands in modest contrast to the person we actually are. The faint tickling of that disconnect, like the moment you first feel an ant's tread halfway up your calf, is part of the human condition. It's normal. Natural. Commonplace.

But that doesn't mean it's okay.

Because others see us not through the gauzy glow of our own self-regard, and not just through our words and actions, but also through the words and actions that we don't take. The latter is especially pernicious because of a little flaw we've all got in our brains called the "fundamental attribution error."

Here's how it works. Think about the last time you were rushing through traffic, cutting lanes, zipping around the cars ahead of you. Maybe you couldn't wait to get to a party, or were late for the airport, or had a sick child to get to the doctor.

Now think about the last time some jerk cut you off on the road. (Don't those people just drive you crazy?)

This is the fundamental attribution error. When I do something that's aggressive or offensive toward you, there's a perfectly reasonable explanation. When I see you do something, it's because deep down you are—in my estimation—just that kind of jerk. I can know the factors shaping my actions, but because I don't know the ones shaping yours, I assume it's just because of who you are. And I forget that you might also have a sick child.

If I fail to stand up for you, you are likely to perceive me as simply not caring. Or worse, that I condone or even agree with whatever bias or abuse you've just endured.

The Person You Mean to Be is Dolly's road map from the messy, imperfect, conflicted person that each of us is today toward becoming a little more perfect, a lot less conflicted, and meaningfully more active and impactful on the world around us.

What Is Special About This Book and Its Author

Dolly Chugh is one of those people whose résumé intimidates and overpowers. She was a varsity collegiate tennis captain, holds degrees from Cornell and Harvard, and worked in banking, consulting, and publishing before earning a tenured professorship at New York University. She still finds time to work with the faculty and leaders of the KIPP schools, volunteer in prisons, and—as you'll read—sneak in a little holiday shopping for her family.

But if you're lucky enough to meet her in person, you'll find someone so warm, gracious, generous, and laugh-out-loud funny that you can't help but want to be near her.

Dolly comes through in every page of this fantastic book. One of my favorite lines from *The Person You Mean to Be* comes just a few pages in: "The person I mean to be stands up for [equality and equity and diversity and inclusion]. The person I mean to be fights bias. Sometimes, I do. Sometimes, I don't."

And then she proceeds to explain, drawing on research, anecdotes, and a bracing honesty and openness about her own life, how to take this reality and move from "believer to builder."

She continuously surprises by describing concepts like "cookie seeking," using it to explain why allies can inadvertently burden those feeling the weight of oppression just when that weight is at its heaviest. She reframes the discussion about "growth mindset" to introduce the best way to react—and build bridges—when you are at your most upset and defensive. And she arms the reader with a lucid narrative for explaining how so many of us benefit from "ordinary privilege," including the simple fact of having white skin, or being straight, or being a man.

The benefit on this front, for many readers of *The Person You Mean to Be*, will be a deeper understanding of the science behind why bias exists, why society seems to tolerate so much of it, and why even 1 percent bias in a system leads to wildly disproportionate results for winners and losers.

Why I Know This Book Will Make a Difference in Your Life, and in the World

The benefit for each and every reader, however, will be a path to self-acceptance and action.

Acceptance is vital to address all those moments of self-doubt and questioning, those instances when our fingers hover above the keyboards, or when we wonder if we have the standing to intervene when we see small slights in our daily lives. Accepting that these hesitations are universal means accepting that they are also unimportant. Everyone behaves imperfectly sometimes. Everyone pauses sometimes. Therefore, don't beat yourself up over it. Get on with acting.

Dolly offers a wide range of ways to act in the latter third of the book, but her message is a pragmatic one. We can still be good people, indeed we can be better people, as long as we do more. Not everything. *Just more.*

She shows how builders use whatever power and stature they have to amplify the voices of others, to encourage, to educate, and sometimes to confront. And she offers the reader clear, actionable techniques to do the same, often in the form of small nudges.

Google, for me, was a tremendous learning experience. One of the biggest lessons was about the power of "nudges," a term coined by professors Cass Sunstein and Richard Thaler, and which I described in my own book as something that "influences choice, but doesn't dictate it." At one point we observed that female engineers were being promoted at a lower rate than male engineers.* At the time, engineers could nominate themselves for promotion, in addition to being nominated by their managers. We found that while women were slightly less likely to nominate themselves, when they did they were actually more successful than men in being promoted. We also found that with a small nudge—an email from Alan Eustace, then senior vice president of engineering, to all technical employees describing this finding and encouraging women to nominate themselves—the promotion gap went away.

It was more than just a simple email. It came from an executive. From a white, male executive. The email didn't prescribe, but rather encouraged: "Any Googler who is ready for promotion should feel encouraged to self-nominate. . . ." And it nudged

---

* I hope the reader will forgive the binary—that's how the data were coded at the time.

managers and shaped norms as well: ". . . and managers play an important role in ensuring that they feel empowered to do so."

I believe so deeply in the power of these small interventions that I left Google and in 2017 co-founded a company, called Humu, with a goal of making work better through machine learning, science, and a little bit of love. Central to our technology is the idea that small nudges have a profound ability to increase employee happiness and productivity, and reduce employee bias and attrition.

The Person You Mean to Be is replete with small interventions you can make in your daily life that will have a disproportionately positive impact. For example, Dolly reports that people approach interracial interaction differently, depending on whether they are instructed to "avoid prejudice" or to "enjoy the opportunity to have an intercultural dialogue." A tiny shift in language with a tremendous impact.

Similarly, she shows why it's powerful to downshift from "I just want to explain where I'm coming from" to "Help me understand what I did that upset you." Same conversation, different words, vastly different outcomes.

Why This Book Is Worth Reading Today

The perceptions of the majority always seem to lag the experiences of the minority. As Dolly points out, in 1963, 80 percent of white Americans felt that racial minorities were treated equally—at a time when it was illegal for whites and blacks to marry in sixteen states, from Florida to as far north as Missouri and Delaware, and as far west as Texas.

On September 1, 2016, the San Francisco 49ers quarterback Colin Kaepernick began to kneel on one knee during the playing of the national anthem. "I am not going to stand up to show pride in a flag for a country that oppresses black people and people of color," he explained. He later continued: "This is because I'm seeing things happen to people that don't have a voice, people that don't have a platform to talk and have their voices heard, and effect change. So I'm in the position where I can do that and I'm going to do that for people that can't."

Kaepernick's actions were controversial. In 2017 he was both awarded *Sports Illustrated*'s Muhammad Ali Legacy Award and vilified online using the harshest, crudest language possible. A CBS News/YouGov poll in September of that year found that almost 75 percent of black Americans approved of football players protesting this way, but only about 30 percent of white Americans did. How will Kaepernick's protest—and the fact that he was joined by thousands of professional, college, and even high school athletes—look in five or ten years?

Recent years have been exhausting for those who believe in— as Dolly says about herself—equality and equity and diversity and inclusion. Yet many Americans (and citizens of many other countries) tell pollsters that people are treated equally today. That is simply not true.

Reading *The Person You Mean to Be* is like having a conversation with Dolly herself, and I suspect after reading it you'll feel as much affinity and affection toward her as I do. She'll help you to see how to do just a bit more, and how to *be* a bit more of the person you mean to be.

Laszlo Bock, October 2017
CEO and Co-Founder of Humu
Former SVP of People Operations, Google, Inc., and author of *Work Rules! Insights from Inside Google That Will Transform How You Live and Lead*

Preface

We will have to repent in this generation not merely for the hateful words and actions of the bad people but for the appalling silence of the good people.

—REVEREND DR. MARTIN LUTHER KING JR.,
LETTER FROM BIRMINGHAM JAIL

I was lying on the ground, playing dead, in the Times Square Toys "R" Us store. With at least one hundred other people, I was part of a Black Lives Matter "die-in" in the toy gun section. It was December 2014 and we were protesting yet another police shooting of an unarmed black person, this time a twelve-year-old boy named Tamir Rice, killed while playing in a Cleveland park with a toy gun. "Silent Night" played over the speaker system while I lay still with tears in my eyes.

I was terrified, but not because of the protest, which I knew was necessary for change. It was organized, peaceful, and disciplined, unlike many negative media portrayals of the Black Lives Matter protests and protesters.* While I was proud to stand with them and lie beside them, I felt out of place. I had never participated in a protest before, though I am grateful for those who protest. I am scared of controversy, though I respect those who

---

* The origin story of the phrase "black lives matter" begins with activists Alicia Garza, Patrisse Khan-Cullors, and Opal Tometi in 2013. Today, the phrase has come to refer to at least three different things: a decentralized social movement, a formal organization with official chapters across the United States and Canada, and a social media hashtag. More on this history can be found in the book *When They Call You a Terrorist: A Black Lives Matter Memoir* by Patrisse Khan-Cullors and asha bandele as well as the article "The Matter of Black Lives" by Jelani Cobb, published in the *New Yorker*.

can handle it. I am not anti–law enforcement (nor is the Black Lives Matter movement), though I believe that abuse of authority needs to be addressed. Nor am I an African American who bears the burden of racism, though I know the burden is great. I was terrified because I am a not-very-bold, suburban, middle-aged, Land's End–wearing, Ivy League–educated, married-to-a-doctor mom of two, not your standard protester identity. This was not my usual Saturday night.

Still, none of us are only one thing. I am also an expert in the psychology of bias. As a professor and social psychologist, I use data, experiments, writing, and teaching to explore the unconscious biases held by good people like you and me.

And, I am a female, foreign-born person of color. I am a daughter of Indian immigrants who left everything and everyone behind in a tireless pursuit of a better life for their children in America. I am the Hindu wife of a brown-skinned, bearded Sikh man who wears a turban. I see our country through my proud perspective as an American with a fierce love for this land, and through my pained perspective as a person of color who is not always seen as "one of us."

Sometimes, I am described by a well-meaning white friend as her "Indian friend." Sometimes, I am handed a dirty plate by a polite parent at a kids' birthday party who assumes that I am there to clean up after the guests. Sometimes, I walk into a restaurant with my husband and children and pretend that I do not see other customers staring or glaring. America is not always the country it means to be.

To tell the truth, I am not always the person I mean to be, either. Yes, like you, I am a believer in the American values of equality and equity, diversity and inclusion, the values underlying the founding of this country and many major spiritual teachings. Race, religion, ethnicity, sexual orientation, gender,

gender identity, ability—I believe bias of all forms is wrong. I am a believer.

Still, the person I mean to be is more than just a believer. The person I mean to be stands up for those values. The person I mean to be fights bias. Sometimes, I do. Sometimes, I don't. Sometimes, I want to, but don't know where to start. Sometimes, I don't notice bias and am surprised or defensive when others point it out. Sometimes, I—the one who studies bias for a living—*am* the problem. I am that well-meaning friend, that polite parent, that staring customer. I mean to do better. As a believer in these values, I need to do better.

Not Everyone Is Ready for This Book (but You Probably Are)

Not everyone is a believer. Being a believer requires more than believing in the values. It also requires us to believe in the reality of a crushing volume of scholarly studies, research papers, and firsthand reports that offer excruciating detail on how we devalue the bodies, minds, souls, careers, incomes, life spans, and humanity of people who are not white, or male, or straight, or gender-conforming, or Christian. I am not writing a book that summarizes that voluminous evidence, though I have read a lot of it, experienced some of it, and done scholarly research that supports it. If you are absolutely convinced that these biases are not serious issues in America today, my book is not the place to start. My book is for those who have at least a vague belief that this reality might exist for some people and who want to understand and do something about that reality.

What makes things messy is that there are many people who are believers in the values but not in the evidence about the reality of bias. As an example, let us stick with racial bias. In 2011, psychologists Samuel Sommers and Michael Norton asked Americans to share their perceptions of the extent to which black and white Americans were the targets of discrimination. The average white respondent felt anti-white bias was *more* prevalent than anti-black bias. According to a more recent Reuters poll, only 37 percent of Americans believe minorities are not treated fairly. In another study, participants overestimated by 25 percent the progress our country has made in narrowing earning and wealth gaps between blacks and whites. Despite the evidence otherwise, not everyone is a believer.

Maybe this is to be expected. According to antiracist activist Tim Wise, "In every generation, white people have said there is not a racial problem and people of color have said there is. History has proven [the people of color] right. What are the odds that white folks are suddenly getting it right this time?" Wise, who is white, reminds us that two-thirds of whites felt that Reverend Dr. Martin Luther King Jr. was pushing too hard and too fast for change. They said this in the same month as the 1963 March on Washington where King delivered the "I Have a Dream" speech. During that same time period, four years before the Supreme Court declared that whites and blacks could legally marry in every state, 80 percent of white Americans said they felt racial minorities were treated equally in their community. It is predictable, then, that our generation—like every generation—should have its nonbelievers.

According to the Roper Center for Public Opinion Research at Cornell University, we have forgotten white Americans' resistance to the civil rights movement in the 1960s. Peaceful protests, which we revere now, such as the March on Washington and the lunch counter sit-ins, were viewed negatively by the majority of white Americans. Three years after the "I Have a Dream" speech, only 36 percent of white Americans believed King was helping the cause of civil rights; 14 percent were not sure and 50 percent said he was hurting the cause. In roughly the same time frame, 94 percent of black Americans felt he was helping. The stark contrast between the views of white and black Americans—36 percent versus 94 percent—washes away with the passage of time.

Consider that Muhammad Ali was once "the most hated man in America." Even Jackie Robinson was mad at Ali in 1967. Ali refused to go to war for a country that had "called me n——. . . lynched me . . . put dogs on me . . . robbed me of my nationality, raped and killed my mother and father." Yet, within fifty years, the majority of Americans regarded Ali with affection, not hatred. People would not only give him humanitarian awards, they would even name humanitarian awards after him. What appeared to be radical change at the time seems more moderate and even inevitable-sounding within a generation.

The Number of Believers Is Growing

Some say that 2016 was the new 1968. The 2016 presidential election generated and unlocked deep divides. These divides are bringing some people from the mainstream into discussions of inequality and injustice for the first time. I don't think being a believer is a partisan issue. Conservative columnists Matt Lewis and Leon Wolf note an emerging interest among white Americans in issues facing African Americans. I have lived in some of the more politically conservative areas of America (including the Bush family's hometown of Midland, Texas) and some of the more politically liberal areas (including Cambridge, Massachusetts, known to some as the People's Republic of Cambridge). I have learned that believers, and nonbelievers, can be found everywhere, and that the number of believers is growing across party lines.

Between the World and Me, *Hillbilly Elegy*, and *The New Jim Crow* are bestselling books whose white, middle-class readership is learning about and addressing class and racial justice. The documentary about mass incarceration, *13th*, found a mainstream audience on Netflix. Organizations like Google and Goldman Sachs have had discussions about allyship. Terms like "male privilege" and "white privilege" each generate a half million Google search hits. The relatively new use of the word "woke" was heralded by a *New York Times* piece about the cultural importance of signifying someone who is "hip to the realities of inequality."

We are also living in a time of unprecedented integration. This is not our parents' or grandparents' America. If your grandparents were living in the United States in the twentieth century, it was possible, even probable, that they would have gone through most days not interacting with someone of a different race or ethnicity, contradicting the melting-pot narrative. They probably worked in single-gender workplaces. They were unlikely to know—or be—someone who was openly gay or gender-nonconforming.

Today, Americans are experiencing a different reality. Seventy percent of Americans, according to a Reuters poll, interact with people of a different race in their circle of friends, coworkers, and relatives. Among people under thirty, this number rises to an astounding 90 percent. According to a CBS poll, 77 percent of us now personally know someone who is openly gay (compared to only 42 percent less than twenty-five years ago). Our workplaces are less gender-segregated. Our definitions of gender fixed at birth are evolving. So we are more diverse, and more divided, than ever before. Believing in the values of equality is no longer enough. We need to be people with the skills to make it better. We need to learn how to fight bias.

Using Science to Move from Believer to Builder

Where do we begin? If you need to drop twenty pounds, or your marriage is failing, or you hate your job, there are a million books filled with evidence-based research. If you care about fighting bias against groups marginalized in American society, there are fewer evidence-based options. Plenty of books address the structural, political, and macroeconomic solutions for inequality. Few offer individuals a social psychologist's expertise about how to fight bias at the person-to-person and person-to-system levels. Yet the research is there to help us move from having the identity of a believer to having the skills of a builder.

This insight first hit me when my amazing MBA students organized something called Ally Week at the New York University Stern School of Business. They created a week of programming to which hundreds of time-crunched students voluntarily came to learn how to act as allies for students different than them (e.g., white students for nonwhite students, non-veteran students for veterans, straight and gender-conforming students for LGBTQ+ students, male students for female students). The Ally Week organizers asked me to be the keynote speaker. I spend my days conducting and reading research on bias and related topics. Still, as I looked at this research through the lens of how to help people be better allies, even I was shocked at how much useful, eye-opening, and relevant research is buried in academic journals. As social scientists, we can help people become more skillful builders.

Fortunately, social science is playing a larger role in our national discussion. Many social psychologists, including me, have been studying, discussing, and debating implicit (also known as unconscious) bias for years, even decades. Many activists have also been having similar conversations. Psychologists Mahzarin Banaji and Anthony Greenwald recently published the authoritative book on the topic, *Blindspot*. During the September 2016 presidential debate, Hillary Clinton said "implicit bias" five times. In the vice presidential debate one week later, Mike Pence questioned whether a black police officer could show implicit racial bias. (Pence was incorrect. Research shows the majority of white Americans show implicit race bias favoring whites, while black Americans' implicit race bias ranges from showing implicit bias favoring whites to implicit bias favoring blacks. Similarly, I have published coauthored work that shows that women tend to show stronger implicit gender bias than men.)

Implicit bias research is just one slice of the science that can help us. Research from psychology, sociology, economics, political science, and other disciplines reveals ways that believers like you and me can become builders. The research also reveals ways we can do harm despite our best intentions. I have curated the most actionable and robust of these research findings—the good news and the bad news. Sure, science is dynamic, some answers are incomplete, and there is much more research to do. No single study or research finding offers an airtight solution. But as a scientist living in a bias-packed world, I believe we know enough to act on the science in hand.

Builders Need Both Heat and Light

The week before the Black Lives Matter protest at Toys "R" Us, I happened to reread Dr. King's pointed 1963 *Letter from Birmingham Jail* where he spoke of the "appalling silence of the good people." That was not the person I meant to be. I knew that research said that protests made a difference, so I found out when the next Black Lives Matter protest was taking place and rallied some friends and family to join me. So there I was, no longer silent. As I lay there, I also realized that this was not my voice.

As it turned out, I am a bad protester. As we chanted our way up the escalators in the 250,000-square-foot Toys "R" Us store toward the toy gun section, my mind raced with inappropriately off-topic thoughts. I am a working mom with limited opportunities to get to brick-and-mortar stores in the two weeks before Christmas and now I unexpectedly found myself at a Toys "R" Us. I could just pull out my holiday shopping list and multitask my chanting and shopping self through the store (without holiday crowds, even, since the protest had scared them off). These were real thoughts that I had. Oh my God, what could be less appropriate? Multitasking during a Black Lives Matter protest and then having the gall to update my to-do list: *Star Wars* Legos—check, *Frozen* dollhouse—check, civil disobedience—check. Protest movements deserve better.

I wondered if the only way to build a better world was through the building of movements and protests. I wondered if there was work for people like me who do not like controversy, who will rearrange the dishwasher but never openly debate which way the forks should go (pointing down, obviously). I admire the temperament and courage of people who are willing to have the acrimonious argument and stage the defiant protest. They apply heat and they take heat.

The truth, however, is that I am better at the teachable moment and the patient partnership. I am good at talking with people. I am good at asking questions. I am good at listening to people. I am good at learning new perspectives. These are the skills that help generate light. Maybe I, and others looking for their place in the work, was overlooking the importance of light.*

There are many opportunities to generate light in our homes, in our communities, and in our workplaces. We can be inspired by the research of organizational scholar Debra Meyerson on "tempered radicals." Tempered radicals are insiders in organizations who do not present as rebels and are often successful in their jobs. They are catalysts for change by challenging the status quo in small, cautious ways. Meyerson writes, "Tempered radicals push and prod the system through a variety of subtle processes, rechanneling information and opportunities, questioning assumptions, changing boundaries of inclusion, and scoring small wins." While no individual action is a revolution, the sum of their daily efforts leads to real evolution. Said another way, tempered radicals follow the advice of author and activist Silas House, "Be revolutionary, every day."

To be clear, research shows that turning up the heat is also essential work. Social movement scholar Jo Freeman found that more extreme feminists served as a "radical flank" in comparison to more moderate feminists. Herbert Haines extended this work in studying the civil rights movement, noting that moderate black organizations saw increased rather than decreased funding as the radical black movement emerged. Light is not an alternative to heat in social movements. It is a necessary partner. For some of us, light is our entry point into the work.

This book brings together stories and science that can help us create that light. We will meet people from across the country and from multiple industries, each experimenting with what he or she

---

* I find the heat and light metaphor to be powerful and others seem to agree. While I have not been able to trace its original source, I have seen it used in sources ranging from *The Unitarian Register/The Christian Register* to Cathy Young in the *Observer* to Barack Obama's speeches.

can do to build a better workplace and world. Some have been thinking about things like diversity and inclusion for a long time and others have just joined the conversation. Some are thinking about person-to-person dynamics, while others are thinking about systems that shape our societal lives. Their stories are less about solving and saving and more about growing and grappling. Like me and you, they are good people looking to do better, trying to be the people they mean to be.

The Person You Mean to Be

Introduction: Good-ish People

The three hardest tasks in the world are neither physical feats nor intellectual achievements, but moral acts: to return love for hate, to include the excluded, and to say, "I was wrong."

—SYDNEY J. HARRIS

On Sunday, June 12, 2016, Rachel Hurnyak woke in her Bay Area home to horrific overnight news from Orlando, Florida. As bartenders at a popular gay nightclub shouted "Last call," a man had walked in with multiple firearms. He killed forty-nine people and injured fifty-three others.

Rachel was shocked, and as someone who self-identifies as queer, she was terrified. She knew it could have been her—or anyone in her community. Rachel was once my student, and when I heard the news, I had the same thought.

As Rachel thought about going into work the next day at a Bay Area technology company, she knew her stress level was dangerously high. It was not the good kind of stress that makes employees more focused, motivated, and creative. She was grieving. The Grief Index study captures data from more than twenty-five thousand people collected over several decades. The study reports that, at any given moment, approximately one in four American workers is experiencing grief.

Rachel was feeling "hidden grief," which specialists say emerges from negative events and relationships outside of work, such as family deaths or illnesses or national tragedies. Hidden grief costs U.S. companies as much as $75.1 billion in lost productivity per year due to employees who have difficulty concentrating, make errors in judgment, and experience accidents. Sometimes, the source of the hidden grief, such as the death of a family member, is relatively straightforward and easy to share, but hidden grief can also be more complex and difficult to share with others.

Unable to sleep that night, Rachel decided to make her hidden grief visible to the world. She blogged, "This week and beyond will be difficult for your LGBTQ and/or Muslim colleagues . . . one community grieves because our members were killed in one of the first safe places we ever knew. The second community grieves because they're being blamed for those killings."

Much as she loved her job and her colleagues, Rachel was dreading being at work the next morning. It was just going to make things harder, even though work colleagues are a critical component of many people's support systems. In Rachel's case, most of her straight colleagues were good, well-intentioned people who would seek to comfort her. They might call themselves allies.

I imagined myself as one of those colleagues reaching out to Rachel that Monday morning, filled with sympathy and outrage, overflowing with good intentions. We might mention our donations to The Trevor Project or the Human Rights Campaign. We might fill her in on the minutiae of each breaking news story about the shooter. We might tell her about a gay family member or college friend or former colleague. We might recall Matthew Shepard, or Tyler Clementi, or another victim of a terrible hate crime. Our eyes would well with tears.

Yet, instead of finding comfort in such good intentions, Rachel was filled with dread. This surprised me. She is one of the most appreciative people I know, the type who makes you feel heroic for the smallest of kind acts. Clearly, I was missing something.

"What they are saying is more for them than me," Rachel says.

"You go to a lot of funerals when you're a pastor's kid and you hear the same conversations every time. It is almost a competition to see who was the most relevant. 'Well, I saw Jim on Tuesday at the store and he looked okay.' Or, 'I saw him the following morning and he didn't look okay.' Meanwhile, Jim's family is sitting alone in the corner. We make it about ourselves."

Rachel feared that she would need to set aside her grief to make room for her colleagues' emotions. Their grief—my grief—would be genuine. Her colleagues and I cared about her well-being *and* we wanted something as well: We had an urgent desire for her to see *our* grief. We saw ourselves as the good ones, as believers on the right side of history. We needed her to validate us. At some unconscious level, we craved affirmation that we were good people, and that she knew it.

Claiming an Identity

In speech and action, we express how we see ourselves and how we want to be perceived by others, a process that organizational scholars Caroline Bartel and Jane Dutton call "identity claiming." Psychologically, identity claiming is an ordinary and universal process. Each of us claims multiple identities. My husband, my children, and I all claim an identity as Indian Americans. My daughters also claim identities as Mets fans and as girls-but-not-girly-girls. My husband claims identities as a physician, a Punjabi Sikh, and a devoted dad. I claim identities as a woman of color, a do-gooder, and a loving mom.

Each of us has an intense craving for others to see and ac-knowledge our various identities, a phenomenon that Bartel and Dutton call "identity granting." They compare the interplay be-tween identity claiming and granting to a public performance and audience reaction. Tina Fey may claim an identity as a funny person, but if audiences don't find her funny, her identity as a funny person has not been granted.

We are vigilant for clues about whether our identity has been granted. Psychologist William Swann has studied how much we care about this affirmation of ourselves, including one study in which participants were even willing to pay for affirmation. How people treat us and what they say to us affirms us.

When we are unsure of whether an important identity has been granted by others, our craving for affirmation becomes more intense and urgent. Psychologists call this a moment of self-threat— our identity is being challenged or dismissed. Just as moments of physical threat trigger a hyperfocus on self-preservation, moments of psychological self-threat do the same. If I value being seen as a do-gooder, then I feel self-threat when people judge me as a greedy person, based on stereotypes of my résumé. If I value being seen as a loving mom, then I feel self-threat when other mothers judge me for working full-time outside the home. Once I am in self-threat mode, other problems follow.

Along with organizational scholars Mary Kern, Zhu Zhu, and Sujin Lee, I studied what happens when we construe an external situation as a threat. We asked participants to do a word scramble task and told them we would pay them based on their performance. We also measured whether they saw the task as more of a threat or more of a challenge, which potentially suggests a self-threat. Our prediction was that people who saw the task as a threat would be more likely to morally disengage or turn off their conscience, which keeps us from doing unethical things. As predicted, participants were more likely to morally disengage when they (believed they) faced a threat.

Then we used a simple intervention to bring this threat down. We asked participants to remember a situation in which they fel secure, able to depend on someone and have that person depend on them. Even though this intervention had nothing to do with the threat of the word scramble task, we suspected that it would be affirming and reduce the threat that people felt in the situation. The affirmation made them less likely to morally disengage after the self-threat, as we predicted.

Threat, especially self-threat, is stressful. Threat-motivated stress can lead to bad performance, negative health consequences, and poor behavioral choices. We do not feel good and we usually do not treat others well. We become defensive. Our hopes of being a good person are diminished at times like these.

In summary, we each have identities we claim. We look to others to grant those identities. When we don't get that affirmation, we feel threatened, which is stressful, and we do things we would not normally do. Under self-threat, we become less of the good people we mean to be.

Research reveals how our need for affirmation overrides our genuine desire to be a good colleague, friend, and ally. One study found that we value boosts to our self-esteem, such as compliments, even more than our favorite sex acts and foods. Given that it is socially taboo to openly covet compliments, these study participants probably underreported how much they value that affirmation.

We all fall into this pattern. We fish for affirmation. We center our needs, nudging away the needs of others. We seek what activists call "cookies," acknowledgments of our good intentions, even when the impact is costly to the cookie giver. We especially crave that affirmation when faced with a situation that challenges the believer identity we are claiming. The affirmation relieves the self-threat, but ironically, we end up acting less like—not more like—the people we mean to be. The pattern is both heartbreaking and exhausting.

Believers were the people most likely to be Rachel's allies. We were also the people most likely to leave her hanging emotionally. When she needed us most, we were inclined to hit her up for cookies of affirmation.

Chimamanda Ngozi Adichie writes of the dangers of cookies in her novel *Americanah*. The protagonist leads several diversity workshops until she realizes that the workshop attendees' primary motivation is not to learn but to feel better about themselves. Craving cookies, they sacrifice the opportunity for meaningful change.

The cookie craving intensifies when self-threat hits, as with the tragic events in Orlando. Many of us want to support Rachel and others who are marginalized. Yet we come up short. We want to do better by Rachel, but we might be unsure about how to do so. We might feel as if we are damned if we say something and damned if we don't. Many of us believe in the promise of equality and equity, diversity and inclusion, but do not know how to build those beliefs into reality.

Rachel will return toward the end of the book to describe where she found the support she needed. First, we're going to learn the four ways in which builders are different than believers. Let's begin by exploring how good people like you and me think.

The Psychology of Good People

I study the psychology of good people. I see myself as a good person and yet my behavior is filled with evidence to the contrary. I cling to antiquated gender stereotypes. I defend systems that favor well-off, well-connected families like mine. I misidentify people of the same race. I let homophobic jokes slide. I am judgmental of people whose gender identities confuse me. None of this makes me proud.

At the same time, I fight for equality, donate money to social justice causes, spend time supporting individuals from marginalized groups, and challenge the status quo. So my mind flips between a belief that I am as good as they come and a belief that I am no good at all. In the end, the belief that I am a good person always wins.

I am not alone. Most of us have what psychologists Karl Aquino and Americus Reed call a central "moral identity." Moral identity is a measure of whether I care about being a good person, *not* whether I am a good person. Their research reveals that most of us want to feel like good people. This is an identity we claim and want granted.

Now, just because many of us have a highly central moral identity does not mean that we agree on what is and is not moral. In fact, moral identity does not appear to be unique to any particular political affiliation, generation, gender, or belief system. While you and I may disagree on what is and is not moral, we both would bristle at any accusation that we lack morality. Even people who are engaging in crimes or bullying that others view as immoral may still see themselves as moral. A recent *Washington Post* story offered an in-depth profile of former white nationalist Derek Black, revealing that even KKK affiliates do not necessarily self-identify as racists.

While none of us are good all the time, and some of us are far from good a lot of the time, we still see ourselves as good. How do we sustain this view of ourselves? We hold a faulty assumption that our behavior pivots around our ethical standards and our moral values. That is not how our minds actually work. Our behavior pivots around our identity. I want to see myself as a good person, which I can accomplish by being a good person (doing X) or by convincing myself that I'm a good person (while doing the opposite of X). Even when we fall short, our reflex is to claim an identity as a good person. Evidence to the contrary is a self-threat.

It is difficult to overstate just how quickly and seamlessly we deal with self-threats. Our bodies are built to fight off bacteria and our minds are built to fight off self-threat. This does not make us bad people, but it does make us unlikely to recognize when we do bad things. The result is that all of us, even the "good people," do bad things. It is easy for us to see this in other people and much harder for us to see it in ourselves. Through it all, we cling to an illusion of being a perfectly ethical and unbiased person and to the idea that such a "good person" can exist. This illusion is problematic.

As a result, good people are prone to what my mentors—business school professor Max Bazerman and psychology professor Mahzarin Banaji—and I call "bounded ethicality." Bounded ethicality is the psychology of "good-ish" people. Good-ish people are sometimes good and sometimes not, sometimes intentionally and sometimes not, like all of us. This model of bounded ethicality challenges ways of thinking and talking in which you are either a good person or not, a racist or not, an unethical human or not. We argue that this binary notion is seductive but misleading and scientifically inaccurate. We do not need to fall for this false notion.

Mary Kern and I expanded on the model of bounded ethicality and have developed a model of "ethical learning" which takes the psychology of good-ish people into account. We redefine what it means to be a good person as someone who is trying to be better, as opposed to someone who is allowing themselves to believe in the illusion that they are always a good person.

This psychology of good people explains our need to be affirmed by Rachel. We care a lot about our good-person identity; we erroneously see this identity as either/or; we want the identity to be granted by Rachel; and we especially need that affirmation under self-threat. This way of thinking is very human and very costly to the people we care about supporting. It is possible to break free of this psychology. We see what that looks like next.

"I Didn't Want to Offend Her"

"It was so embarrassing," recalls author Sarah Weeks. Sarah had no idea how to say her student's last name: Gita Varadarajan. Sarah was Gita's instructor at Columbia University's Teachers College; Gita was an experienced educator enrolled in the Reading and Writing Project, working on her own writing to help her elementary-school students work on theirs. Sarah was thrilled when she had students like Gita who fell outside of the white, American-born norm in her classroom. Still, as a self-described "white girl from the Midwest," she did not want to "offend" Gita—a recent immigrant from India—by shredding the pronunciation of her last name.

Sarah understood that knowing and using someone's name was critical to building meaningful relationships. Dale Carnegie, author of the classic *How to Win Friends and Influence People*, once said, "A person's name is to him or her the sweetest and most important sound in any language." A Google search for "how to remember people's names" yields almost three million hits. But this was an issue of pronunciation, not memory. So Sarah simply called Gita by her first name and avoided the problem.

After the course ended, Sarah encouraged Gita to expand a story she had written into a book, which they decided to write together. Sarah has published more than fifty-five children's books, including *So B. It* and *Pie*, which has sold more than three million copies. Gita is an experienced teacher and a first-time author with a fresh voice. As collaborators, Sarah often introduced Gita to people in her publishing network. Still, Sarah avoided saying Gita's last name.

As Sarah and Gita developed the story, they focused on how Gita had written about twelve-year-old Ravi Suryanarayanan,* a middle-school boy whose family moves from Bangalore to New Jersey. Ravi was frustrated that none of the teachers and students in his new school had tried to say his name. Sarah had privately winced when she read Gita's draft, seeing herself in the fictional teachers. Sarah asked Gita about the characters' motivations, specifically why no one tried to learn how to say Ravi's name. Gita's analysis was immediate and unflinching. "Arrogance," she said. "I don't think they care."

Sarah was stunned. Arrogance? While they were discussing fictional characters, Sarah's self-threat meter went into the red zone. This was not the identity Sarah intended to claim or the identity she thought Gita had granted her. Sarah confessed. The issue was not that she cared too little but that she cared too much to risk embarrassment or offending someone else.

Like so many of us in an uncomfortable situation, Sarah's good intentions weren't enough and the impact was clear. Gita did not grant Sarah her desired identity or the affirmation she craved. Sarah had no idea how Gita perceived the intentions and beliefs of people like her, and the impact of those perceptions.

That's when Sarah moved from believing to building. She asked Gita if she would teach her the correct pronunciation of both Varadarajan (Gita's surname) and Suryanarayanan (the main character's surname, and also Gita's maiden name). Gita readily agreed. Sarah realized that when a native speaker said the name quickly, she needed help hearing each distinct syllable. She asked

---

* Sarah and Gita experimented with the main character's first name. Earlier drafts referred to Ravi as Suraj.

Gita to say it more slowly. Again, Gita agreed as she saw Sarah was willing to put in the work.

Sarah wrote out the names phonetically. She practiced saying them. Once she stopped worrying about self-threat, she was surprised to realize that the names were not that hard to say semi-correctly, albeit in an American accent. (She's right. If you can say "supercalifragilisticexpialidocious" or the names on *Game of Thrones* or Arnold Schwarzenegger, you can probably say "vuh-ruh-dhar-AH-jhun" and "sur-ee-ah-neh-RI-ya-nan.") She just had not tried before.

A week later, Sarah called Gita. When Gita answered, Sarah asked, "May I speak with Gita Suryanarayanan Varadarajan?" Gita cried. It was the first time anyone had tried to say her name since she had moved to America several years before. "The *first* time," Gita emphasizes.

Higher Standards

No one would have confused Sarah's pronunciation with that of a native speaker. Her American accent did not disappear. But one need not have Meryl Streep's capacity for accents to do a vague approximation of native pronunciation. Maybe we cannot roll our *r*'s, but we can strive to put the emphasis on the correct syllable and leave the correct letters silent. In pronunciation, perfection need not be the enemy of progress.

I have been slow to learn this lesson. Like Sarah, when a name looked "hard" on paper, I did not say it aloud. Even worse, I just blew by it in my mind, not even fully reading it. My standards for effort were selectively low. My family is from northern India and I have lived in the United States since I was six months old. "Normal" Indian names to me are the ones I grew up hearing, like Raj,

Gupta, Singh, or my own, Chugh.* I had never learned or tried to say longer, south Indian names. I admit it: Through the process of being interviewed, Sarah taught this brown woman how to say Varadarajan.

Sarah's efforts were meaningful to Gita, but Sarah was also redefining the norm for herself. Names with one or two syllables that "sound white" may seem normal to some Americans. Some people may regard other types of names as "hard to say" or reasons to ask "can I call you Sue?" or even to assign a nickname to the person, without permission ("We'll just call you Sue"). What are we saying about who belongs and who does not if we treat white-sounding names as the norm and other names as the variants? After all, these names are not the norm for many Americans, most non-Americans, or the original Native Americans.

Sarah's identity as someone who believes in diversity survived, not despite her confession, but *because* of it. Her shift from believer to builder started with educating herself. She asked for help, without demanding or presuming it from Gita, who might have not wanted to go down this road. None of us should be obligated to educate others. In this case, Gita wanted to help Sarah learn. Their conversation grew from there.

Gita suggested they tell each other the worst stereotypes their respective cultures held about the other. They decided to write their thoughts down on an index card and then exchange cards. Gita's list included "Divorced. Obsessed with meat. Feeds kids out of cans." Sarah's list read something like "Pushy. Dominated by men. Obsessed with education."

They asked each other awkward questions. They talked about models of good parenting in each of their cultures, noticing simi-

---

* Pronounced with a *u* that sounds like the *oo* in "good" and a hard *gh* at the end.

larities and differences. They compared what was "normal" versus "weird" in their worlds.

Notably, they had different experiences of these candid exchanges. Sarah still cringes when remembering her awkward entry into these conversations, while Gita remembers far less discomfort. In fact, she remembers the pleasure she felt that somebody wanted to know and understand her. Sarah was processing her self-threat while Gita was feeling seen and heard.

As Sarah built her capacity and Gita supported her growth, their collaboration grew deeper and richer. The best evidence lies in the book they cowrote, *Save Me a Seat*, a widely acclaimed book filled with humor and humanity. It features two middle-school students named Joe and Ravi. Joe and Ravi are quick to stereotype each other but also share a common enemy, the class bully. The book has resonated with reviewers, parents, teachers, and kids—and Rhode Island adopted the book as a statewide read.

Both Sarah and Gita cite the name pronunciation conversation as the gateway to the book. From there, they both reflected on what they assumed to be "normal." They took chances and trusted each other with their mistakes. There were more questions than statements. There were, and still are, awkward moments. To their mutual delight, the awkward moments unlocked something powerful. When I independently asked each of them to capture their conversations in one word, I was surprised that Gita said "laughter" and Sarah said "fun."

The story of Sarah Weeks and Gita Varadarajan highlights our missed opportunities at an individual-to-individual level. Throughout this book, we will see examples of how people grapple with the relationships in their work, personal, and community lives. Their story suggests what else might be possible if we can engage in those relationships as builders. We will also see examples of how individuals grapple within social systems—the cultures, laws, institutions, and traditions of our lives.

"I'm Not That White Person"

Lorri Perkins is that empathetic friend who celebrates your promotion as if it were her own. She cries when your dog dies. She can't wait to hear about your big date. She can relate to people from seemingly every background, which I have seen her do for the twenty years of our friendship.

As an organizational facilitator and consultant, Lorri had led workshops for a corporate client on topics like goal setting, problem solving, and communications. When the client hired a diversity consultant, he asked Lorri to work with the new consultant to ensure that the new workshops were aligned with Lorri's previous work.

These new workshops covered topics new to Lorri, who is white, like systemic racism and white privilege. "I was now part of a conversation that most of my suburban white friends were not," Lorri recalls about her experience sitting in the workshops. "It was uncomfortable. It created a lot of self-reflection. I felt myself wanting to explain that I'm not that white person you're describing."

To her, the session with the diversity consultant felt divisive and counterproductive. "I wanted to explain how I grew up. My parents did not have college degrees. That's not privilege the way I, and so many others, define it." Faced with self-threat, Lorri was tempted to shut down and tune out and defend herself as a "good person."

Lorri decided to speak to a trusted black friend from church, though they had never talked about these topics before. She was surprised to learn that the bucolic roads she loved were the same ones her friend's family avoided at night, fearing interactions with the police. Lorri had heard about these issues on the news but had never considered them as a possibility in her town. She wondered what else she did not know about her friend's experiences and perspective.

"I don't even think of myself as white," Lorri says, a sentiment expressed by many white people. Now she was realizing that if being black meant having a race, so did being white. She began listening more to conversations about systemic bias, trying to understand what the term meant. Filled with questions but unsure with whom she could discuss these issues, she contacted me. Despite our long friendship, we had never discussed race or gender or any of the social issues I am writing about in this book.

At first, I resisted. While Lorri was a believer, I was one of her few close friends of color. It is hard to explain things that are visible to you and invisible to others, which is how systemic bias works. In my life, I felt like I was already doing this exhausting explaining work with a lot of people, more than any one of them realized. The national climate felt very hostile to me, and I needed my emotional energies to focus on my family, not on educating others who did not feel targeted. I told Lorri this and gave her books to read and people to follow on social media.

After she did her homework, she came back to me, and this time, I agreed to talk. A swirl of events had brought Lorri to think differently about the world: the 2016 presidential campaign, videos of police officers killing unarmed black people, the conversation with her friend at church, challenging questions from her children, and the diversity workshop. "I'm just starting to realize that the people that I'm sitting side by side with at church, at work, at my kids' school are dealing with problems that I had assumed just don't apply to them," Lorri says.

"I am one of those people that had to work hard to under-stand this word 'privilege,' to get past this word," Lorri recalls. "I had to reframe what that word means. I realized that even though I did not have a red carpet laid out for me, a black person walking that same path of nonprivilege would certainly have less opportunity or less going their way, less wind at their back than a white person on that same path." Lorri kept reading and listening more.

"I'm not an activist," she says. "But I am thinking about what are the subtle but consistent things I can do to not turn my back. It can be overwhelming. Sometimes I get lazy. What's my role?" That question has been asked by many people who do not identify as people engaged in social justice or social movements.

Even for those people, research tells us that small steps are crit-ical to longer-term and larger progress. The narrative of big, bold action in social change is largely mythical. Contrary to the my-thology about her, Rosa Parks had engaged in many small acts of resistance before that famous day on the bus, as detailed in Jeanne Theoharis's biography *The Rebellious Life of Mrs. Rosa Parks.*

I turned the question back to Lorri. How might she engage? She thought for a moment. "I think my role is to initiate as many conversations as I can with those who are open and will-ing to having the conversations. I can break the silence. I can pop the bubble a bit." In her roles as a consultant, as a parent, as a church member, as a family member, and as a neighbor, the opportunities for conversation—the opportunity to create light—were everywhere. She could learn about the experiences of people with different backgrounds than hers and prompt thought in people with similar backgrounds to hers. Lorri could engage herself and others to see the systems they are all part of. As we will explore, her privilege, ordinary as it is, gives her a natural role.

What to Expect

This book is for and about people of all races, ethnicities, genders, religions, physical and mental abilities, and sexual orientations, good people who believe in building a better workplace and world. As we move from thinking about being a good person to being a good-ish person trying to be better, we can expect certain emotional reactions. Good people like us are especially prone to feelings of shame. Shame is a tricky emotion. If and when shame strikes while you are reading, do not feel ashamed of the shame. Instead, I encourage you to consider the difference between shame and guilt. When we feel shame, we feel as if "I am wrong"; it is a high-self-threat emotion, which we want to make go away by blaming others or shutting down. When we feel guilt, we feel as if "I did something wrong"; it is less about the self and more about the behavior.

Shame is paralyzing. If we do act when we feel shame, whatever we do usually makes things worse, not better. In contrast, guilt is motivating. When we feel guilt, we are more likely to make positive changes in our behavior and to engage in interpersonal problem solving. As shame researcher, author, and popular TED Talk speaker Brené Brown says, "I'm pro-guilt. Guilt is good. Guilt helps us stay on track because it's about our behavior." If you are a believer who is trying to be a builder, shame gets in the way. We have too much hard work to do.

I encourage you to begin that hard work with the approach you take in reading this book. Let yourself feel both inspiration and unease. Toggle between feeling misunderstood and trying to understand. Balance the impulse to judge others with my invitation to reflect on yourself. If you can fight through the ugliness of shame, you will have the emotional openness you need to manage these contradictions.

Most important, consider the possibility that the thoughts and feelings that arise for you while reading this book are the same ones that arise for you when confronting these issues in the real world. Pay attention to the reactions you have while reading (maybe even jot some of them down). Consider that these may be the same reactions you have to issues of diversity and inclusion in other parts of your life. Do you feel offended and misunderstood when I mention the group you belong to? Consider how members of other groups feel when their groups are discussed. Do you want to stop reading, especially when we talk about bias in good people? Stay with the issues, even when things get uncomfortable. Do you wait to be educated by others rather than educating yourself? Take responsibility for looking up unfamiliar ideas or names you may encounter in this book. Do you question the realism of the real-world examples in the book? Consider that the status quo is being challenged. Do you have the urge to give this book to other people in your life, rather than read it yourself, because you think they need it more than you? Consider that you may be missing opportunities to be more of the person you mean to be. All of us have some of these reactions (including me, while writing this book). Notice which ones you have.

When you have the reactions above, the tools in the book are ready for you to use them. You do not—in fact, should not—wait until you are done reading the book to begin applying them. Practice in your own mind and heart while reading so that you will be better able to do so out in the world.

And when you are out in the world, you can expect to use these tools in many parts of your life. I hope this book helps you to talk effectively about LGBTQ rights at holiday gatherings or address a racist joke at work. I hope it helps you respond to a coworker who calls you sexist or figure out what to say to your immigrant neighbor about news of hate crimes. I hope it helps you to think about what you can do to make your next meeting a more inclusive one or decide what you think of protests and protesters.

I also hope to surprise you with research that reveals the selfishness of the urge to "save" people in need, the inefficacy of sympathy and "white tears," and what people may be thinking when you say you do not see color. Our intentions and our impact are not always the same, and research can help us fine-tune the assumptions we make about ourselves and others.

In the chapters that follow, science will guide us and stories will bring the science to life. We will unpack the work believers need to do to become builders in four phases:

1. ACTIVATING A GROWTH MINDSET of being a good-ish work-in-progress, not a premade good person;
2. SEEING THE ORDINARY PRIVILEGE we hold and putting it to good use on behalf of others;
3. OPTING FOR WILLFUL AWARENESS, though our minds and lives make willful ignorance more likely; and
4. ENGAGING the people and systems around us.

We begin by exploring the mindset that liberated Sarah and Gita to deepen their collaboration and liberated Lorri to see more clearly the people and systems in her life. It is a mindset in which the less we worry about being good people, the better people we will be.

Part I

Builders Activate a Growth Mindset

I embrace the label of bad feminist because I am human. I am messy. I'm not trying to be an example. I am not trying to be perfect. I am not trying to say I have all the answers. I am not trying to say I'm right. I am just trying—trying to support what I believe in, trying to do some good in this world, trying to make some noise with my writing while also being myself. . . .

—ROXANE GAY, *BAD FEMINIST*

1

Stumbling Upward

Early in his career, Hollywood executive Perrin Chiles was searching for the right subject for his first documentary film. Autism diagnoses were skyrocketing and a groundswell of science was emerging. Stereotypes about children with autism and judgments of their parents were also on the rise. Empathy was in short supply. Perrin did not know much about autism, nor was he close to any parents of children with autism. Yet he believed that he could tackle his ignorance through effort and the help of others. He did not assume that he knew what he needed to know or that he needed to prove to others that he already knew the answers. When it came to his knowledge about autism, he viewed himself as a work-in-progress. He had what psychologist Carol Dweck calls a growth mindset.

Growth Versus Fixed Mindset

Mindset refers to our belief about our capacity to learn and improve. If I have a growth mindset about drawing, I believe that I can improve my stick figures with effort, time, and feedback. The alternative, a fixed mindset, is where I see myself as fully formed—either as someone who is terrible at drawing or wonderful at drawing or somewhere in between—and destined to stay that way. The fixed mindset is an "either/or" mindset because it allows no room for being a work-in-progress. Our mindsets vary across the different parts of our lives. I might believe my drawing skills to be set and my math skills to be malleable.

Perrin's belief that he could learn about autism allowed him to enter unfamiliar territory with humility, take risks, and learn from others: "I came into the experience just knowing that I didn't have the answers." Directed by Tricia Regan, *Autism: The Musical* was Perrin's first documentary film, following a group of children with autism and their parents over several months as they staged a live musical. The film premiered at the Tribeca Film Festival in 2007, aired on HBO, was short-listed at the Oscars, and won two Emmy Awards. It is filled with heart-warming euphoria and heartbreaking pain, with the parents and children centered in the telling of their stories. I doubt even the most stoic parent—or human—has ever watched this movie without a lump in his or her throat. Many families affected by autism recommended the film to friends and family members. Perrin believed he was a work-in-progress in his understanding of autism and tried to listen to those who knew more. The results were powerful.

After *Autism: The Musical*, projects came and went. Perrin now had a family and a mortgage, and his eyes were open for new opportunities. He noticed that many well-vetted scripts, pilots, pitches, and stories in Hollywood had been "back-burnered." These abandoned intellectual properties could be purchased for pennies on the dollar. They were seeds that needed attention, maybe a new pot or fresh soil. With two co-founders, Perrin started Adaptive Studios to buy and grow those seeds, one of which was *Project Greenlight*.

"Talent Can Come from Anywhere"

Before *American Idol* and *The Voice*, *Project Greenlight* was an innovative film-writing and filmmaking talent discovery competition. In its original form, the contest generated a television program, which showed the behind-the-scenes process of selecting a contest winner and making a movie. Judges picked the winner and then mentored the winner through the moviemaking process.

Before Perrin got involved, the show first aired in 2001 and was led by actors Ben Affleck and Matt Damon. *Project Greenlight* was an attempt to replicate their surprising rise from unknowns to Oscar winners for the script of their first movie, *Good Will Hunting*. The show was ahead of its time, airing before DVRs, social media, crowdsourcing, and widespread broadband Internet. Contest participants stood in line at the post office to mail in VHS tapes.

In the first three seasons of the show, the judges picked three talented, up-and-coming filmmakers and writers as winners. *Project Greenlight* ran on HBO and then on Bravo, before being canceled after three seasons as other reality talent competitions entered the landscape. It sat on the back burner for almost a decade.

Enter Perrin and Adaptive Studios. The time was ripe to modernize *Project Greenlight* for a digital age, by reviving and modernizing its original spirit—"given the opportunity, talent can come from anywhere and go everywhere." In those first three seasons, the panels of all/almost all white male judges had also selected three consecutive white male winners. Despite the intent to find new voices from different communities, Perrin could see that the insider system was still replicating itself. He wanted to revitalize the show's original ethos.

Perrin, also a white male, knew Hollywood. The statistics are striking. If an alien were to stumble upon an archive of American film and television, this alien would conclude that we are a mostly male, overwhelmingly white, overwhelmingly straight population, with few people over sixty or with physical disabilities. Female speaking characters are only 29 percent of those in film and 36 percent of those on television. These statistics have not changed meaningfully in more than half a century. Whites are overrepresented, comprising 72 percent of speaking parts (versus 62 percent of the population). In a study of the top one hundred films of 2015, forty-eight did not include a single black character with a speaking part (defined as one word or more). Seventy films did not include an Asian or Asian American character. Across film and television, only 15 percent of directors are female and 29 percent of writers are female. In film, women are even harder to find in director's chairs; about 4 percent of movies are directed by women. Media scholar Stacy Smith, who leads the massive research effort that produced these findings, calls this an "epidemic of invisibility." Perrin realized that *Project Greenlight* had fallen into similar patterns.

The revived season four of *Project Greenlight* was an opportunity for change. The contest was still structured around the discovery of an unknown director/writer. This winning filmmaker would receive a $3 million budget and a deal with HBO. Still, the judging panel remained mostly white men with the addition of one white woman and one black woman.

HBO would film the judging process and the winner's attempt to make his or her first feature film, creating the behind-the-scenes content. The result would be a reality series—featuring the judges, the contestants, the winning director, multiple mentors, Damon and Affleck, and the crew—plus the resulting movie itself, featuring its cast and crew. Viewers of the reality series would see "the drama behind making a comedy."

Project Greenlight's star digital expert, Brittany Turner, led the revamp of the contest engine. The key innovation was that anyone, anywhere, with a Facebook account, could enter the contest. At first, the new contest engine appeared to be a massive success, generating five thousand submissions, perhaps the largest-scale video contest submission ever. Talent was apparently coming from everywhere and the *Project Greenlight*/Adaptive Studios team was optimistic.

Time to Activate

Upon closer examination, however, something "crushing" became clear. Of those five thousand submissions, fewer than 15 percent were from women and fewer than 5 percent were from people of color. Brittany, who is African American, says with a sigh, "You didn't have to go through a gatekeeper. We thought if the contest was open to everybody, then everybody would apply." Everybody did not apply. Like so many organizations, Adaptive Studios wondered why.

"There's the issue of access to technology and privileges like an expensive film school," Brittany speculates. But she also had an additional hypothesis. "The legacy of *Project Greenlight* was Matt Damon and Ben Affleck," she says. "My perception of that, especially as a woman of color myself, is that I think people see those two guys and they assume 'This contest is not for me' or 'They're not gonna get my perspective.'" In other words, while they may be big names, they were not necessarily big draws for everyone, or big names everyone could see themselves in.

Researchers have studied the role of "representation" in talent-search processes and the findings support Brittany's instincts. Black and Hispanic job applicants are more likely to apply for jobs when black or Hispanic representatives are depicted in company recruitment materials. It also matters how those representatives are portrayed. In one study, black undergraduates were more likely to apply for jobs portraying black company employees, especially if the employees were in supervisory positions. If you are underrepresented, you are more likely to look for representation clues, however superficial, and take them into account.

Everyone was frustrated. "By the time we arrived to do our judging, we knew we had blown it," Matt Damon would later tell the *New York Times*. This frustration flowed into the judges' discussions in the first episode. A controversial exchange about diversity erupted on camera between Damon and fellow judge Effie Brown during the judging process. An edited clip of the exchange aired in the HBO series, went viral, and sparked a nationwide discussion. Many viewers of the clip condemned Damon for "mansplaining" and "whitesplaining" to Brown, an experienced and respected black female colleague, about diversity when she tried to raise issues. Some observers wondered how challenging the diversity and inclusion issues must be off camera, if this happened on camera and survived editing. Others wondered what nuance was omitted in the editing process. Nevertheless, the judges picked a winner: another white male.

From there, the controversy grew. Once the winner was selected, Brown's role was to serve as the film's line producer. In the making of a movie, the line producer is accountable for keeping the movie on schedule and within budget, particularly important for a director working on his or her first feature-length film. Despite Brown's significantly longer and more successful track record, the inexperienced director was frequently shown questioning her decisions, competence, and intentions.

The director then wrote and made a movie titled *The Leisure Class*. The movie featured a 100 percent white cast and a subservient, one-dimensional female lead character. At multiple points in the series, Brown is the sole voice challenging the racial makeup of the cast and crew and the flatness of the female lead character. Brown's colleagues ranged from inconsistent in their support to undermining of her work. The story line of the movie focused on a family from the "1 percent" striving to protect its multigenerational wealth and reputation. It was a fine script and a fine movie, but given the stated goals of this particular competition, the outcome was disappointing.

The whole endeavor became a high-profile lightning rod. Numerous postmortem interviews reflect that many people had good intentions going into this project. They were believers. Still, these intentions did not translate into their becoming builders, or prevent them from choosing a winner from the most overrepresented profile in Hollywood: a straight white male director with film-school training. Brittany winces as she remembers, "It felt like taking a big punch for all of us."

Psychological Safety in Teams and Growth Mindset in Individuals

Workplace teams require patience and flexibility under the best of conditions and the *Project Greenlight* scenario was hardly ideal. The Adaptive Studios team consisted of mostly white men and a sole black woman in the national spotlight, trying to navigate racially charged fallout. Such a scenario is known to especially deplete and alienate the woman or the minority in the "hot seat."

I asked Brittany what it was like to work in that context, on issues of race and gender. "As a woman of color, a part of me felt 'I should've known this.' I should have known how to 'formally do diversity,' but it is something you have to learn." She was highlighting the difference between being a believer and a builder. Her experiences as a black woman had given her first-hand reasons to be a believer, but they did not equip her with the skills to be a builder. She, too, needed to have a growth mindset.

Brittany's beliefs about her ability to grow were necessary, though not sufficient. The beliefs she had about the people around her also mattered, specifically, her belief about what business school professor Amy Edmondson calls "psychological safety." Edmondson studies teams and has shown that when a group believes they can speak up, ask for help, admit mistakes, propose ideas, take blame, confess uncertainty, and disclose inability, they learn more and perform better.

Consider the teams where you have held back from asking questions, because you did not want to seem stupid. Maybe you made suggestions and felt they were dismissed without any real consideration. You may have been slow to reveal mistakes, even when it would have been useful for others to know about them, because you did not want to be judged negatively. You tried to hide your weaknesses. These are all normal responses to low psychological safety, where interpersonal fear is high. Now think about a team where you were less likely to behave in these ways and notice what changed in your growth and performance. Low psychological safety teams foster fixed mindsets and are less likely to perform well. When a team's psychological safety is high, however, it is easy to imagine how growth mindsets, and performance, will flourish.

Edmondson finds that the most important influence on psychological safety is one's manager.* For Brittany, Perrin's behavior was critical. As he had done with the topic of autism, Perrin

---

* This finding reminds me of the words said to me by a former client manager from my days in consulting, Dave Kuhlman. When we started working together, Dave told me, "There is no mistake you can make that I haven't already made." He made himself vulnerable so that I would be willing to do the same.

decided he had room to grow on the topic of diversity and inclusion. This topic and situation was more threatening to his identity than autism. In fact, self-threat could not have been higher on a topic like racism and sexism and therefore the importance of his work-in-progress mindset could not have been greater. His mindset would shape what he did and what he learned during this time of controversy and crisis.

Consider what happened when researchers created a high-self-threat situation in a lab experiment. They tested participants on their general knowledge and then put electrodes on their heads to measure their attention levels to the feedback on their performance. The electrodes measured event-related brain potential, which reveals how much attention people are giving to particular tasks and information. Participants in a fixed mindset paid close attention when told which answers were right versus wrong, but when they were given the chance to learn by seeing the correct answers, they tuned out. Participants in a growth mindset paid close attention to both types of information. In other words, they were willing to learn.

Perrin had essentially been told he got the answer wrong. In a fixed mindset, he would tune out, while in a growth mindset, he would tune in. In her book *Teaming*, Edmondson recommends that leaders foster psychological safety by acknowledging the limits of their current knowledge, displaying fallibility, highlighting failures as learning opportunities, and inviting participation. If Perrin did, it would liberate Brittany to do the same.

"Before season four, the conversations [about race- and gender-type issues] weren't at the level that I would have preferred them to be," Brittany says. "Now, I genuinely feel like I can have an open dialogue about race [and gender]. I've worked and lived and gone to school in places where that hasn't been the case. What happened with season four opened that door even further. It doesn't mean that they're always going to understand immediately but they will put in the work to understand. That way, I can meet them halfway." This sharing of responsibility so that people from marginalized groups are not always doing all of the work is critical.

Together, Perrin and Brittany scoured Twitter feeds, read think pieces, and reflected on their role in unintentionally replicating the problem they were trying to address. "We had to take a step back, listen, not get defensive, and try to take the lessons learned and apply them to the next thing," Brittany says. At a time when an either/or mindset would have doomed them to a defensive stance, they tried to stay in their work-in-progress mode. Brittany says, "Perrin is a great listener. He did a ton of reading and listening and talking with people. It is so easy to get defensive and say 'Well, we tried. All these people are mad for no reason.'"

When people are angry at you, activating a growth mindset is critical to learning why they are angry. It is easy to write off the anger as sour grapes, as Brittany pointed out. This defensive dismissal—typical in a fixed mindset—is unwise. Research shows that people are far more willing to accept bad outcomes if they view the outcomes as fair. A funny example lies in a TED Talk by biologist Frans de Waal about the moral life of animals. Capuchin monkeys behave in many humanlike ways and thus are a popular way of studying humanlike behavior. In the video, researchers work with capuchins trained to exchange a rock for a food reward. One capuchin dutifully exchanges a rock for a cucumber and happily eats the cucumber. Then the researcher moves to the next capuchin and switches to a sweeter and juicier reward, a grape. The first capuchin sees the whole thing, tries for a grape, and once again is given a cucumber. The now-furious capuchin shakes the bars of the cage and throws things at the researcher. It was not about the grape; it was about the inequity.

As believers, we know that inequity is real in this country. Inequity triggers anger. Therefore, anger is a natural response from people from marginalized groups—whether they be women, or people of color, or gay people, or immigrants. However, the resulting anger can generate heat and self-threat. It can confuse or shut down fixed mindset observers.

As builders, our opportunity is to learn from this anger, not to recoil from or "tone police" it. When people are expressing anger about something being unfair, consider listening with the intent to grow from what you hear. Even if the anger makes you uncomfortable, do not let it stop you from listening. Perrin and Brittany understood that they had things to learn from the anger.

When Growth Mindsets Matter the Most

It would have been tempting for Perrin to defer to Brittany, which happens so often in organizations. "They didn't put it on me as the woman of color. In fact, they were really cognizant of avoiding a whole 'Brittany knows the answer' or 'Let Brittany go figure out this diversity thing' type of approach." This leadership move was important, as it signaled that the problem was everyone's to fix. It is at these moments when mindset shapes leadership response. In a fixed mindset, a leader might feel pressure to have all the answers rather than be a work-in-progress. So, rather than risk being exposed, he or she pushes the problem to someone else, or denies the problem. When psychological safety is needed most, a fixed mindset approach from leadership will shut it down.

Just as Perrin had activated a growth mindset to learn about autism, he needed to activate a growth mindset to learn about bias. "There are things in Hollywood that a lot of people have just taken for granted, or not thought about," he says. "People like me, I should say. Blind spots in our own life experiences, our own perspectives, and how those perspectives inform our actions and what we do. We saw that, as well intentioned as we were, this is a systemic problem and it's something we need to figure out how to better address if we are going to continue to do this."

When it comes to issues like bias, it is more likely than not that our mindset will be fixed. In our national discourse, we stick to either/or labels: racist or not, sexist or not, homophobe or not, good person or not. The goal is to dodge the negative label. The psychology of good-ish people says otherwise. Our bounded ethicality means that all of us have blind spots. In fact, if you find yourself thinking or saying "I don't think I have any blind spots," then *that* is your blind spot.*

The difference between a fixed mindset and a growth mindset lies in whether we believe we have blind spots. As builders, we should never make claims of not being racists, sexists, etc. These claims are rarely accurate and usually lower our credibility. Rather, we should say, and believe, "I know that I have work to do in this area." That statement, if made with sincerity, reveals movement from a reflexive fixed mindset to a more intentional growth mindset.

When we are in a fixed mindset, we are walking on I'm-a-good-person eggshells. We are in a constant struggle to not say the wrong thing or do the wrong thing. I call this overwhelming feeling the "fixed mindset tax" because it is taxing on our attention. We focus less on the project, person, or policy at hand and more on not being wrong. Furthermore, our preoccupation with not being wrong means that we will not learn from our mistakes, which means we are even *more* likely to be wrong. The fixed mindset tax can be costly.

---

* I am not sure where I first heard this line, but it is advice that I repeat often. Thank you to the unknown original source.

High-stress, high-self-threat moments trigger these reactions. Research shows that we are more likely to try to prove that we are right or to withdraw effort when we are in a fixed mindset and challenged by others. We are then in a worse position when we next say something, second-guessing how it will be received without the insight to help us improve.

In contrast, in a growth mindset, we still make mistakes and we learn from them, which makes mistakes less likely in the future. In a growth mindset, it is possible to make good mistakes. Some people worry that if mistakes are accepted as part of learning, then we give people a free pass to make mistakes. Yet research says that when we view ourselves as works-in-progress, we are more willing to hold ourselves accountable for our actions. We are more likely to apologize to people we have hurt and we offer better, more complete apologies. Accountability is higher, not lower, when we give ourselves room to grow.

Listening to Your Mindset Voice

Thankfully, psychologists such as Carol Dweck and others have tested a host of ways to help us activate a growth mindset. The gist of these interventions lies in listening to what our "mindset voice" tells us about who we are and our capabilities. Let's say you make a comment that you feel is legitimate and inoffensive. To your surprise, people are offended and you are told that your comment is racist. Your fixed mindset voice might lead you to think, "That is ridiculous. I am not a racist. I should have kept my mouth shut. I will just say that I am sorry the other person was offended and get out of this conversation as fast as possible." Try to activate a different voice, which leads you to say, "That was not my intention. Would you be willing to tell me what I did wrong?"

An inspiring example of how to do this well took place on live television in 2016. Heather McGhee, president of the public policy and advocacy organization Demos, often appears on national television providing thought leadership on equity issues. In this segment, McGhee (who is African American) was taking live viewer calls about race. A caller named Garry Civitello from North Carolina said: "I'm a white male. And I'm prejudiced. What can I do to change? To be a better American?"

Such openness to growth on the topic of race is rare. The clip went viral, with more than eight million views. That call started a conversation between McGhee and Civitello that continued long after the show was over. McGhee reports that Civitello has been enjoying the work of renowned black social activist and scholar Cornel West. Learning and growing is the work of builders.

The impact of growth mindset on psychological safety is significant. If Brittany had perceived her team as low in psychological safety, based on Perrin's behavior, she would have been taking a massive career and interpersonal risk to speak openly to her white male boss about race and gender issues. If Perrin had perceived his team as low in psychological safety, he would have been far less likely to discuss his blind spots with a black female subordinate. While reacting to the fallout of season four, Perrin and Brittany could have turned up the psychological safety or shut it down. They had a choice.

Psychological Safety and Experimentation

Adaptive Studios had many projects beyond *Project Greenlight*. As it turned out, they had already been planning to launch something new the day after the final airing of *Project Greenlight*'s season four. The initiative, Project Greenlight Digital Studios

(PGDS), would channel the *Project Greenlight* original spirit and mission into a 24/7 contest engine focusing on emerging talent and emerging technologies. A TV show would not necessarily be part of the equation, allowing for more contests and more experimentation. Brittany had been tapped to run PGDS, long before the fallout of season four. Now, the project's mission made more sense than ever. Brittany realized that the approach would need to be refined to "dig into communities that are often silent or not heard, to find talent which is there and just needs to be nurtured."

The team decided they needed to re-engineer the contest engine, to run more contests, and to leverage the timing flexibility of a digital platform. They did not have to wait for Hollywood gatekeepers to move forward. While the public controversy and spotlight had focused on the show, they saw deeper, more systemic issues. Waiting until people had already applied (or not applied) to create opportunity and access was waiting too long. "We can't just run this contest and after the fact realize, Oh shoot, there are no minorities, there are no queer people," Brittany says. "It doesn't work that way. You have to know where the pain points are and then attack them—hypertarget them—with all your might."

With each subsequent contest, they tried new things. In the first filmmaker contest after *Project Greenlight*'s season four, Brittany noticed an increase in submissions from people of color and women, seemingly from the inspiring impact of Effie Brown's presence and courage. Representation alone had seemed to attract new viewers and new contest participants. The winners were a team of Haitian American filmmakers. "I don't know if our winners, Josh [Jean-Baptiste] and Edson [Jean], would have applied otherwise," Brittany recalls. "And they were, by far, the standout submission."

Next, in the New Normal contest, they partnered with YouTube star-turned-HBO star Issa Rae, who served as the executive producer and face of the contest. As a black woman creator known for challenging the Hollywood status quo, Issa actively promoted the contest to her huge fan base. Like season four, the New Normal contest was an open submission process through a widely available technology platform. Both contests had backers interested in nontraditional and underrepresented voices. Both had a Hollywood outsider-turned-insider at the helm.

Upon closer examination, the New Normal contest reflected key lessons from season four. The New Normal contest put an underrepresented voice at the helm and was explicit in its invitation to specific, underrepresented voices. They did not assume those applicants would find the contest; they went and looked for the applicants. The resulting application pool looked far more like the one they had been hoping for in the season four contest. In the end, the judges selected three female winners—one Asian Canadian, one Indian American, and one African American. The contest brought many new people into the PGDS community, which now leans female, based on social media followership.

PGDS still needs to work on better tracking of their progress. Data collection of contest participation demographics, aside from gender, has been uneven. The eyeball method suggests much progress has been made, but going forward, they are working on developing benchmarks and measurements to accurately track their alignment with their mission. "It's really easy to say 'Yeah, it looks more diverse,' but what does that mean?" Brittany wonders.

Her worry is well founded. For example, my coauthors—Edward Chang, Katherine Milkman, and Modupe Akinola—and I studied the gender balance of corporate boards. Corporate boards are under scrutiny and face pressure to increase gender diversity. To no one's surprise, our analysis found that most boards were predominantly male. But, more surprisingly, we found that many boards had exactly two women on them, more frequently than would happen by chance. Through several studies, we found that what used to be tokenism (one woman) was now "twokenism" (two women). Boards appear to be defining gender diversity through the lens of what the social norm is, rather than through the lens of what would actually constitute gender balance. In this particular context, two women met the social norm, especially relative to past board composition. As Brittany speculated, "looking diverse" does not necessarily mean diversity has been achieved.

Organizational scholar Miguel Unzueta further notes that perceptions of diversity are fluid. What we perceive as diversity does not necessarily line up with the actual numbers because "diversity is what you want it to be." People will perceive a group as more diverse if they tend toward a more hierarchical view of the world. They will perceive a group as more diverse if they are feeling motivated to protect their own group. Members of minority groups will perceive more diversity if their own group is represented, versus if other minority groups are represented. Similarly, Brittany and her colleagues were prone to perceived diversity distorting their true progress. While our categories of race, ethnicity, sexual orientation, gender identity, and more are imperfect and convoluted, they still offer us important measures. The numbers do not tell the whole story and yet they are needed in the story if we are to track the impact of the work.

The Adaptive Studios team also concluded that marketing and outreach to underrepresented communities require money and resources. Finding new voices would require a committed search. Brittany stresses that money is needed for targeted marketing through social media, film schools, community-specific presentations, and production budgets, as well as cash to help with liquidity, relocation support, and an attractive prize purse for contestants and winners.

We Need to Find, and Center, Our Partners

The team reached another critical conclusion: They needed partners. "It's really important that we don't center ourselves and pat
ourselves on the back for our efforts," Brittany says. "It's important to center the people who are representatives of that group.
We're not saying or doing anything that people of underrepresented groups haven't been talking about forever."

Perrin explains his view on partnerships. "For me, being white,
being male, being straight, it was very important that we find
partners and that they were well represented in terms of making
the right decision on what content we greenlight. A lot of Hollywood is driven by ego and power and all of those things, and
our approach is almost the exact opposite. We would rather lead
with great material and great partnerships and be good long-term
partners."

Enter Allie Esslinger. In 2015, she was working in the indie film
space as the founder of a digital streaming platform and content
creator network called Section II. Section II, named after a law
that once outlawed portrayals of homosexuality in film, was Allie's
response to the dearth of LBTQ women in film. For example, in
2014, 1,633 films were released, only 6 of which featured LBTQ
women. Allie described Section II to me as "Netflix for lesbians."

While season four was unfolding amid great public scrutiny,
Allie sensed through Perrin's social media comments that he was
listening with an intention to learn, not to defend or dodge. At
this point in her career, Allie had tried to explain the goals of
Section II to many straight white men in power positions like
Perrin. It had not gone well. She was used to pushback or su-
perficial responses ("Maybe you should try to reach out to Ellen
[DeGeneres]"). She typically braced herself for disappointment or

for empty PR-driven promises. Nonetheless, she decided to reach out to Perrin via Twitter. To Allie's surprise, Perrin wrote back immediately and suggested they meet.

"A lot of times, it's really hard to explain or tell a story to someone who isn't affected by the outcomes of the story, but he got it," Allie recalls. "He asked a lot of questions, but he didn't question the philosophical or business validity of what it means to have better representation, in front of and behind the camera. He sees entertainment as transformative."

Perrin saw the meeting with Allie as an opportunity to learn and partner in new ways. "We rolled up our sleeves and talked to leaders of different communities, saying 'This is our intent. Help us think about a contest or think about a greenlighting process that would benefit your community.'" Both Perrin and Allie came away from the conversation feeling hopeful, and Perrin introduced Allie to Brittany.

Allie feels timing worked in her favor, on the heels of great cost to others. "I got the benefit of the mistakes they made on *Project Greenlight*," she says. "I think that must have been a traumatic experience for Effie. No one wants to be someone else's learning curve. I benefited from their desire to do better after that."

One year later, Section II and Project Greenlight Digital Studios launched the See Yourself filmmaker competition. Absent the lessons of season four, they do not think they would have done this contest. In marketing the competition, PGDS used the normal film and indie film trade magazine outlets. They also designed specific outreach efforts at LGBTQ film festivals like Outfest, using Section II's database of filmmakers, and in media outlets like *The Advocate*. By launching the contest at Outfest, they hoped to center people from the target community, not themselves. The result was a dialogue within (rather than outside and about) the community.

The outreach effort showed up in the submissions. At least 20 percent of the people who were present at the event applied for the competition. PGDS reports that they saw more women, people of color, and LGBTQ submissions than in the past.

As always, there were more lessons to learn. While their applicant pool had more LGBTQ applicants than previous contests, male applicants still dominated. "We had more of the elements in place with the judging panel and the outreach, but . . ." Brittany's voice trails off. "I think the targeting was still too broad. Were we targeting queer women, particularly knowing that they tend to be underrepresented? It's so many layers and layers and you really have to crack open each one. We haven't even scratched the surface."

The result has been a series of contests over the past two years, each experimenting with new forms of judging, outreach, mentorship, and selection. Perrin reflects, "I'm really proud of what we've been able to do, but it really is an evolving process. I often say in the best way I can, we are stumbling upward."

How to Activate Your Growth Mindset

Everyone stumbles. Let's say someone suggests that you have said or done something racist or sexist or homophobic, or you are wrestling in your own mind with something you might have done. Be on the alert for the fixed mindset voice declaring: "I'm not a racist!" When this happens, you are probably slipping into an either/or mindset. If you find yourself telling others how you support people from marginalized groups, that is another possible sign of a fixed mindset (especially if the people you are telling this to are from a marginalized group). If you keep repeating what you "really" meant, that is another possible sign.

When you activate a growth mindset voice, you are more likely to respond, "I don't really understand what I did wrong, but I would like to understand," or to take the time to figure it out on your own. You are more likely to apologize by saying "I am sorry, I was wrong" than by saying "I am sorry you were offended," which points the finger at the other person for taking offense rather than at ourselves for delivering the offense. In a growth mindset, you are more likely to accept that your apology may not erase the damage done, and to refrain from reburdening the other person by asking them to make you feel better or put their anger aside. If these are new ways of responding, you may feel uncomfortable. Keep trying. Like all habits, these get easier with practice.

As builders, we are ready to look at ourselves as individuals who carry unconscious biases and examine ourselves as part of systems in which biases are baked in culturally, legally, and structurally. To confront both unconscious and systemic bias, we will need to keep our growth mindsets activated.

2

One of the "Good Guys"

At first glance, Rick Klau seems like the prototypically successful, straight, white Silicon Valley guy. He has had a bunch of cool jobs at Google, including working on their Blogger, Google+, and YouTube products. He is now a partner at an offshoot of Google called GV (formerly Google Ventures) that invests in and helps launch tech startups.

Rick's work straddles two industries that many people want to break into: venture capital and technology. He hires, manages, and evaluates the potential and performance of many ventures and people. In that capacity, Rick says, "I felt strongly that women and underrepresented minorities should have equal opportunities in the workplace. And I would have told you that, as someone in a position to hire people, I had done a good job of ensuring equal opportunities. I would have told you that I was one of the good guys." Like so many of us, Rick is a believer.

Unconscious Bias

I first met Rick at a conference hosted by Google. His humor and warmth saved me from that awkward moment when you stand alone at a conference, wondering if you can still flag down the taxi that just dropped you off. While we collected our name tags and chatted casually, Rick asked me about my research. When I said "unconscious bias," the look on his face said that the small talk was now transitioning into big talk. Rick looked at me with sincerity and said, "Unconscious bias training changed my life. Literally." I do not hear that every day, especially from straight white guys.

The change began when Rick's boss insisted that he and his peers attend an unconscious (sometimes, also called implicit) bias training. Google, like many organizations, was (and is) trying to address the overwhelming whiteness and maleness of their organizations. Some companies have been shamed by the media. Some have been condemned by the courts. Some are motivated by the performance benefits of diversity or winning a war for scarce talent. Some simply want to do the right thing. Few organizations can afford to be complacent.

Rick told me about his experience. At first, he did not think he needed the training. As a team player, he still went to the session, not expecting much, given that he was already a believer when it came to diversity and inclusion issues.

The session was not what he expected. He learned about the automatic, mental shortcuts needed for the human mind to process the eleven million bits of information received every moment. Of those, we only consciously process forty bits of information, meaning that 99.999996 percent of our mental processing takes place on an unconscious level.

Some of that unconscious processing includes implicit biases. Rick took the Implicit Association Test (IAT) and received his implicit bias score. The web-based IAT was developed by the world's experts in unconscious bias, psychologists Mahzarin Banaji, Anthony Greenwald, and Brian Nosek. Anyone with access to a computer and an Internet connection can easily and anonymously take it at https://implicit.harvard.edu.* Millions of people have taken the IAT on this public website.

Taking the test is like playing a video game in which you need to be both fast and accurate. The goal is to quickly categorize words and pictures, with less than a second allowed for each response. There is little time to think, which is the point. The test is not measuring what you would do if you had the time to think it over. It is measuring what your brain associates with what when you are on autopilot.

To illustrate, let's say that when I say Romeo, your brain immediately goes to . . . Juliet. I say twinkle twinkle . . . you think little star. I say peanut butter . . . you think jelly. Now what if I try to get your brain to do something different. When I say peanut butter, I ask your brain to say . . . mayonnaise. Your brain slows down to sort things out. Maybe your brain still thinks jelly, despite your attempt to override it. (Your brain also prays that you are not planning a PB&M sandwich for lunch.)

It is this extra hundred milliseconds or so that the IAT captures. The IAT Rick took did not actually use words like "peanut butter" and "jelly." It used words and pictures related to common gender stereotypes. In the Gender IAT, the test taker is asked to associate words like "male" and "female" with words related to family and career, or math and the arts. There are many IATs available on different topics. Regardless of topic, they all use this same basic structure of hundreds of rapid-fire rounds of associ-

---

* When you visit the IAT website, sign in as a guest (no need to register or give your personal information, if you choose not to). Then, when you see the list of possible IATs, look for one that relates to a cause close to your heart. The website is being improved and expanded constantly, but at the time of this printing, you could find IATs on race, religion, disability, gender, sexual orientation, and skin tone (as well as many other topics). The test takes about ten minutes, ideally uninterrupted and with a good Internet connection. You will receive a score at the end. In a perfect world, take it more than once, perhaps a day or two apart, but at the very least, take it once.

ations, half of which support a common stereotype and half of which reverse a common stereotype. In the Black-White Race IAT, the test taker is associating "black" and "white" with words related to good and bad, or violence and intelligence.

When Rick took the IAT, he would have been pecking away at his keyboard quickly. Someone watching him would not have been able to distinguish between his 600-millisecond responses versus his 500-millisecond ones. The test would capture that difference, and it is possible Rick might also feel the extra effort required with some of the trials. After Rick finished the test, the IAT algorithm would compute his score based on both his speed and his accuracy.

Rick did not like his Gender IAT score. Like more than 75 percent of us (myself included), he was faster at associating women with things related to family and home and slower at associating women with things like career and work. On the flip side, he was slower at associating men with things like family and home. This implicit result directly contradicted his explicit egalitarian gender beliefs. He emerged "spooked."

In fact, our explicit and implicit attitudes are related, though not with a 1:1 correlation. Socially charged topics are where explicit and implicit attitudes typically diverge. One way to think about this difference is to think of explicit beliefs as what we cling to as believers. Our work as builders reflects both explicit and implicit beliefs, which is where Rick hit a snag. The correlation between our explicit and implicit attitudes on topics like gender and race in the United States tends to hover around 0.3. This is roughly the correlation between height and income. That is, the two are positively, loosely related. A correlation of this magnitude suggests that most of us have implicit attitudes that differ from the beliefs we consciously understand ourselves to hold.

Consider that 70 to 75 percent of all people who take the IAT in the United States show implicit race bias. They are more likely to associate white with good and with harmless objects, and black with bad and with weapons. Among white Americans, the percentage is around 85. Even now, it is hard to imagine a twenty-first-century America in which three-quarters of Americans openly express explicit race bias. So, explicit and implicit race biases can and do diverge.

Furthermore, our implicit associations have important implications for managerial and other real-world behaviors, as detailed in the excellent research summary "The Existence of Implicit Bias Is Beyond Reasonable Doubt." In this comprehensive paper by psychologist John Jost and colleagues, the authors refute ideological and methodological objections some have raised, using empirical data, and highlight ten studies they say "no manager can ignore." Our behavior seems most prone to our implicit biases when we are under great time pressure or stress. Even when we are more deliberative, we may not realize the extent to which we form judgments based on implicit biases. Rick's implicit gender beliefs could affect who he hires, whose potential he bets on, whose emotional response he trusts, whose ideas he values, and who he views as leadership material. Despite his explicit gender belief, it could affect his perception of men who do take paternity leave and women who don't take maternity leave. While he could not know for sure whether his implicit associations were leaking into his behavior, there was enough research about the relationship between implicit associations and behavior on an aggregate level to make him worry.

Some readers will not see the problem with Rick's results and any potential effect on his behavior. Some people are comfortable with both explicit and implicit gender beliefs that associate women with family and men with office work. Those people do not include Rick (or me). The issue here is not whether you or I would be upset by Rick's Gender IAT results. He was. His moral identity was at stake. Self-threat flooded his mind.

Rick remembers resisting the conclusion that he was part of the problem. I have taught many unconscious bias workshops like the one he attended. Participants frequently question the test and its results, either directly or subtly. Initial resistance is natural. Even when I take the IAT, after administering and studying it for years, I have the same visceral response when my implicit results contradict my explicit beliefs. I really want the result to be wrong. What happens next is a choice between growth and fixed mindsets.

Much as I want to deny it, I have seen my own implicit biases affect people I love. For more than a decade, I have mentored a young first-generation immigrant, Fiona Rodriguez.* Not only will she be the first in her family to graduate from college, she was the first in her family to graduate from *high school*. One day, I attended parent-teacher conferences with Fiona's mother. Fiona's science teacher and I agreed on Fiona's aptitude for science and potential for a career in health care. Enthusiastically, we talked over each other, both saying, "She would be an amazing . . ." We finished our sentence simultaneously, in the exuberant way of people thinking the same thing at the same time, except we were not thinking the same thing. The teacher said "doctor" and I said "nurse."

Wait, what? Both are admirable professions, worthy of her consideration. Yet I had unconsciously stereotyped Fiona, because she is Hispanic and female, as a nurse, not as a doctor. This reality is not changed by the fact that I am a female person of color or that my children have had a female Puerto Rican pediatrician since birth or that I am deeply invested in Fiona's future. Regardless, my unconscious biases leaked into my thoughts and actions.

---

* At her request, not her real name.

Some key questions remain in implicit bias research. As with all science, our knowledge evolves with each new study. Here is what we know so far, as of this writing. First, unconscious bias is both sticky and malleable, meaning it reacts in momentary ways to what is happening in the mind and world of the bias holder and it fluctuates within what appears to be a fairly stable range for each individual. Second, we also know, from the research, that these unconscious biases can leak into microaggressions and behaviors that are consequential in the real world. Some of these behaviors are subtle but meaningful, such as nonverbals and perceptions of others. How far we sit from someone, how long we smile, whether we make eye contact, whether we perceive them as angry—these are all examples of subtle, meaningful nonverbal behavior. Other behaviors may be more directly consequential, such as the people we promote and the medical treatments we deliver.

The IAT and implicit bias were initially controversial and, as a result, are the most carefully studied measures and concepts in modern psychology. The scrutiny has been good for the science, with careful testing and retesting. As a result, many of the concerns raised by Rick, and me, and most test takers, have been carefully studied and addressed through the natural course of science and peer review. Rick's analytical mind was eventually satisfied with the science and the method, which is widely accepted by the majority of the scientific community.

From the start, the creators of the IAT have repeatedly stated that no single individual—including Rick—can or should look at one IAT score and draw a grand conclusion. The creators of the test consistently refuse to endorse any use of the IAT for individual-level, high-stakes decisions, such as jury selection, courtroom deliberations, or employment. They have held a steadfast stance that no single taking of the test for any single individual can be scientifically tied to a specific behavior. In aggregate, the data is useful for looking at trends across a population. Individuals can use their IAT scores as a first step, not a last step, in examining how implicit bias might manifest itself in their work and world, which is precisely what Rick did.

Getting to Work

Given that Rick is an influential voice with an influential job at an influential company, people probably *really* want to be in his network. So he started there. Opening up his laptop and phone, he scrolled through his contacts. The list was too long to count by hand, so he automated the process. He found software that analyzes people's names and profile information to compute gender stats. He ran his contact list through the software. To his dismay, only 20 percent of the people in his contact list were women.

Next, he reviewed his connections on Twitter and LinkedIn. Social media posts are a meaningful form of influence in the technology space. Rick tweets often, on a range of topics. He has approximately 25,000 Twitter followers and follows about 2,500 people, some of whom he retweets, amplifying their voices. He fed the list of the people he follows into the gender recognition software. He shook his head at the results. The ratio was the same: 20 percent.

He sifted through his online calendar, looking for industry panels he had sat on. He found panel after panel composed of only men. His contacts and calendar looked so different from who he really was. What he believed and what he built did not match.

One evening, he read a popular rhyming book aloud to his young daughter, only to realize that he had to substitute "girl" for "guy" multiple times in the story. He recalled a conversation with a female colleague who had challenged him not to refer to women as "guys." He had dismissed it with a roll of the eyes. Ever since the IAT, ever since that 20 percent result, he was noticing things that he had missed, or rolled his eyes at, before.

Remember, Rick hired women. He promoted women. He was a believer. His moral identity was tied to being one of the good guys. He *is* a good guy. As psychology has taught us, the unconscious mind is doing the lion's share of our mental work. Our unconscious biases, those attitudes and stereotypes outside of our awareness, may or may not align with our consciously held beliefs.

In her outstanding book *Why Are All the Black Kids Sitting Together in the Cafeteria?*, psychologist Beverly Daniel Tatum describes how these unconscious associations are shaped by what she calls "smog." We breathe in these cultural associations, whether we consciously believe in them or not. Do you remember how you first came to associate peanut butter with jelly? While Rick's explicit beliefs are egalitarian, he breathes in the same cultural biases as everyone else, which may help to explain his contacts, calendar, and eye rolls.

What makes the cultural smog so damaging is its invisibility. A striking example of this can be found in our own marriages. In my research with management scholars Sreedhari Desai and Arthur Brief, we studied how men's attitudes toward working women are affected by the roles of their wives. We found that men with stay-at-home wives undergo a negative change in their (explicit) attitudes toward women in their workplaces. Surprisingly, these men did not show such negative attitudes toward working women before they got married. In fact, they were no more biased against working women than men who selected dual-career marriages. Our data suggests that the division of labor in the marriage subsequently shaped their views about working women, not the other way around. The change in attitudes came after marriage, not before.

Perhaps this was a conscious belief that only happened to emerge after marriage. Alternatively, we can speculate that these were unconscious associations formed after marriage. Remember peanut butter and jelly? Similarly, these men may have unintentionally formed an association between "working women" and "bad." The association was not necessarily because the husband consciously believed it. Nonetheless, within the totally legitimate personal choices of his marriage, the association was made and carried into his workplace views.

Smog surrounds even those of us who are in or care deeply about the stereotyped groups. Our research shows that women, as a whole, show stronger implicit gender bias than men. Black Americans are just as likely to show pro-white implicit race bias as pro-black implicit race bias. These are painful results and it is not unusual for my workshops to prompt tears and anger. A woman who self-identifies as a feminist and working mother is angered by her implicit gender bias score. A black man committed to social justice work weeps when he sees his implicit race bias score. A lesbian woman shakes her head in disbelief at her implicit biases about gay people. Our identities do not necessarily protect us from the smog.

Rick did an audit in which he bypassed the internal debate about whether or not he was unconsciously biased and moved his thought exercise to wondering how and where unconscious bias might show up in his job. Based on his audit, Rick was convinced that he had work to do. He actively sought out connections with people who "didn't look" like him. He shifted the gender ratio of people with whom he interacted on social media. He made himself vulnerable by making that ratio publicly available and by publicly committing to change. He declined invitations to all-male panel discussions and suggested alternatives. He stopped referring to mixed-gender groups as "guys."

Rick knew he was not the only "good guy" with an unconscious bias and 20 percent problem. So he rolled out the unconscious bias training to all of the hundreds of companies in the GV portfolio. He even had the sessions recorded and posted publicly on You-Tube. He encouraged others to take the IAT, study their contacts, and analyze their calendars.

He shared what he was learning in online articles, blogs, and frequent tweets. He shared his slipups and his progress. He took a strong stand that we all could do better. "A funny thing happens when you engage with more women. You become more aware of their experiences, more conscious of their challenges. Read one headline about online harassment and you might think it is an isolated case—follow hundreds of women, you'll learn just how common it is." So he took it upon himself to speak up online about the issues. Ironically, he seemed to face less Internet vitriol than many do when wading into discussions of race and gender. He could not help but notice that he, a white male, was rarely harassed.

The Case for Diversity

For Rick, as a believer, the effort was worthwhile. Did it also make good business sense? The answer hinges, in part, on whether diversity is important to performance. The leading scholar on this question, management scholar Katherine (Williams) Phillips, acknowledges the challenges. In 1998, she and organizational scholar Charles O'Reilly analyzed eighty studies examining the relationship between diversity and performance. Based on the research conducted at that point, they concluded that diversity can "cause discomfort, rougher interactions, a lack of trust, greater perceived interpersonal conflict, lower communication, less cohesion, more concern about disrespect and other problems." So why are people like Rick and so many others putting so much effort into diversity?

Of course, there are legal and public relations motivations. But organizations and individuals motivated only by these concerns are naive, as the economic and performance advantages of diversity are increasingly clear, as Phillips captures in a more recent summary of the research on the topic. Women-run organizations have been shown to be more profitable and racially diverse teams have been shown to be more high-performing. In fact, particularly in organizations where innovation is valued, more inclusive organizations perform better on virtually every measure of success. The list is long: greater innovation, creativity, employee retention, recruiting success, information processing, and bottom-line results. To ignore these well-proven benefits is to be at a competitive and economic disadvantage.

It is intuitive that people with different backgrounds bring different perspectives and ideas, but the positive performance effect suggests that when Rick works with people different from himself, it actually changes how *he* works. The research reveals that he is likely to work harder to process information; he will share unique information more readily; he will generate more nuanced and complex thinking. We not only add different ingredients to the recipe, we also use them in more creative and thoughtful ways. The business case for diversity is substantial.

For many of us, probably including Rick and definitely including me, you can put aside the legal, PR, and business case for diversity. The motivation is more personal. While I believe the business case for diversity is robust, it also makes me uneasy. If a company's clients do not want a gay or nonwhite or female or transgender person working with them, some would argue there is a business case for hiring fewer people from those groups. Relying exclusively on the business case for diversity corners us into the status quo, because some of the revenue we earn as a business will always come from people who do not want things to change. The business case for diversity should be part of our motivation for moving from believer to builder, not all of it.

For many of us, the moral case for diversity is the most robust and reliable of all. Our moral identity is a vibrant part of who we are. We are not always aware of ways in which we are not being the person we mean to be, but once we are made aware, we feel like Rick. We want to do something. We do not want to be known merely as believers, people who say the right things but do not make those things a reality. However imperfect in our efforts, we want to be good people who do more than only talk and believe. We are motivated to do better and need a place to start.

How to Examine Your Own Unconscious Biases

To start, learn more about your own unconscious biases. Take the Implicit Association Test at https://implicit.harvard.edu. If you have already taken the IAT and remember your results, then you may want to take it again. Because you have activated your growth mindset, you are also now more likely to select the IAT that makes you feel anxious, maybe because you think you will not like your result or because you care so much about that issue. Your growth mindset enables you to go into spaces you might not have been ready for in a fixed mindset.

It also sets you up well for a self-audit. To do this, assume your IAT results are right (even if you do not believe this yet). Then imagine what behaviors, decisions, and judgments in your life would be prone to those biases. My unconscious gender biases show that I associate men with math and work more than I associate women with those things. This infuriates me. If I assume it is true, I can imagine that I would call on men more than women in class and interrupt women more than men. With a teaching assistant's help, I gathered some observations, and sure enough, even when I was being watched, my biases surfaced.

Where might your biases show up? Map it out, based on how you spend your days. If you are a product designer, look at who tests your products and what conferences you attend. If you are an independent tax accountant, look at what assumptions you make about your clients when inquiring about possible deductions and how often you receive inquiries from clients who do not look like you. If you are a physical therapist, look at how you respond to complaints of pain from patients and how much scientific language you use in your explanations. If you are a parent, consider what books you read to your children and what household tasks you expect of them. Our roles will shape where we look for the leakage of our unconscious biases.

We want to understand our unconscious biases and delete the ones we don't like. Unfortunately, researchers have yet to figure out the easy delete solution. Still, we can make different decisions. To correct for my bias, I now make a point not to call on too many men consecutively during class. I sometimes ask students if there is anyone whose hand has been up that I keep missing; often, that hand belongs to a woman. As an individual within a workplace and a world, you can examine how your unconscious biases are perpetuating systems that go against your beliefs.

Many of our unconscious biases show up beyond our minds, in the culture, law, history, and organizations we are a part of. We often think of the system as bigger than and separate from us. The system may be biased, but we are not, we imagine. As with unconscious biases, much is hard to see. Now we are going to look at how we are part of the problem, a step that should be welcome to those who want to be part of the solution. Many of us are part of—even beneficiaries of—systems in surprising ways.

3

If You Are Not Part of the Problem, You Cannot Be Part of the Solution

How difficult was your childhood? Wait, before you answer, read this: "Most social scientists agree that, even today . . . White Americans are advantaged in the domains of academics, housing, healthcare, jobs, and more compared to Black Americans." Now back to that question about your childhood.

If you are white, your answer may depend on whether or not you read the sentence about the advantages of being white before you answered the question about your childhood. Psychologists Taylor Phillips and Brian Lowery found that a white person typically reported an easier childhood when the group advantage for whites was not mentioned. When they read the statement in the paragraph above, they reported a harder childhood, and life.

Of course, their childhoods did not get harder. Nor, the data shows, did their belief in the degree to which group advantage exists change. What did change is whether they believed the group advantage applied to them. Phillips says people actually "rewrote their personal histories." They did not change the events of their lives, but they told themselves a different story about how much and which of those events mattered. The same personal history can be told—and believed—as ranging from a "tough childhood" to a "happy childhood," depending on whether one focuses more on the bad days versus the good days.

The Hard-Knock Life Effect

Phillips and Lowery call this the "hard-knock life" effect. The heart of the effect is the distinction between group (dis)advantage and personal (dis)advantage. Participants were able to simultaneously believe that others in their group were advantaged while also believing they had not had it as easy. We point to our parents' divorce (personal disadvantage) but do not take into account that the divorce might have taken a greater toll if we were black (group disadvantage).

The hard-knock life effect is not unique to white people. It refers to a psychology of privilege, which can affect any group who is motivated to deny a claim that their privilege is unearned or lacking legitimacy. This natural psychology emerges when we fear others will view our advantage as unearned. In one study, wealthy employees were reminded of the advantages of being wealthy in getting health care and legal help. Those same wealthy employees then reported that they worked harder in their jobs than those who were not reminded of their group advantage. Similarly, people who leaned on family connections to get a job reported themselves as equally qualified for the job as those who did not use inside connections. Yet when those same people are told that someone else was hired through inside connections, they evaluate those employees as less qualified.

Our reality distortions even convince ourselves. Researchers find that we actually have an easier time remembering our disadvantages than our advantages. We believe our rewritten personal histories. Self-threat plays a starring role in the hard-knock life effect. When we counter the self-threat by highlighting our personal disadvantage, we give ourselves a cookie.

While the hard-knock life effect appears to be a natural human reaction to being told our group enjoys an advantage, we need not feel defeated. There is an intervention to counter the hard-knock life effect, so that we can have a clearer appreciation of our experiences, both advantageous and disadvantageous. It comes back to cookies. Phillips and Lowery found that participants who reflected on their personal values or a past accomplishment were less likely to rewrite their personal histories and more likely to recognize both group and personal advantage. Other researchers have found that cookies in the form of positive feedback on an intelligence or personality test can also be effective.

So rather than feeling helpless about how our brains work, we can use the science to interrupt this natural reflex. Think about what is important to you. Reflect on your accomplishments. Recall positive feedback you have received. In other words, proactively give yourself the cookie before your cravings send you searching for one.

When you see someone else falling into the cookie-seeking pattern, you have a choice, depending on how you feel that day and how you feel in general about cookie seeking. One choice is to give them the cookie before you try to talk to them about group advantage. Applaud their hard work. Acknowledge their progress. True, some of us will not be in the mood, that day or maybe ever, to concede to cookie seeking. This approach is understandable. The difference between being proactive in affirming others versus not being willing to do so is akin to the light versus heat difference. Neither is better or worse, but should you be willing to hand out cookies, the research suggests they will help the listener hear what you have to say next.

As we move into a discussion about privilege, now is a good time to reflect on the steps you have taken to activate your growth mindset. We are about to make the invisible systems of privilege more visible, which means you are doing something most people have not even tried to do. As self-threat arises, hold that thought in mind.

Systemic Headwinds and Tailwinds

We return to that charged word: privilege. Recall that privilege has a very specific meaning in this context, which is not the same socioeconomic meaning it carries in daily conversation. In this context, privilege may or may not have anything to do with money. Calls to "check your privilege" are intended as calls for greater self-reflection about the ways in which one might have relative advantage related to one's identity.

On college campuses and in school districts and communities around the country, misunderstandings have run rampant. A telling example occurred in an affluent, mostly white Connecticut town that voted two to one in favor of Hillary Clinton over Donald Trump. An essay contest invited high school students to consider the extent and role of white privilege in their lives. While the students seemed comfortable with the topic, some of the town's adults took issue. Comments about race baiting, black privilege, and "what is stopping nonwhites from moving to town" erupted on social media. The contest sparked so much controversy that the story was picked up by the Associated Press and the *New York Times*. The hard-knock life effect was in full force.

Group advantage is perpetuated through systems. Systems are the ways in which things happen, whether on a small, family scale or a large, societal scale. Each of us deals with systems constantly.

Some systems are formal, such as the public transportation system I use to commute to work. Other systems are informal or cultural, such as the chitchat between parents about the best back-to-school supplies for their children. Anything that involves more than one person probably involves a system.

Privilege is about whether cultural, legal, and institutional systems are experienced equally by everyone. The key insight is that many systems privilege some people over others. Scholar and activist Peggy McIntosh, who is white, looked at her own life to craft a list of how white privilege shows up. In her well-known article "White Privilege: Unpacking the Invisible Knapsack," she lists fifty examples. They range from "I have no trouble finding neighborhoods where people approve of our household" to "I can choose blemish cover or bandages in 'flesh' color and have them more or less match my skin."

The concept of privilege is not limited to white privilege. For example, the dress codes of many organizations require someone to be clean-shaven. How is this system experienced by my bearded, turban-wearing husband? Health care often requires long, unpredictable waits in doctors' offices. How is this system experienced by an hourly worker missing work for an appointment? Parents are often invited to events during their children's school day. How is this system experienced by children whose parents and guardians are unavailable during those hours?

Few leading ladies or supermodels have olive skin and thick, curly dark hair. How is this system experienced by my non-blond, non-fair-skinned adolescent daughters? Pictures of significant others are often displayed at work. How is this system experienced by a gay employee with a homophobic supervisor?

Multiple forms of widely used technology (electronic soap dispensers, photo recognition software, and video game consoles) have high fail rates with darker-skinned users, which suggest that some tech companies are not testing their products on a broad range of customers. How is this system experienced by African Americans? Many companies offer cash bonuses to employees who refer friends for potential jobs. How is this system experienced by employees whose networks do not "fit" in at the company? In other words, just as white privilege is the underpinning of systemic racism, other forms of privilege create systemic forms of other types of isms and phobias. All of these systemic differences are examples of privilege.

One of the best-documented examples of a system that treats different groups of people differently is the American criminal justice system. Stunning amounts of data reveal that the whiter and/or wealthier a person is, the more favorable the system will be. This data is so vast that it is difficult to summarize. One stark example: Psychologist Jennifer Eberhardt finds that more stereotypically black-looking people are more likely to get the death penalty. In her influential book, *The New Jim Crow*, legal scholar Michelle Alexander has meticulously documented the legalized ways in which this white and wealth privilege is baked into our systems of law and law enforcement. Despite this trove of data, many remain unconvinced that the system is privileged for some groups more than for others.

Have you ever flown east-west versus west-east in the United States? You may have noticed a difference in flight times. It takes as much as forty additional minutes to go from New York to L.A. versus L.A. to New York, for example. The difference lies in the headwinds one faces going west versus the tailwinds going east.

Antiracist educator and author Debby Irving uses an often-cited headwinds and tailwinds metaphor to explain the invisibility of these systemic, group-level differences. Headwinds are the challenges—some big, some small, some visible, some invisible—that make life harder for some people, but not for all people. When you run against a headwind, your speed slows down and you have to push harder. You can feel the headwind. When you have a tailwind pushing you, it is a force that propels you forward. It is consequential but easily unnoticed or forgotten. In fact, if you are like me when I jog with a tailwind, you may glow with pride at your great running time that day, as if it were your own athletic prowess. When you have the tailwind, you will not notice that some runners are running into headwinds. They may be running as hard as, or even harder than, you, but they will appear lazier and slower to you. When some of them grow tired and stop trying, they will appear self-destructive to you.

The invisibility of headwinds and tailwinds leads us to vilify people facing headwinds. It is no coincidence that the groups facing great headwinds in our society are also the most negatively stereotyped. Psychologist Susan Fiske and her colleagues have analyzed a wide range of stereotypes and found that they have a common set of features, which break down into two dimensions: warmth and competence. These two dimensions produce a two-by-two matrix: low versus high competence and low versus high warmth. Someone who is viewed as a competitive threat is considered low warmth versus someone who is viewed as a communal being, who is considered high warmth. Someone who is viewed as low in status is considered low competence while someone who is respected is considered high competence.

Low competence/low warmth groups tend to be ignored or attacked by others. Fiske and her colleagues found that stereotypes of blacks, homeless people, and drug addicts fall into this category. Disgust is the most common emotion people express toward groups in this category. Our failure to see systemic headwinds and tailwinds in the world around us leads us to blame the people facing the headwinds.

As a result, we confuse equality and equity. Equality says we treat everyone the same, regardless of headwinds or tailwinds. Equity says we give people what they need to have the same access and opportunities as others, taking into account the headwinds they face, which may mean differential treatment for some groups. We see a meritocracy where one does not exist.

This illusion of meritocracy gets even stronger over time. We're about to look at how multiple headwinds and tailwinds unfold over time and accumulate across generations. To do this, we will consider a family who may remind you of families you know. This is a blended case study, based on three real individuals.* It gives us a glimpse into family histories shared by a significant portion of Americans and an understanding of how systemic forces operate and accumulate over time.

The Bootstrap Narrative

Colleen had her own room and computer growing up in the 1980s, as did her siblings. Her family took both "fun" (e.g., Disney) and educational (e.g., Washington, D.C.) vacations. She attended "good" schools and grew up in a "good" neighborhood. She had friends from school and the neighborhood, almost all of whom were white like her.

Colleen's father was a regional sales manager for a components company. Her mother was a nurse who stopped working outside the home when Colleen and her siblings were born. She helped with homework and drove the children to sports and other extracurricular activities. Colleen worked occasional babysitting and part-time jobs, scheduled around family vacations and her social

---

* Colleen is a composite of three anonymous individuals, each of whom is a descendant of a white WWII veteran who benefited from the GI Bill (all of the quotations are from a single individual).

life. Colleen recalls, "We had tons of books, tons of activities, and from a young age, college and postcollege degrees were an expectation."

This upwardly mobile life did not come easily. Colleen's maternal grandparents were born into immigrant families and faced great struggles. When their families originally arrived in America, they were met with overt bias and discrimination. They eventually stopped speaking their native language and married people from other groups, blending into white America. Colleen grew up with stories of how her grandparents and parents had pulled themselves up by their bootstraps. "Part of my growing up and loving America is this narrative that everyone is created equal and everyone has opportunity," she explains. She embraced the bootstrap narrative and all it implied about meritocracy.

One of Colleen's grandfathers served in the U.S. armed forces, where he made great sacrifices for his country. Thankfully, when he returned alive from World War II, his service qualified him for the GI Bill (formerly known as the Servicemen's Readjustment Act of 1944). The GI Bill was passed by Congress less than three weeks after D-day. This legislation was enacted to help military veterans rapidly adjust to civilian life. Five million new low-interest/zero-down-payment mortgages allowed veterans to buy their first homes and move to a new thing called the suburbs. Loans with low interest rates generated two hundred thousand new businesses. More than eight million veterans, including Colleen's grandfather, attended college or technical school for free. The number of college graduates in America tripled within a generation.

Because of the tailwinds of the GI Bill, Colleen's family, and many others, fast-tracked into middle-class America. Vast data shows that owning assets (such as a home) or holding a college diploma moves the starting point forward for future generations.

Colleen's great-grandparents had determined the starting point for her grandparents. Via the GI Bill, Colleen's grandparents then moved that starting point far forward for her parents, and her parents moved that starting point forward once again for Colleen. The tailwinds grew stronger with every generation.

In high school, Colleen was a high achiever. Her school selected her to attend a statewide student leadership conference. There, she found herself informally debating the merits of affirmative action with another participant. Colleen remembers thinking, "I don't even understand what she is saying. If everyone is equal, then everyone is equal." Colleen argued passionately that slavery had ended in 1865 and the civil rights movement had ended racism in the 1960s. After all, her family proved the American dream was possible for anyone willing to pull themselves up by their bootstraps. When the other girl argued that the dream was more attainable for white families than black families, Colleen doubled down on her descriptions of her family's hard-knock life.

Meanwhile, Colleen's college-educated parents had earned enough and saved enough for her college education. They would not qualify for need-based financial aid. Colleen remembers resenting that some students with the same qualifications as her would pay less tuition. She ended up attending a college that offered her a full tuition ride. She was proud of her merit-based scholarship, which reflected her academic and extracurricular accomplishments in high school.

Her parents paid for her room, board, and other living expenses allowing her to focus on schoolwork, extracurriculars, volunteer work, and friends. She occasionally drank alcohol (with a fake ID), but never worried about legal consequences. She did not have a part-time job or commute to school. Her parents owned their home and earned enough to save for their retirement, so she did not worry about supporting them or her siblings now or later.

She also did not need to navigate college on her own. Her college-educated parents knew the ins and outs of higher education. If needed, they were able to encourage her to meet with an undergraduate adviser, or drop a course, or enroll in a summer session. Even if Colleen had a bad semester, they knew enough to help her contain the damage.

After college, Colleen was debt-free, so she could pay for many of her living expenses. Occasionally, she turned to her parents for help with security deposits, first and last months' rent, and a place to stay in between leases, which allowed her to live in apartments she might not have been able to afford. She drove her mother's old car, and she also received generous holiday gifts that helped pay for work clothes.

As a naturally curious person, Colleen went into her first job as a teacher in an underserved community eager to learn. She remained committed to the bootstrap narrative, but also knew that she was "going into a community where no one looked like me and I didn't look like anyone else. Even as a twenty-two-year-old, I knew that I needed to listen and I needed to learn."

Colleen's growth mindset would prove pivotal. Despite the poverty she expected to see in the community, she also found beauty and humanity. She found many people working as hard as her grandparents and parents to build a better life for their children, but the bootstrap narrative did not seem to apply. A few "made it," but many seemed to struggle with no reward.

She rattled off some of what she saw. "I realized that the barriers facing these kids and families were ridiculous. Some of it was historical and some of it was happening right now." Kids went to schools that lacked libraries and sat in classes with thirty or more kids. They were more likely to know someone incarcerated than a college graduate. Parents worked two or three minimum-wage jobs and still did not earn enough money to cover their rising living expenses. Older siblings took care of younger siblings while their parents worked, leaving limited time for academic or extracurricular activities.

Law enforcement appeared quick to stop, search, and arrest members of the community, but slow to help when they were in need. Minor, nonviolent offenses led to arrests rather than the warnings typically given in the community where Colleen had grown up. An arrest for something minor often meant weeks, months, even years in jail awaiting trial, even if that person was innocent, because bail was unaffordable. Previously incarcerated parents had to reveal their records on job applications, making legal employment unlikely, even after their dues to society had been paid. To feed their children, some earned income however they could, risking another arrest. The headwinds were relentless.

Colleen realized that even if everyone in the community had her family's work ethic, they still might not be able to overcome all the headwinds they were facing. Colleen remained in awe of her grandparents and parents and their accomplishments, and yet something about the bootstrap narrative was no longer making sense. "Remember that movie *Sliding Doors* where they showed how the main character's life was changed radically when she made the subway versus missed the subway by mere seconds? What if I had been born black instead of white?" she wondered.

She walked me through her thought experiment: "I began to break this down. This is when I started to see the systemic piece of the story," she says. What if her grandparents had been black? Colleen asked herself.

In his excellent book *When Affirmative Action Was White*, historian Ira Katznelson lays out much of what Colleen's black family would have faced. First of all, her black grandparents would have most likely lived in the South. Three-quarters of the nation's African Americans lived in the South at the close of World War II, due to the fresh legacy of slavery. In fact, her grandparents' grandparents and maybe her grandparents' parents might have been enslaved. In that case, her family would likely have been torn apart as mothers, fathers, and children were bought and sold separately. Her black grandmother's grandmother might have been raped by her white owner and borne his child into slavery.

Her black grandfather would have been far more likely to be rejected from the military than her white grandfather, as blacks were often deemed unsuitable for service. For the sake of argument, she assumed luck was on his side. Her lucky black grandfather would have been allowed to serve his country, would have survived the war, and thus would have been eligible for veteran benefits when he returned home.

The GI Bill offered full tuition for veterans, so he might have tried to go to college. After all, college attendance was a key component in the rise of her middle-class white grandfather. At the time, however, few colleges admitted black students. Those that did imposed highly selective criteria on black applicants. Again, Colleen's black grandfather would have had to be far luckier than her white grandfather, even if he was equally or more qualified for college.

Few black students would have met the extra-stringent admissions criteria and had the good luck to fall into the quota. For those who did, the reception was hostile and threatening. If Colleen's black grandfather had, he would have faced restrictions on where he could walk or eat. He would have been forced to take on the expense and inconvenience of living off campus. He would have been jeered by chants like "2, 4, 6, 8—we won't integrate."

These harsh restrictions and hostile receptions were not limited to colleges in the South. Even in the North or the West, he would have found significant student opposition and de facto segregation. Regardless of which white college he attended, he would not have seen a black professor. In fact, he would have been unlikely to have a white professor who had ever had a black student, classmate, or professor himself. College is difficult for most people. He would have had to be far stronger than most people to adjust to life at a white college.

Colleen wondered if she would have been willing to endure such danger and isolation for an education. She wondered if her real grandfathers would have had the fortitude for such a hostile environment. She could imagine few people who would. Average white people could attend white colleges, but only exceptional and lucky black people (men, for the most part) would be admitted and able to survive them, regardless of who paid the tuition.

Instead, her hypothetical black grandfather may have considered a black college or university. The vast majority of black colleges and universities had fewer than one thousand students, about half the size of today's Colby College in Maine or Connecticut College. They only had room for a fraction of those applying, regardless of qualifications. So Colleen's grandfather might have been one of the twenty thousand black veterans eligible for college, but not lucky enough to find a spot in a black school. In fact, historians estimate that an additional fifty thousand African Americans would have applied, had there been spots.

If he was one of the lucky few who got into one of the overcrowded, underfunded schools, he would not have gotten a PhD or certified engineering degree. None were offered at any black colleges, which had meager offerings in comparison to their white counterparts. Despite all the luck and hard work required to get him to this point, he would still have had very limited resources at the university and very limited options of fields of study—mainly lower-paying fields like education, theology, and various trades.

Maybe he would have tried to purchase a home, a robust predictor of financial security and a widely used benefit by white veterans. However, as historians have carefully documented, the GI Bill was deliberately designed to give states control over who received the benefits. Southern states, in particular, insisted that they determine the eligibility requirements for the loans. The GI Bill was drafted to accommodate the Jim Crow system of segregation in the South and yet appeared to be color-blind legislation on paper.

As a result, of the first 67,000 mortgages insured by the GI Bill, fewer than one hundred were taken out by nonwhites. Many localities excluded black neighborhoods from the loan criteria and excluded blacks from moving into white neighborhoods via deed covenants and discriminatory behavior. Neighborhoods were coded as "greenlined" or "redlined," the latter being those with minority populations.

For example, the "first suburb" emerged when Levitt and Sons innovated mass production of affordable single-family tract homes in 1947, beginning with Levittown on Long Island, which then led to similar suburbs across the country. At one point, they produced thirty-six homes per day. From the start, William J. Levitt designated that the homes could not "be used or occupied by any person other than members of the Caucasian race" and continued to enforce the rule unofficially when the courts outlawed such restrictions. He argued that he was acting in the best interest of his business, because white buyers would be deterred by black neighbors. His view highlights the risks of relying solely on the business case when arguing for diversity. These views were found in lenders and developers in suburbs across the country.

Today, suburbs are overwhelmingly white, with a tight correlation to the greenlining and redlining done decades ago. Such redlining shaped the demographics that persist in the neighborhoods where we live today. As a result of that redlining, Colleen's grandfather would have been unlikely to qualify for a loan to buy a home when he emerged from WWII.

While his white veteran peers fast-tracked into the middle class via education and homeownership, Colleen's black grandfather would have been excluded from these opportunities, even in the best-case outcome, which assumes he was exceptionally talented, resilient, lucky, and hardworking. A black peer of average talent, luck, resilience, and work ethic would be unlikely to have a college education or own a home, while a white peer of similar averageness would be a home-owning college graduate, catalyzing future generations.

Colleen's hypothetical black grandmother would not have fared any better. Like 85 percent of black women of the time, she might have worked in either an agriculture-related or domestic-related job, the only positions open to her. Unfortunately, this meant that she would have been excluded from two of the most important laws of the time: Social Security and minimum-wage laws. By not covering lines of work that were disproportionately populated by people of color, these laws systemically privileged white people. In the 1950s, the laws would be modified to be somewhat more inclusive by allowing farm and domestic workers to qualify for Social Security and minimum wages. Still, these changes did not fully "catch up" those who had been originally excluded or even include all of them. This means that Colleen's black grandmother likely worked long hours for low wages, with little safety net for a rainy day or retirement. Colleen's black parents would likely have had to spend some of their income supporting her grandparents as they aged. Her actual white parents used that money to save for their children's educations and their own retirement.

Where would that leave Colleen today? Colleen speculates, "I can't imagine that a black version of my family would have been able to provide for us materially in the same way that they did. That is neither good nor bad, but it makes me rethink the whole bootstraps story. Did they pull themselves up or were they pulled up?" She tears up a bit. "I love my family. They worked so hard. But if they had been black, there is a much, much lower chance that their hard work would have mattered."

Colleen's thought experiment is important because of its rigor. To understand white privilege, systemic racial bias, and the disadvantages of headwinds, the most useful comparison is between "white me" and "black me." Yes, some African American families overcame the headwinds, at one key juncture after another, but their success does not mean that they would not have gone even further if they were white. Yes, many white families started from very little and faced many obstacles, but their success does not mean that things would not have been even harder if they were black.

The bootstrap narrative ignores the crucial role of headwinds and tailwinds. Colleen says, "I can actually remember what I learned about the GI Bill in high school. It was definitely the American dream narrative. It was about a long-term economic boom, but that is not what happened for all of America." With a quick Internet search, she easily found vast documentation of a more complete and accurate history of the GI Bill, none of which she had learned in school. In recent years, she started tracing the genealogy of her family, which led her to read more about American history. Again, the facts she had not heard growing up were easily found.

Like many of us, Colleen grew up believing in the idea of America as a meritocracy. Headwinds and tailwinds were not part of her thinking. This misunderstanding of her own personal history is consequential, according to studies about how we process our own good fortune and who we blame for the bad circumstances faced by others. In research led by psychologist Chris Bryan, Stanford undergraduates were asked to write about their academic success. Half of them were asked to focus on their good fortune and the other half were asked to focus on their personal merits. The personal merit group was more likely than the good fortune group to support policies such as tougher restrictions on unemployment benefits and college admissions criteria favoring white private-school students with higher test scores from affluent towns over black students with slightly lower scores from a low-income public high school.

What makes this study so fascinating is the malleability of these views. A simple temporary shift in focus from personal merit to good fortune, or vice versa, changed their views on important societal issues. It suggests that being a believer does not immunize us from the meritocracy belief. The visibility of headwinds and tailwinds, even from the past, is critically important to the decisions we make about the present and future.

While writing this book, I was struck by how often I spoke to a white or black American whose stories resembled Colleen's real or imagined family. Some of the white families were financially worse off than Colleen's actual family, with poverty within the past generation. Many had endured great hardships and I felt great compassion for them. Still, I could not help but wonder if they were not *as* worse off as they would have been without the tailwinds.

Colleen's life today reflects those tailwinds. Differences from one generation reverberate into later generations through what philosopher Ron Mallon calls "accumulation mechanisms" that need not even be as significant as the GI Bill. He says that "we know with certainty (from math and formal models) that if we add up a bunch of small things, we can get a big thing." Sociologist Robert Merton calls this the principle of cumulative disadvantage, or the Matthew Effect (named after the rich-get-richer/poor-get-poorer story in the Bible).

Computer simulations illustrate how slivers of bias can lead to huge advantage gaps. Psychologists Richard Martell, David Lane, and Cynthia Emrich ran a computer simulation that assumed an organization of five hundred people for whom performance ratings determined promotions. Half could earn a performance rating on a scale from 1 to 100. Half could earn a performance rating on a scale from 1 to 101; this is the sliver of bias in their favor. The simulation ran through twenty promotion cycles to mimic twenty years in an organization. That teeny advantage made a huge difference in who rose through the ranks. By the end, only 35 percent of the senior employees came from the 1-to-100 group while two-thirds came from the 1-to-101 group. This "meritocracy," with just a sliver of bias, generated exactly the type of systemic effect that disadvantages entire groups in the real world. If such a sliver can create such a gap, imagine what hundreds of years of widespread systemic bias will do.

We can apply this principle to Colleen's family. Even if the world were to become magically egalitarian today—both in terms of systemic and unconscious biases—we would still expect to see Colleen's white family earning more money and living longer lives than Colleen's black family. The differences of the past still form a gap in the present. The differences of the present widen the gap. Colleen had directly benefited from the systems that had privileged her family. Meanwhile, in the popular narrative, her white family was praised for their "hard work" while her black family was vilified for their "laziness."

Colleen began to regret that bootstrap conversation at the high school leadership conference. "I wish I knew that girl's name. I wish I had just asked questions and listened instead of trying to talk. I was a naturally curious person, but my curiosity did not show up in that one moment." The bootstrap narrative had blinded Colleen to the systems narrative.

She is not alone in her way of thinking. In fact, studies have found that people view identical evidence as more convincing when it is paired with a bootstrap narrative than when it is paired with a systems narrative. Reminding people of the bootstrap narrative even leads people at the short end of inequality to defend the inequality. The bootstrap narrative warps our perceptions of ourselves and the world.

Colleen paused, tears filling her eyes. Because fewer of her hypothetical black family members could access benefits, homes, places in college, and so on, she saw that there were more opportunities for her real white family. They benefited as black Americans subsidized white Americans, through both tax dollars and forgone opportunities. Regardless of her family's socioeconomic class, they benefited from the tailwinds at their back and the headwinds slowing down others. Even if Colleen's family did not espouse racism, they had improved prospects because of racism. "In other words," Colleen says, "I am the direct beneficiary of those racist systems."

Demos, a public policy organization focused on issues of equality, set out to quantify those tailwinds. In "The Asset Value of Whiteness," they report that individual differences in education, family structure, full- or part-time employment, and consumption habits did not compensate for a century of accumulated wealth. The study tested whether any or all of these individual choices could "erase a century of accumulated wealth." The answer was no.

Another research study, conducted by the Corporation for Economic Development and the Institute for Policy Studies, considered the role that the accumulation of wealth plays in creating financial security and opportunity across generations. They estimated that, at current rates, it will take black families 228 years to amass the same amount of wealth that white families have now.

Even if we assume that the headwinds and tailwinds of the past have disappeared (which every measure says is not true), we would not expect to see equivalent assets or life expectancies between blacks and whites. In other words, no amount of bootstrapping could make up for the difference something like the GI Bill and multitudes of other tailwinds would have made.

Patriotism à la Carte

Something else was still bothering Colleen. If the bootstrap narrative was so easily disproved, why didn't she know any of this? Her question echoes the work of historiographers. Historiography is the study of how we study history. Historiographers ask whose viewpoints are presented and whose viewpoints are omitted. They examine which events are analyzed for cause and effect and which are simply stated as inevitable. They consider what facts are included and excluded from history books—and why.

In his book *Lies My Teacher Told Me*, scholar James Loewen did an extensive analysis of eighteen popular high school history textbooks (each approximately one thousand pages long). While he did not cover the GI Bill specifically, he analyzed the coverage of racism, which offered clues as to the narrative of the texts. Loewen found that only about half of the books listed racism or a similar term in the index. Only three discussed what might have caused racism. In addition, most of the books "present slavery virtually as uncaused, a tragedy, rather than a wrong perpetrated by some people on others. Somehow we ended up with four million slaves in America but no owners. This is part of a pattern in our textbooks: anything bad in American history happened anonymously."

Additionally, he noticed that textbooks about subjects like chemistry or English or math tended to have neutral, "boring" titles like *Principles of Chemistry*. Almost all of the widely used history textbooks he studied included euphoric language (like "song," "adventure," or "triumph") in their titles. So Colleen's ignorance about the GI Bill was an example of yet another tailwind in how history is told. It was not just that headwinds would have slowed her hypothetical black ancestors; it is also that those headwinds were not described and documented for future generations. The gaps between blacks and whites would appear to have emerged in a meritocracy.

In fact, Colleen's sliding-doors understanding of her family's history only scratches the surface of the systemic racism that would have faced her hypothetical black ancestors. Ta-Nehisi Coates's extraordinary article in *The Atlantic*, "The Case for Reparations," summarizes historical scholarship and provides a comprehensive and compelling overview of what has confronted the previous three generations of African Americans. His in-depth article goes well beyond the narrow set of issues presented in Colleen's story. His conclusion about how we typically encode our past as a nation is withering: "To proudly claim the veteran and disown the slave owner is patriotism à la carte."

Loving America is the most American of things to do. Why does loving America preclude an honest understanding of our history and its influence in our lives? Patriotism à la carte ignores headwinds and tailwinds, which makes it impossible to see the problems we face, which makes it impossible to be part of the solution. Without a systems view, Colleen becomes a deeper part of the problem. She defends and benefits from a system that she does not even see.

How to Go to the Systemic Level

In chapter 2, we traveled with Rick Klau through an individual perspective on how inequality emerges through unconscious bias. In this chapter, we traveled with Colleen through a systemic perspective on how inequality emerges through the group advantages of privilege. These two levels—individual and systemic—are rarely addressed jointly. In fact, the individual perspective dominates our current national dialogue and mental attention. Activist and writer Tim Wise notes that we take greater notice of a single victim of a hate crime than of one million victims of systemic injustice. As journalist Greg Howard wrote, "Racism ceased to be a matter of systems and policy and became a referendum on the root of the individual soul." Most Americans think about bias through this individual perspective.

I am guilty as charged and probably guiltier than most. As a social psychologist, I am trained to think about individuals and their biases, conscious or unconscious. The individual perspective is so ingrained that I was not thinking about the systemic level as I set out to write this book. As I did the research, particularly the interviews, it became clear that erasing all the individual "rot" in the world would not lead to equality until our systems were also debiased.

Physician and researcher Camara Jones argues that we can only understand bias when we consider the three interdependent levels at which it occurs: the systemic level, the individual level, and the internalized level.* There is not enough empirical data yet on this topic, but the connections between the three levels are intuitive. For example, systemic racism leads to lower levels

---

* Jones uses slightly different language, which I have adapted using synonyms so that it is consistent with the terms I have been using.

of education and thus lower earning potential in blacks versus whites. This disparity leads to individual biases (perhaps unconscious) that blacks are less smart and more lazy. This bias contributes to internalized stereotypes among some blacks about themselves. The system becomes localized in the form of our conscious and unconscious biases. It all happens in reverse, too. Our individual biases make us less forgiving of mistakes and more likely to blame victims for misfortunes, which makes us less likely to create equitable systems. The levels are intertwined and reinforcing.

The cost to us and what we believe in is great. When the tailwinds remain invisible, we forget that there is a system at work. We look for the bias in individuals and forget that the system itself is biased (and that we are part of the system). We reap its benefits and condemn those running into the headwinds as lazy, unworthy, and less human.

There is hope. I predict that social scientists may eventually find that debiasing the systemic hard-knock life effect is easier than debiasing individual unconscious bias. Yes, the individual perspective is less threatening than the systemic perspective, and yes, we are more able to see disadvantage (headwinds) than advantage (tailwinds).

However, research has shown that our avoidance of self-threat does not have to win. Systems that support whiteness over blackness are hard to see, and when they are made visible, it is normal for self-threat to kick in. Research finds that when white people feel self-threat about their whiteness, they turn to one of three strategies. They may deny the privilege, like antibelievers. They may distance themselves from other white people, akin to the hard-knock life effect. Or they may work toward dismantling inequality and promoting change, the approach of moving from believer to builder.

If you are drawn to either of the first two strategies, you are missing an opportunity. In the first strategy, you do not see the need for change. In the second strategy, you see the need but are less likely to engage in work that makes meaningful change. In the third strategy, you are able to see what is happening and participate actively.

A bit of affirmation and we can better see the systems, the privilege, the personal advantage. In fact, scholars Miguel Unzueta and Brian Lowery got white people to think of racism in systemic terms by explicitly affirming the individual first. While we will not always have a researcher on standby to do this, we can do it ourselves. In other words, if we can find our own cookies without burdening other already-burdened people (remember Rachel from the beginning of the book?), then maybe there is more hope than we realized. We can see the systems view.

As diversity educator Vernā Myers describes in her popular TED Talk, the challenge is to "stop trying to be good people. We need real people." So far we've focused on activating a growth mindset. A growth mindset allows us to think of ourselves as works-in-progress rather than premade good people, and to confront bias on both an individual and systemic level. Having worked through the debate about the word "privilege" and its actual systemic meaning, we can explore research findings about how we can see and use privilege to make positive change.

Part II

Builders See and Use Their Ordinary Privilege

It's not that I'm blind. Sometimes, I'm just not paying attention.

—JUSTIN SIMIEN, *DEAR WHITE PEOPLE*

4

Knowing It When You Don't See It

When executive Kimberly Davis walks into a room, people notice. When she speaks, people listen. Her presence has served her well in multiple senior positions at big-name organizations, including her current role as an executive vice president at the National Hockey League. Still, as a black woman, she has faced headwinds throughout her climb to the executive ranks.

At one financial services firm, Kim attended a networking event for senior female executives. The purpose of the event was to bring together individuals who might not otherwise cross paths. When she arrived, some of the other attendees had already informally gathered in little groups. As was often the case, she was one of the few people of color in the room, but this did not faze Kim. She took the initiative to approach a group and introduce herself.

She had assumed they would pause their conversation, open the circle, and welcome her, a basic etiquette norm. She stood there, waiting to introduce herself. No response. Undiscouraged by their rudeness, she moved to another group. Same thing. She approached three different groups and not one group acknowledged her. "They just continued to talk. I just stood there. It felt like hours, though I'm sure it was a matter of just seconds." Kim, who has a presence many of us aspire to, went completely unseen.

Did these other women deliberately exclude Kim? Undoubtedly some did, absurd as that behavior is. But it seems unlikely that all of them acted deliberately, given the expectation of politeness in such organizations. It is possible that they did not even "see" her—even though she was standing right in front of them—because they had a particular world view and she, as an African American female executive, did not fit into it.

A World View Takes Shape

Joe Lentine grew up in the suburbs of Detroit in a middle-class, Italian American family. He looks back at his all-American childhood and hometown with affection. He was close to his family, went to church, loved his country, and was an Eagle Scout. He liked people and people liked him.

What Joe did not notice at the time was that he had no substantive interactions with nonwhite people. All of his classmates and neighbors were white. According to the Detroit Area Study, a longitudinal set of surveys and interviews with residents, Joe's experience was not unusual for a white resident around that time. Even among the small percentage of white respondents who grew up in "mixed" neighborhoods (at least 20 percent nonwhite), almost none of them had meaningful interactions with their black neighbors. The survey also found that 42 percent of white respondents disapproved of interracial marriage.

Growing up, Joe remembers that racial slurs were commonplace. "I participated in racist jokes," he confesses. "I held unfounded opinions." His world view was taking shape as he entered adulthood. When Joe was eighteen years old, he had an internship at General Motors and worked with two black high school students in a cooperative work program. "We had arguments about simple things. The topics escape me now, but I do remember it was not a good first experience." It was his first meaningful contact with African Americans and his world view was being confirmed, or so it seemed.

Joe then attended General Motors Institute, now known as Kettering University, a mostly white, middle-class engineering school with only slightly more people of color than his high school. "My first and only black friend was a fraternity brother I met during sophomore year of college. It was not until I bonded with him that I began to change my views. In hindsight, I began to soften my prejudices, coming to terms [with] that it is wrong to classify all in the group with the same, mostly negative, characteristics." He began to reflect back on his experience with the two high school students as well, wondering if his negative interactions were better explained by their relative inexperience and youth rather than by their race.

Seeing It

Joe joined General Motors full-time after college. He became friends with a fellow employee who was born in China and had lived in the United States since he was twelve. His friend wanted to see his parents' new restaurant, near Seattle. Both of them wanted to see the country, so they decided to take a road trip.

"It was a fantastic vacation," Joe remembers, but also an eye-opening one. He remembers the stares his friend sometimes got, and at one particular restaurant, the hostile mumbling about Pearl Harbor. They got pulled over by border agents who suspected Joe's friend of trying to sneak across the United States/Canada border. "I felt awful for him. I was mad at the bigotry. These are some of my first memories of awakening into my own white privilege, into having empathy for my friend, and the start of empathy in general for marginalized groups."

Two weeks after this trip, Joe packed up his 1971 rusted-out black Mercury Cougar and headed to business school. Many of Joe's classmates (including me) affectionately nicknamed him "GM Joe," because of his passion for manufacturing, General Motors, and Detroit. Joe was especially enthusiastic about participating in as many overseas school trips as possible—including trips to South Korea, Hong Kong, India, and Japan—even if he had to go deeper into six-figure debt. At the time, I did not think much of his travels. Joe was a people person, quick with a smile and a kind word, so I just assumed he was one of those open-minded folks with a love for travel.

I know now that the cross-country trip had changed Joe's world view and that he was making an intentional choice to expose himself to people and experiences that would stretch his views. The more of the world that became visible, the more of the world he wanted to see. He knew it would not happen unless he made it happen.

Joe returned to GM after business school, where he rose into the executive ranks before turning thirty-five, among the youngest of GM's executives. During this time, at the age of thirty, he came out to himself as a gay man. He was wary about how people at work would react, so he only came out to a few mentors and colleagues. As he traveled his own journey as a gay man, he began noticing more about the experiences of people from other marginalized groups, things he had missed before. The bigotry of the slurs and jokes of his youth came into view. He became uncomfortable with the racial slurs around him at work, particularly as competition from Japanese automakers grew. Research shows that Joe's experience is typical of people who have privilege in one identity and disadvantage in another. According to organizational scholars Ashleigh Shelby Rosette and Leigh Plunkett Tost, the disadvantaged identity helps the person see his or her privilege, especially when he or she has not fully overcome the disadvantage.

Joe recalls being on a five-person executive team reporting in to an "old-fashioned, hard-core manufacturing executive." The team included a black man and a white woman. "I noticed we would have completely different staff meetings if either of them was not present. If the woman was not there, the swearwords and sexist comments would flow from my boss's mouth. And if my black colleague was there, my boss would relentlessly pick on him, undeservingly. I was embarrassed.

"In hindsight, I wish I had had the courage to speak up and defend them. I can use the excuse that I didn't because I lacked authority, but there were avenues that I did not use," Joe reflects. "I did, however, become friends with these colleagues. We had many open discussions. I learned about their experiences." Through these conversations and observations, Joe was seeing his privilege.

While Joe was thriving at GM, his father was thinking about selling his dental insurance business and turned to Joe for business advice. As they discussed his father's options, Joe became excited about the company's potential and the prospect of working with his dad. After twenty years at General Motors, GM Joe joined DENCAP Dental Plans in 2006. In 2009, he became the company owner and president.

A New World View

Joe brought his characteristic smile and cheer to DENCAP. He cared about both results and process, so he evaluated employees on what they did and how they did it. They celebrated every birthday, with public remarks from Joe about the celebrated employee—a favorite memory, an anecdote of when they first met, a funny story or two. Joe talked about the office culture as much as the bottom line.

The bottom line rested on DENCAP's service to the people of Detroit, well beyond the white suburb in which Joe grew up. Many of DENCAP's customers and health-care providers come from Detroit's African American, Middle Eastern, and Hispanic communities, so Joe wanted his employees to reflect those communities. Many of DENCAP's customers are also on Medicaid. "Detroit is 80 percent poor. I want employees who understand what my customer base is struggling with." From a business perspective, building a diverse and inclusive workforce was a competitive advantage. Even more urgently, Joe felt a need to establish the kind of work environment in which every one of his employees would feel respected and seen. The memories of the racist jokes, staff meetings, and road trip ate at him.

As DENCAP grew, Joe decided that he would not wait for résumés to arrive from people of all races and genders. He was going to find the people and make the effort to learn about them. He went to the Arab Chamber of Commerce. He reached out to an urban dental assistants program. He partnered with an organization placing transgender youth in jobs. "Sometimes, people are transitioning from working in a factory to working in a professional office environment. It can be a tough transition for all of us. But employees who make that kind of transition are the most loyal and grateful and dedicated employees." A younger Joe might not have seen these possibilities.

In his childhood years, Joe did not notice headwinds or tailwinds. In his young-adult years, they started to become visible. In his managerial years, Joe was recruiting, leading, serving, and partnering with the people facing the headwinds. He had chosen to tackle a profound professional and personal challenge. He had not been sued or accused of anything. He just knew he could do better.

Noticing has been a big part of the journey. Joe began paying closer attention to experiences he may have missed or dismissed in the past. He grappled with the "unfounded opinions" of his youth. "I experienced the judicial system by going through it with an employee who had unpaid parking tickets," Joe recalls. He could have just loaned her the money (which he did do), but in addition, he seized the opportunity to see a system usually hidden from him. "Sure, she should have paid her tickets, but the system is really a complete trap for those who cannot pay that one first ticket, which leads to a suspended license, and then more violations. Plus, what I did not know was that she had literally been brought up to discard tickets and not pay them if she did not have the money."

In the provocative book *A Colony in a Nation*, journalist Chris Hayes chronicles the trap of traffic and parking tickets. Hayes argues that revenue generation on the backs of the poor, more than public safety, guides the enforcement of these rules. When viewed through the eyes of the poor, the system is booby-trapped. Discarding tickets is neither an ideal nor an irrational response. The situation faced by Joe's employee was not as preventable as it might have appeared. What one saw in the system depended on what one noticed in the system.

While Joe's company has come a long way, there have certainly been bumps in the road. Two years ago, a white employee used the n-word in a joke told to another white employee. A black employee heard her and reported the incident. Joe was furious and disappointed in the white employee. He knew he had to act swiftly to ensure that his employees understood his stance. He decided to confront the employee who had told the joke and ask her to speak directly with the black employee who had heard the joke. "I know she didn't mean anything by it, but that is not okay, even in private and even as a joke," Joe says. "I was vocal about my path to fire her should this go sideways with her attitude in response to speaking to me and to the person who heard her joke. Word spread quickly." Ultimately, Joe decided not to fire her because she showed a willingness to listen and learn. "In the end, it was a big learning moment for her. I cannot see her ever saying that again."

Joe went from not noticing bias to taking a stand. "I have to defend marginalized groups in an active, aggressive manner," he says. "I am starting to understand what they mean when they say white privilege. There is so much poverty and you think you know why. You think you know why 80 percent of kids in Detroit are arriving at school hungry. Then you get into the system and you start questioning things, why are things that way, why? The more I expose myself to these issues through my employees and my customers, the more I realize there are some injustices here. Put yourself in their shoes. I didn't have any sense of this growing up. I am figuring this out now."

Bounded Awareness

Kim's and Joe's stories remind me of a teaching exercise I often use, borrowed from the work of psychologists Ulrich Neisser, Dan Simons, and Chris Chabris. I play a video of people in white and black T-shirts passing a basketball.* I ask the students to count the number of times the players in white T-shirts pass the ball,

---

* Multiple versions of this video exist. Here, I describe one by psychologist Ulrich Neisser, and I have also used other versions by Dan Simons and Chris Chabris in my teaching, an idea I learned from Mahzarin Banaji.

and the students do so dutifully. Then I ask them if they noticed anything unusual about the video. Most say no, except one or two students who mumble something about a woman with an umbrella walking through the players. The other students scoff. I play the video again; this time, we watch without counting.

Sure enough, a woman with an umbrella walks across the screen in the middle of the video, "impossible" to miss. The majority of the students missed her the first time they watched the video. This video has amazed not only my students but people all over the world. Consistently, almost 80 percent of viewers miss what is right in front of them. I sometimes use other versions of the video, which feature gorillas and other shockingly obvious things. Same story. These videos and the related research demonstrate that we can miss what is right in front of us.

Visual attention researcher Jeremy Wolfe and his colleagues say we see what we expect to see. They re-created the airport security screening process in a lab and had study participants screen bags for "weapons." When the participants were told that the dangerous objects would appear 50 percent of the time, participants had a 7 percent error rate. When the participants were told that the dangerous objects would appear only 1 percent of the time, their error rate increased to 30 percent. They did not expect to see something, so they did not see it, even when it was right there.

This research might help explain Kim's and Joe's situations from earlier in this chapter. These studies are examples of what Harvard Business School professor Max Bazerman and I call "bounded awareness." Bounded awareness is our tendency to not see, seek, or use readily available and relevant information. Sometimes, we do not perceive readily perceivable information. Other times, we perceive relevant information but miss its obvious relevance. In his excellent book *The Power of Noticing*, Bazerman explains that we are better at focusing than at noticing. The question is not whether we are failing to notice things we should; the question is what we are failing to notice that we should.

You might wonder if bounded awareness is the result of information overload. Sometimes, maybe. Yet even with all the time and bandwidth in the world, we still fall victim to our own bounded awareness. Something else explains these breakdowns in our awareness. We seem to be motivated to see, and not see, certain things. Nobel Prize winner Daniel Kahneman and his collaborator Amos Tversky demonstrated that our eyes and ears and minds approach the world with a point of view. Then we (unconsciously) set out to find evidence to confirm that point of view. This "confirmation bias" is the natural reflex to pay more attention to the stuff that supports your point of view while discounting or not even noticing the stuff that contradicts your point of view.

To see a simple version of how the confirmation bias works, try this exercise with a friend or colleague. Write this sequence on a piece of paper: "2–4–6." Then ask your friend to guess the rule you used to come up with the 2–4–6 sequence. She can try out other sequences of three numbers, and you will tell her if her sequence follows your rule. She can try out as many sequences as she likes but will only get one actual guess of the rule.

If she proceeds as most people do, she will offer a few sequences like 6–8–10 or 12–14–16 and you will say "yup" for each. Her excitement will be visible, as she concludes that she is ready to make her guess of the rule! She will say something like "Numbers that increase by two" and will look at you, anticipating a "That's it!" response. When you tell her that she is wrong, she will look shocked. After all, every response until that point confirmed what she was thinking. However, notice what she did, and did not, ask you. Her questions asked you to confirm what she believed to be true. She did not give you questions that might disconfirm what she believed to be true. If she believed "numbers that go up by two," a confirming guess would be 8–10–12, but a disconfirming guess would be 10–20–30 or 12–10–8 for a rule that was "increasing numbers."

She, and we, fall prey to the confirmation bias. We are drawn toward information that is consistent with our world view, not inconsistent. Our minds do not search for new data that might challenge what we believe, but for data that will confirm it.

Stereotypes, both conscious and unconscious, also trigger the confirmation bias. Studies show that we are more likely to notice, remember, and search for additional information when it confirms a stereotype. Psychologist Anthony Greenwald sums up this psychological tendency. He says that we like to think that our mind is like an impartial judge in search of the truth, but it is more like an attorney searching for evidence to support her case. When all of the information we are using confirms our point of view, we are falling for the confirmation bias. That is a red flag of bounded awareness.

Let us retrace where we have been. We know that we have unconscious biases and systemic privilege in play. Now we know a bit about how our minds work, busily legitimizing those unconscious biases and privilege rather than challenging them. And even when evidence challenges them, we may literally not see or hear it because it does not match our expectations.

Kim's colleagues may not have intended not to see her. Joe may not have realized what he was failing to see. Their eyes and ears "confirmed" their world view. The result, however unintended, was exclusion rather than inclusion. We become part of the problem and we miss things that are easily seen and heard, especially if those things contradict our world view. We can move from believer to builder when we see what is not visible and challenge it. One world view is particularly important to challenge: the meritocracy belief.

Meritocracy Belief

One of the most salient world views held by many Americans is a belief that the American dream is a meritocracy, within equal reach of people from every race, ethnicity, gender, sexual orientation, and income level. The meritocracy belief is the bootstrap narrative Colleen embraced in chapter 3. Those of us who are "successful" want to believe that we worked hard and earned our success in a fair system.

Psychologist Alison Ledgerwood and colleagues demonstrated the power of this meritocracy belief on our bounded awareness. As we touched on in chapter 3, they recruited undergraduate students to read a psychology study and then evaluate the methods and conclusions of the study. The (fake) study either supported or refuted the meritocracy belief in its conclusion, but the rest of the study was identical. The undergrads judged the quality of the study more favorably when it supported the meritocracy belief. This finding was especially true if they had first read a passage challenging the legitimacy of the status quo in society. They literally saw what they wanted to see in the study.

Seeing what we want to see affects our understanding of the world we live in. Behavioral scientists Michael Norton and Dan Ariely asked a nationally representative sample to estimate the current distribution of wealth in America. They found that people believe wealth inequality is far less pronounced than it actually is. Then they gave the participants the chance to construct their ideal distribution of wealth in America. It turns out that people do believe some inequality is desirable; even the lowest-income respondents did not think perfect wealth equality was ideal. Overall, Americans prefer something closer to Sweden's level of inequality (not much) than to the United States' (quite a bit). In other words, what people perceive is both incorrect and much like the world they want to see.

Our tendency toward bounded awareness is also affected by where we sit in society's formal and informal hierarchies. Power reinforces bounded awareness. Even a minimal amount of power and a minimal reminder of that power have profound effects on human thinking and behavior. A vast research literature shows that power shifts our focus from others to ourselves. We become more egocentric and are less likely to see the perspectives and emotions of others.

By power, I do not mean anything elitist or unattainable. I mean any control over any resources or outcomes. When study participants are asked to write a few sentences about a time when they had control over resources or outcomes, they write about times when they could hire and fire people, or save someone's life with their medical skills, as well as about being an older sibling, being in charge of reconciling the cash box at work, or being the one friend with a car. The more power we feel, the more bounded our awareness becomes.

Some research suggests that money has similar bounded awareness effects, leading us to focus more on ourselves than on others. Let us consider how power and money reinforce our meritocracy belief. The more power we have and the more money we have, the less likely we are to see our own privilege in the system. The more power we have and the more money we have, the more likely we are to cling to the meritocracy belief and the more likely we are to believe that the poor and powerless do not deserve power and money. We may have good intentions in the same magnitude as our power and money, but we are still prone (maybe more prone) to the psychology of bounded awareness.

In essence, we fool ourselves, and the consequences are significant. Sociologists Emilio Castilla and Stephen Benard have demonstrated the "paradox of meritocracy in organizations." It began when Castilla was studying a company that had put a merit-based compensation system in place. He was perplexed to see that women, minorities, and people born outside of the United States had to earn higher performance scores to get similar salary increases to white men. He and Benard decided to examine this pattern in a controlled laboratory setting, where they could eliminate any other explanations for the surprising pattern. They found the same pattern: When an organization labels itself as a meritocracy, male employees were given higher raises than women employees with the same job, same supervisor, and same performance evaluation than when meritocracy is not mentioned.

It is clear that merely believing in diversity and inclusion does not mean we are building diverse and inclusive organizations. In fact, the believing may be fooling us into seeing the world as more fair than it really is. Comforted by our beliefs, we do not realize our biases are exacerbating the very problems we wish to solve. When we don't see what is in front of us, we strip ourselves of the ability to address it. Psychologists Colin Wayne Leach, Nastia Snider, and Aarti Iyer speak of the need to "poison the consciences of the fortunate" (quoting Nietzsche) in order to move those in advantaged positions to challenge inequality. They find that when privilege is seen as changeable and challengeable, then we are more likely to act. To get to that point, we have to know privilege is there, even when we don't see it.

It Is Really Loud in This Echo Chamber

When we only perceive what we expect, we create an echo chamber where there are few surprises. We do not look for or notice disconfirming information. Beliefs become more deeply held. What makes these psychological echo chambers even more problematic is that we also live in social and media echo chambers. These echo chambers are more willfully created than our psychological echo chambers. These are the ones we choose.

I learned this accidentally at a young age. When I was a kid, I had a clock radio that I used for music and as an alarm clock. My parents handed it down to me when they bought one of those fancy duo-alarm models for themselves. The first night, I turned the station-changing dial too far, leaving the dial stuck to the far right. The station where the dial got stuck happened to be 107.5 FM. As a result, during those formative childhood years, I was exposed to only one radio station—WBLS FM, New York's most prominent "black radio station" in the 1970s.

I listened to that radio every morning when I woke up and every night as I fell asleep. While I listened mostly for the music, of course, I also heard DJs and newscasters and radio talk. I did not think much of it at the time; it was adult talk that you had to plod through to get to the next song. What I did not realize was that I was learning that there are as many versions of the black experience as there are black people. I heard a slew of concerns and experiences that people in my mostly white school and entirely brown family did not seem to know. None of these issues were being discussed at my school lunch or family dinner tables.

Several years later, I reached middle school and got a new alarm clock. As I flipped between different stations (still searching for my favorite songs, no doubt), I realized that the conversations I was hearing on WBLS were not happening on other "nonblack" radio stations. If someone was only listening to the "mainstream" radio stations, one would have no idea that one was in an echo chamber.

A PRRI (Public Religion Research Institute) American Values Survey asked participants to name up to seven people with whom they regularly discussed important matters. Participants were asked, "Looking back over the last six months, who are the people with whom you discussed matters important to you?" Respondents could name friends, family, coworkers, and so on, and then they were asked for demographic data about each of those people. The researchers used this data to calculate the racial breakdown of individual people's networks, an analysis known as egocentric social network analysis. They found that 75 percent of whites, 65 percent of blacks, and 46 percent of Hispanics had homogenous networks composed exclusively of people sharing their own race.

They also found that the average white person's network is 1 percent black while the average black person's network is 8 percent white. Said another way, the average white person's network was 91 percent white (with the balance including 1 percent black, 1 percent Asian, 1 percent Hispanic, and 1 percent mixed race). Meanwhile, the average black person's network was 83 percent black (with the balance including 8 percent white, 3 percent mixed race, 2 percent Hispanic). So most of us—regardless of race or ethnicity—build echo chambers in our closest relationships, but whites in America have the loudest echo.

Research by psychologist Drew Jacoby-Senghor looks at how implicit bias shapes our echo chambers in unexpected ways. He found that implicit bias predicted how much indirect contact white women had with black friends of white friends on Facebook.* It is intuitive that we hang out with people similar to ourselves. But Jacoby-Senghor shows that we are not simply drawn to people of our same race, but to people of our same race who share our implicit biases. So we do not just create demographic echo chambers. We also create bias echo chambers. As a result, not

---

* He did not find the effect for white men, interestingly, which may have to do with differences in male and female friendships. Further research is needed.

only do we miss out on direct contact with people different than us, but also on indirect contact, via friends of friends, which has also been shown to reduce prejudice.

The consequences are significant. White Americans are less likely to hear or participate in conversations about race, as their echo chamber amplifies their own experience within a system that privileges them. Studies show that black people discuss race in person and on social media far more than white people do. For example, 68 percent of black survey respondents said most or some of the social media posts they see are about race or race relations, versus 35 percent for white survey respondents. The definition of "most" and "some" were left to the respondent to decide, suggesting that this gap might be even greater than it seems. Racial issues are not on the radar for many white people and we can imagine that a similar pattern exists for gender, gender identity, religion, sexual orientation, and so on.

The implication of our echo chambers on our bounded awareness is severe. We are less likely to have encounters that challenge our unconscious biases and systemic privilege. And we are less likely to perceive those challenges when they do occur, even if they are right in front of us.

Eavesdropping on Other People's Echo Chambers

By day, Felicia Fulks uses her advanced training in library and information science to help biologists and others in the life sciences conduct their research. By night, Felicia wants to help people see and hear what is in front of them. She uses her experience as a woman of color and a community builder to help other women of color and white women find and learn from one another in an online community.

The impetus for starting the group was Felicia's experience in the high-profile online community Pantsuit Nation. Pantsuit Nation was formed prior to the 2016 presidential election. It is now composed of millions of people who were disappointed by the election of Donald Trump (full disclosure: I am a member of this group). It has offered hope, encouragement, and validation to many people (including me).

But while the group gained momentum and members quickly, it also began to fracture. Felicia remembers feeling "horrified" (as did I) at how women of color were treated when they would post a comment explaining how their experience differed from those being shared by white group members. Felicia remembers, "Inevitably, there would be a list of white women saying 'Why are you dividing us? We should all be united right now.'" These attempts to "unite" were far from uniting, effectively silencing those women rather than learning from different experiences. Many women of color recoiled after being silenced and shamed, simply for sharing an experience that challenged those of the majority.

"They kept using that trigger word—'divisive,'" remembers Felicia, echoing a sentiment I heard from multiple people about this particular word while writing this book. When women of color were accused of being divisive, simply by sharing their experiences, women of color came to understand the intended meaning behind "the d-word." Because the majority do not share the experience or understand the emotions the experience was generating, they were denying it by labeling it "divisive."

Felicia wanted to challenge this view of what is divisive. If you are in the sun and I am in the rain, why is it divisive for me to point out this difference? What is really divisive is telling someone who is standing in the rain that it is not raining. We forget that the civil rights movement was divisive, as the statistics earlier in the book demonstrated. Here, the word was being used to silence people. Felicia says with a sigh, "As long as you say that d-word, you are erasing someone's experience."

This erasure is the motivation of the growing and long overdue attention to intersectionality. While the word "intersectional" strikes some as academic or tangential, it is exactly the opposite. We set the stage for thinking about intersectionality earlier in the book when we talked about all the different identities each of us claims. Intersectionality is about taking into account these multiple identities that every person carries, particularly when some of the identities are marginalized.

Race and law scholar Kimberlé Crenshaw developed intersectionality theory (and the term) in response to a specific legal case in 1964, which is a stark example of nonintersectional thinking. In the case of *Degraffenreid v. General Motors*, five black women sued GM for race and gender discrimination. At the time, women were only considered for front-office jobs and African Americans were only considered for heavy machinery work. If you were an African American woman, you were considered for neither type of job. Women meant white women. Blacks meant black men. The court ruled that the plaintiffs could not prove gender discrimination because not all women faced discrimination and they could not prove racial discrimination because not all black people were discriminated against. The nonintersectional laws let black women fall through the legal cracks.

When a law, policy, or way of thinking assumes a single dimension of identity, usually the majority identity, then it is failing to be intersectional. Said more simply, if we only take some people into account in our fight for equality and inclusion, we are not actually fighting for equality and inclusion.

Another example lies in the contemporary pay gap between men and women. Women are often said to earn 79 cents for every dollar earned by men, but there is also a significant pay gap between white women and nonwhite (black, Hispanic, or Asian) women. If we focus on closing only the gender pay gap in our diversity initiatives, new laws, and data analyses, we will think we have solved the problem when in fact we still have an unaddressed pay gap.

When we are not intersectional, we are assuming everyone in a group comes from the same mold and is receiving the same treatment. When we assume this, we generalize the experience of white middle-class women to represent all women, for example. Our tendency is to assume the whole group looks like us or like the majority group, which surrounds us, and we dismiss other perspectives because they do not match the dominant perspective. While this initial reflex happens to all of us, what is problematic is when we insist on defending that dominant perspective as being universal for everyone in the group. Not being intersectional is the same as saying you believe in equality for all . . . as it applies to some people. It is an oxymoron.

Felicia was also confused. "It didn't make any sense to me that we couldn't work together, women of color and white women." They shared many common concerns and also had unique concerns. The women using the d-word were opting for willful ignorance.[*]

So Felicia created a private online group, separate from Pantsuit Nation, to foster a more willful awareness. In less than a month, sixteen hundred people joined the group (full disclosure: I am a member). Intersectionality was a core motivation. She believed there were white women ready to see more, even if it meant hearing perspectives that felt self-threatening.

---

[*] Willful ignorance originated as a legal term describing an individual's choice to be unaware of information that would threaten his claim of innocence. In the more colloquial use of the term, which I use here, willful ignorance describes an individual's choice to be unaware of information that makes her uncomfortable.

"One of the goals of the group was to have a safe place for women of color to actually just talk and get things out. That is ultimately our goal," Felicia explains. "But I also thought when I started the group that it was a learning experience for white women, that they would be able to hear our stories and our experiences and be able to actually understand what we go through." Maybe the d-word would stop being used if she could help people see what was outside their bounded awareness.

The group has a unique structure, analogous to the structure of someone's home. The home belongs to women of color, with allies explicitly welcomed as "guests." Some "rooms" are shared spaces open to all; other "rooms" are designated for women of color; still others are for allies only. The unique feature of the digital forum, however, is that one is welcome to listen to conversations in other rooms, as long as one respects the rule that one doesn't participate in the conversation by posting comments. By design, this structure allows white people to eavesdrop on conversations that typically take place exclusively in black communities and black people to eavesdrop on conversations that typically take place exclusively in white communities. The group includes a number of white women who self-report that they do not know any black people outside of this online community.

The group is led by administrators, all women of color recruited by Felicia. Their role includes holding members accountable for honoring the guidelines and mission of the group. New members are asked to spend their first few days only listening in shared spaces. White women are encouraged to practice listening more than they share. They are counseled that this may feel uncomfortable, as they are typically in spaces where white perspectives are the dominant voices.

When someone missteps, the admins intervene and ask the individual to join them in a separate space. In that processing space, people can debrief what happened without hijacking discussions taking place in other rooms. This design feature is an intentional departure from our usual response to such incidents, where "you just get hurt and walk away," says Felicia. "It is about dealing with the hard stuff." There is no option not to see and hear.

Felicia stresses that "we need to be willing to own our impact regardless of our intent." This sometimes leads to tough exchanges in which the impact of a well-intended but misguided comment is made clear. These include calling out "little pinpricks of pain from having microaggressions every day, which add up to a lot of pain."

Felicia does not pretend the group offers 24/7 "sunshine and happiness" and says that they have lost members as a result. It is not a place flooded in confirmatory data for the meritocracy belief. Felicia explains, "It's almost like they don't want to believe that the things that they think are true—like people are treated equally—might not be true. They want to believe there isn't that much racism." In the end, she hopes to "convince white women in the group that our cultures are different, our experiences are different, but ultimately we pretty much want the same stuff. We should be united, but united based on fully understanding everyone's experiences and understanding why some people have come into the group with all this anger and rage or why some people are just really depressed."

Felicia is hopeful about the impact of the group and its emphasis on awareness building. Ultimately, the goal is allyship in the form of action, but for those in the earlier stage of awareness building, she sees them as "in training, on their way to being an ally." About the white women for whom the group is their only contact with women of color, she says, "Hopefully, it makes them more comfortable with going out in the world and also meeting women of color and being okay with it. There are a lot of [white] women who would never have approached a [white] family member or coworker [on a race-related issue], but now it's happening. Maybe nothing changed but they had the talk and I think they wouldn't have had it before." Felicia, too, has gained greater insight into what happens to her in real life in her interactions with white women.

How to See More, Respectfully

Felicia's group is a powerful mechanism for countering the confirmation bias, for looking beyond the "sunshine and happiness." As you make your own efforts to counter the confirmation bias by entering conversations and spaces where people from marginalized groups are speaking more freely than usual, be prepared. Know that you will feel self-threat and that affirmation will not always be provided. You may be turned off by the anger some people express or you may feel that the demographic you are part of has been unfairly characterized or mocked. Many of us have the instinct to exit or fight this conversation. Remember, that you are a work-in-progress and consider these principles on how to see more, respectfully.

First, recognize that you are in a space where people are speaking more freely than you are used to. In many spaces, people from marginalized groups temper their emotions and withhold their true thoughts. As a result, some of us are accustomed to emotionally comfortable spaces and may bristle when authentic emotions and thoughts are shared. That moment of bristling is a sign that you have unusual access at the moment. You are hearing what some people really think and feel. Do not allow yourself to write off what you are hearing as "divisive." Stay where you are, so you can learn more, rather than exiting. Don't give up that access.

Second, avoid jumping into others' conversations, arguing for your perspective, or sharing your views and experiences. You will feel self-threat that will make you crave affirmation. Don't let that cookie craving lead you to crowd out or hijack the discussion. Third, notice the judgments you are having about other people. Take note when you have thoughts like "She would be a lot more effective if she said . . ." or "He is making things worse the way he is going about this." Challenge yourself to hear their experience without questioning its expression. Avoid being the tone police.

Fourth, whether or not you believe what you are hearing to be true, assume half of the statement is true. Let's say someone says that "black people are never given a chance" and you can immediately generate a dozen counterexamples to reject this claim. Avoid rejecting the point because of your reflexive analysis. Imagine what the world would be like if it were halfway true. Do not lose the opportunity to learn by getting caught up in an argument. In fact, these are the moments when your opportunities to be a builder will be unusually visible.

As builders, we need to make the invisible visible. We need to know it, even when we don't see it, because we are going to use its power. Too much is at stake in our culture, our democracy, and ourselves. We need to train our eyes to look for the things we do not see by seeking perspectives from people different than us. We need to ask the questions we are intuitively not going to think of, those that might prove us wrong rather than right. We need to ask for people outside our echo chambers to share their experiences by earning their trust that we will listen fully to what they have to say. We need to keep asking questions when there is consensus in the data or in the room by resisting the urge to assume that the majority speaks for the minority. Doing this reveals our privilege, which allows us to use it for good. That power is what I call ordinary privilege.

5

The Power of
Ordinary Privilege

African American spoken-word artist Christopher Owens could not believe his white friends had done it again. For the twenty-seventh time (not a typo), a white friend had tagged him on Facebook with a request. "My friend will say 'Hey, my mom's friend is saying racist stuff on my page, so could you explain racism to her? I want to say something, but I know it would resonate more if you said it.'"

After the twenty-seventh Facebook tag, Christopher was done. He explains, "It's exhausting to explain to people who aren't oppressed that you're oppressed." Not only are headwinds exhausting, but trying to make headwinds visible to those propelled by tailwinds is doubly exhausting. Someone else—someone with a tailwind—needed to step up.

Christopher posted, "This is the new racism: You didn't start it, but you for damn sure aren't willing to stop it." His instinct was that his friends were both chickening out and squandering opportunity. Yes, someone needed to challenge that mom's friend. They disagreed on who the mom's friend would take more seriously. Christopher's white friend was betting on Christopher while Christopher was betting on his white friend.

The research says that Christopher is right. His white friend would be taken more seriously in this situation. By expecting Christopher to do the work, Christopher's friends were actually fueling the headwinds. This reality may not be how it should be, but it is critical for believers who want to be builders to know. In this chapter, I will share that research and how it ties to what I call ordinary privilege.

Ordinary privilege is the part of our everyday identity we think least about, because we do not need to. For example, I do not use a wheelchair, but I was recently assigned to a wheelchair-accessible hotel room. In this room, the toilet, sink, and door handle were lower than I am used to. While I rarely give any thought to my ability to stand, I thought about it constantly during this hotel stay. (My thirty-six hours in this hotel room was a microdrop in the ocean of inconvenience a wheelchair user experiences. Nonetheless, I repeatedly swam through bouts of self-pity and frustration followed by waves of self-awareness. Humbling.) My usually invisible ordinary privilege regarding my height and legs was briefly visible to me.

People who can walk are less likely to think about their legs than people who cannot walk. White people are less likely to think about their race. Straight people are less likely to think about their sexual orientation. The upwardly mobile are less likely to think about their economic mobility. Christians are less likely to think about their Christian identity. Native English speakers in the United States are less likely to think about their first language. It is important to realize that this is not because there is anything inherently better about legs, whiteness, straightness, upward mobility, Christianity, or English. Rather, the society in which we live is structured around these identities. Those whose identities do not vary from the norm are lulled into thinking that their experience is universal. People with other identities are reminded of their difference from the norm on a regular basis.

In *Why Are All the Black Kids Sitting Together in the Cafeteria?*, Beverly Daniel Tatum recounts a classroom exercise in which she asks her students to complete the sentence "I am . . ." using as many descriptors as they can in sixty seconds. One pattern she has noticed is that white students rarely mention that they are white and straight students rarely mention that they are straight. She writes: "It is taken for granted by them because it is taken for granted by the dominant culture."

It is also important to notice the wide range of ordinary privileges. Our intersectional identities create unique forms of headwinds and tailwinds for each of us. Since each of us has a multifaceted identity, each of us probably has at least one domain of ordinary privilege. It may not easily and quickly come to mind, however. Of course, that proves the point. What makes ordinary privilege *ordinary* is that it is not something that makes us stand out as an elite or feel special. What makes ordinary privilege a *privilege* is that it usually brings us some influence not easily given to those who lack it. If you want to find the tailwinds in your life, find the ordinary privilege.

The Influence of Ordinary Privilege

Research shows that our ordinary privilege grants us influence. For example, David Hekman, Stefanie Johnson, Maw-Der Foo, and Wei Yang looked at how "diversity-valuing behaviors" are perceived in the workplace. In their first study, they surveyed 350 executives on whether they valued and promoted diversity.* Then they also looked at how these executives were evaluated by their

---

*   These diversity-promoting behaviors included whether they respected differences (cultural, religious, gender, and racial), whether they valued working with a diverse group of people, and whether they felt comfortable managing people from different racial and cultural backgrounds.

bosses to see if there was a relationship between those diversity-valuing behaviors and how their performance/competence was evaluated by their bosses. In other words, how do bosses view diversity promoters?

The answer, it turns out, depends on who is promoting diversity. Diversity-promoting female and nonwhite executives were rated worse by their bosses than their non-diversity-promoting female and nonwhite counterparts. White and male diversity promoters were rated no differently than their non-diversity-promoting white and male counterparts. The researchers found similar patterns when they looked at how people perceive hiring decisions. If a white male manager hired someone who looked like him (or someone who did not), there was no penalty in how his performance and competence were evaluated. If a nonwhite male manager hired someone who looked like him, he was viewed negatively. Only white male managers could hire someone who looked like them and not take a hit for it.

Psychologists Alexander Czopp and Margo Monteith studied even touchier situations. They found that white people who confronted a person expressing racial stereotypes were judged less negatively (by the offender) than black people doing the same. They also found that offenders felt more guilt and were more likely to apologize if confronted about their behavior by a white person than by a black person. Both black and white confronters were equally effective in decreasing the offender's future stereotyping.

Psychologists Heather Rasinski and Alexander Czopp also showed that observers are affected by the race of the confronter. They showed participants a video. Half of the participants watched a white person confront a white person about a racially biased statement. The other half watched a black person confront a white person about the same statement. Both videos were staged using actors so that the researchers could standardize everything except the race of the "confronter." Not only did the white observers report being more persuaded by the white confronter, they also rated the black confronter as more rude. The white confronter was more influential while the black confronter was labeled a complainer, pointing to the power of ordinary privilege.

The effect extends to written feedback. In this study, participants completed a measure of unconscious bias akin to the IAT. They were then given feedback about their unconscious racial bias. All participants were told that they showed an unconscious bias associating whites with intelligence more than blacks with intelligence (note: the experimenters explained that this was false feedback at the end of the study). Then the participants read a short article imploring them to consider their own racism (e.g., "you are part of the problem"), accompanied by a photo of the author, either a black or white researcher. The race of the researcher was the variable of interest. When the feedback came from a white researcher, it was more easily accepted than when it came from a black researcher. Two questions revealed the explanation. First, participants said they were surprised that the white researcher chose to research this particular topic. Second, once again, participants viewed the black researcher as a "whiner" or "complainer."*

The power of ordinary privilege is also evident online. Political scientist Kevin Munger explored this phenomenon through a clever experiment on Twitter. His goal was to confront white male harassers using the n-word and track whether they changed their behavior after being confronted. To do so, he created "bots"—automated Twitter accounts that appear to be real people. He gave these virtual confronters identical profiles and tweet histories but different numbers of followers, to convey high or low status.

---

* The researchers also did a parallel examination of gender and sexism. Interestingly, they found that the sexism issues were not viewed as seriously as the racism issues, a pattern that has been found in other research. This downplaying of the issue may require a different approach in order to be effective.

Those with five hundred followers were more likely to be per
ceived as high status; those with two followers were more likely
to be perceived as low status. Finally, he assigned each confronter
a race: black or white. The result was four distinct profiles: white
male bots with high status, white male bots with low status, black
male bots with high status, and black male bots with low status.

To find harassers, he searched for the specified slur on Twitter
to find a sample of people using the word in tweets. He focused on
those using the word as an overt racial insult and on a repeated basis.
He had no trouble finding harassers. Some harassers offered up their
names and/or photos in their profiles, while others were anonymous.

He randomly assigned one of the four confronters to each harasser. Once a harasser sent a new tweet with the racial slur, Munger's
confronter bots automatically replied: "Hey man, just remember that
there are real people who are hurt when you harass them with that
kind of language." Munger then monitored the confronters' subsequent tweets to see if and when they used the slur again.

The power of ordinary privilege showed up on social media
just as it had in the workplace. Harassers who were confronted
by a high-status white tweeter used the racial slur 0.3 fewer times
per day in the seven days after being confronted. True, the impact
was not permanent, as the harassers seemed to be back at it about
a month later. But if a single tweet from a total stranger curbed
behavior in the short term, imagine the potential impact of an
intervention from someone the harasser actually knows.

The other confronters were not as effective. Being white and
high status was important in this particular context.[*] Interestingly, the identifiable harassers did not decrease their use of the
racial slur; in fact, some stepped it up. Munger speculates that
anonymous harassers may be anonymous because they are more

---

[*] The other confronters did see a drop in the use of the racial slur, but this drop
was not statistically significant.

sensitive to what others think, and thus they were also more influenced by the confronter.

Study after study supports what Christopher was trying to tell his white friends. He says it reminds him of the movie *A Time to Kill*, based on the book by John Grisham. A black defendant, facing a white jury and white judge, tells the white lawyer why he picked him: "You're my secret weapon." Whether in organizations or on social media, ordinary privilege is a secret weapon. When those who are outside of the targeted group get involved, for better or for worse, they will be heard differently. The result of this reality is a great opportunity for each of us to see and use our ordinary privilege, as two white male entrepreneurs have discovered.

The Things Ordinary Privilege Makes It Hard to See

"Unconferences" have taken off. Unconferences are participant-driven gatherings in which the agendas are created on the spot by participants rather than in advance by the organizers. The primary task of the organizers is to determine the who, when, and where. The what and the how are left to the participants. The result is more spontaneous, organic, and interactive than a traditional conference, an "intellectual jam session."

Entrepreneurs Brian Fitzpatrick (who is known as "Fitz") and Zach Kaplan had attended a famous unconference in the Bay Area and craved something similar closer to their hometown of Chicago. Fitz and Zach created ORD Camp, named for the abbreviation for O'Hare International Airport.

ORD Camp took off. In the early years, Fitz and Zach turned to their own networks in prescreening and building the invite list. Fitz explains, "It's effectively kind of a private party." Attendees felt lucky to be invited to the three-day event, intentionally held in the worst month to travel to Chicago (January) to weed out the noncommitted.

Public radio storyteller Julie Shapiro loved her first ORD Camp. She pulled Fitz aside to tell him so. Then she asked if he wanted feedback for the future. Fitz and Zach took feedback seriously, so he said yes. Julie gave it to Fitz straight. "This is really great, but it's all dudes." That year, 118 people attended and only 14 were women. It would have been hard for Julie not to notice. If roughly equal numbers of people attended each of the eight concurrent sessions in each time slot, Julie would have been the only woman or one of only two women in the room in every session. Most of the men were white.

Given that positions of power are disproportionately occupied by white men in many sectors, other groups are less likely to have a member of their group in a position of influence. This reality is made more problematic by the ways in which networks vary by gender, race, and ethnicity. Men tend to have networks composed of mostly men, while women tend to have networks of men for professional support and networks of women for social support. White men tend to receive more informal help from their networks than black women or white women receive from theirs, possibly because of the influence their networks have. People of color are labeled as either "blending in" or "sticking together" based on their networking choices, and women of color face particularly pronounced choices. Typically, the more a group is outnumbered in the larger group, the more likely individuals are to seek network ties with people like them. In summary, networking for people who are not white males—particularly in contexts where white males are more numerous or more influential—is complicated. ORD Camp was replicating the headwinds for those individuals.

Fitz looked around and said, "Oh my God, it's all dudes." It was a classic example of bounded awareness. Invisibility is the very nature of ordinary privilege. In the context of ORD Camp, being male was an ordinary privilege, and thus the identity Fitz thought about least. It was not that diversity had never crossed Fitz's mind. But Fitz recalls, "I think it's a song that's always been there, I've just never heard it. Once you hear it, it really changes a lot of how you look at things. I think I had to hear it a lot of different times from a lot of different people, who were more kind and patient with me than I deserved." Before Julie, Fitz and Zach just had not heard it so clearly.

Zach and Fitz replayed how they formed their invite list. Zach recalls, "We had invited people we worked with, people we were friends with, friends of friends, that kind of thing. Everyone who came the first year knew someone that invited them. From that filter, it ended up being mostly homogenous, mostly male, mostly software developers, and mostly Caucasian." Once again, systems replicate systems and advantage accumulates.

In this case, the replicating system comes in the form of networks. Sociologist Nancy DiTomaso's book *The American Non-Dilemma* argues that we underestimate the extent to which racial inequality in America is driven by whites' preferential treatment of people within their networks. Through 246 interviews with white people across the socioeconomic spectrum, she finds that job searches often rely on "favoritism, opportunity hoarding, and exchanges of social and cultural capital" between white people. Still, she notes that interviewees often attributed their success to hard work and opposed any policy that would level the playing field. The result, DiTomaso says, is "racial inequality without racism."

"In-group bias"—a tendency to be drawn to and help people like ourselves—is human nature, many would say. We are asked to pass on a résumé for a friend of a friend. We learn of a job opening through a parent at our kids' school. We get the skinny on what companies to avoid from our brother-in-law. We go for a job interview and recognize the interviewer as a former classmate. We perpetuate inequality despite our intentions otherwise. Zach and Fitz did not intend for this to happen.

They are not alone in this situation. The White Men's Leadership Study, conducted by Greatheart Leader Labs, asked 670 leaders from eight leading companies to rate the diversity and inclusion effectiveness of white male leaders in their organization. Almost half of the white male respondents felt that white male leaders in their organizations were effective on these issues. The majority of respondents who are not white males disagreed. Fitz and Zach were not unique.

Don't Just Push the Easy Button

Fitz and Zach decided to redirect the headwinds and tailwinds. Fitz confesses that the steps to do this were not easy. "It forces you to admit, 'Hey, I was doing this in the past. It wasn't cool, and now I'm doing something different.' That can inspire shame really quickly and if you start to wallow in that, you're going push back." Earlier, we distinguished between the paralysis motivated by shame versus the problem solving motivated by guilt. Based on how Fitz and Zach moved forward, it appears guilt won. They decided to grow.

Over the next decade, they experimented with broadening ORD Camp beyond their own homogenous networks. They solicited names from prior participants. They asked people to nominate people "more amazing than you." One time, they asked people to nominate "women and minorities." Another time, they asked participants to nominate people "who don't look like you, if you are usually in the majority." No method was perfect, but every attempt was a stumble upward.

Fitz and Zach also looked again at their own networks. The harder they looked, the more names came to mind. Fitz remembers, "There were a billion different people out there that just weren't coming to mind initially. We had sort of been doing the easy-button thing." They were pushing through their own bounded awareness.

In the same way, we can go beyond the easy button. Regardless of whether our networks look a little like us or a lot like us, we can probably still afford to branch out. We can attend different events and talk to different people at the events we already attend. When we ask people if they know of anyone who would be right for a position, we can specifically ask them to think beyond people in their immediate networks rather than asking them to think of someone who might be a "good fit." We can proactively offer to pass on résumés or offer to do informational interviews when we talk to people outside of our natural networks.

By 2017, ORD Camp had almost equal numbers of men and women. The event slowly shed its "bro-fest" feel, with the topics widening. Some attendees applauded the evolution. Others were uncomfortable. They pushed back on "too many women things" or "too much social justice stuff." Despite caring deeply about feedback, Fitz is unfazed by this pushback. "I want people to feel a little discomfort because it's the discomfort that other folks feel all the time."

In the years in which the number of women was rising, new issues floated to the surface, such as sexual harassment at the unconference itself (which, of course, does not mean that sexual harassment of men was not an undiscussed issue before). A female attendee proposed a code of conduct prohibiting harassment.

Both Fitz and Zach immediately bristled at the idea. "These are people we know!" said Fitz. "I can't believe we're even talking about this!" exclaimed Zach. They believed that they had created a space free of such issues. Still, they kept listening and were surprised by what they learned. Fitz's wife told him, "I've never been to a conference where something like that hasn't happened to me or somebody I know."

Despite their initial opposition, Zach and Fitz eventually developed a code of conduct for ORD Camp. They distributed a hotline phone number and explained that if anyone called the number, Zach and Fitz would stop what they were doing and immediately act on the issue. Still, they felt a bit ambivalent.

The first day of the new policy, an attendee pranked the hotline. This flippant response dissolved their ambivalence and steeled their commitment to the code. Fitz and Zach stood up in front of everyone and took a hard, public stand. This was not a joke. While the seismic revelations of sexual harassment and assault, which began with the exposure of Harvey Weinstein, were still years away, Fitz and Zach were no longer unaware or ambivalent. They were prepared to use their ordinary privilege to make that clear.

Psychological Standing

One step at a time, they stumbled upward. They experimented with a zero-tolerance approach and then realized it deterred people from reporting problems. So they tried a more educational approach intended to make offenders more aware of how their blind spots were affecting the experience of others. As they experimented, they took some flak, but research suggests that it was less than they would have if they were female or nonwhite. Ironically, the people most aware of the problem are also the people who will pay the greatest price for trying to address it.

I asked Zach if he felt the benefits of his ordinary privilege in his and Fitz's efforts, if ordinary privilege was a shortcut to equality. Far from it, Zach said. He says that their efforts "have gotten pushback from both directions." The experience of being a builder is not easy for anyone. Even with tailwinds, running still requires strenuous effort. Still, the experience is, objectively speaking, easier and less costly for some people. That is precisely the point.

Both emphasize, without a hint of humblebragging, that they do not see anything "amazing" in their efforts. Fitz says, "The only thing I could say that we did right was we heard feedback and reacted to it." Still, Fitz is confident that if they had not taken the steps they took, nothing would have changed.

When Zach and Fitz decided to see and use their ordinary privilege, they were also deciding that diversity was a white man's issue. "I definitely heard about diversity, but I hadn't engaged with it viscerally before," Zach says. "I'm not even going to claim that we are doing a good job when it comes to diversity. I would just say that we're trying." Fitz and Zach report more progress and data on gender diversity versus race and ethnicity diversity.

Most of us do not get involved in issues that do not (seem to) affect us directly, where we lack what psychologists Dale Miller and his colleagues call "psychological standing." Psychological standing is the feeling that it is "legit" for us to get involved. We do not feel like it is our place to say or do something, even when we are just as outraged about an issue as someone who is directly affected. It is not that we lack confidence or fear punishment. The risk feels great. The consequence of this belief on Zach, Fitz, and all of us is very real when it comes to moving from believer to builder. The challenge may not be a lack of outrage as much as a lack of psychological standing.

Organizational behavior researcher Elad Sherf and his colleagues shed important light on this possibility. In their research, women were twice as likely as men to volunteer to be involved in a gender initiative at work when a generic invitation was sent out. The researchers were able to change this pattern. They simply told participants that senior leadership wanted and expected both men and women to be involved in the gender parity initiative, because they believed both men and women had important contributions to make on this vital issue. Based on this message, psychological standing for men increased. Men and women were equally likely to volunteer to get involved. In fact, women were somewhat less likely to get involved when the messaging gave psychological standing to men (they were still more likely than men, overall). We can speculate that psychological standing both liberated the men to get involved and liberated the women to sit it out. These research findings are consistent with the White Men's Leadership Study, in which the majority of white men reported that they were not clear that diversity efforts included white men.

For those concerned about psychological standing, small steps may be the way to begin. If you are unsure about joining the diversity task force, ask to have coffee with someone familiar with their work. If you are hesitating to attend an allyship training session, consider doing an Internet search about the presenter and his or her work. If you notice a homogenous interview list but are hesitant to say so publicly, pull aside a colleague to discuss it. In other words, give yourself psychological standing. While the risks may feel great to you, the daily risks facing the people you wish to support are far greater. You will probably make some mistakes, but if you are joining the efforts with a growth mindset, you and your ordinary privilege are likely to be welcomed. Avoid letting the insecurity of psychological standing be a barrier to getting involved.

The work of diversity and inclusion has to include people with headwinds and people with tailwinds. We cannot wait for others to give us psychological standing. Zach and Fitz put their tailwinds to work so that others would not have to do all the work.

How to Use Ordinary Privilege to Fight the Headwinds

Subha Barry, former head of diversity at Merrill Lynch and Freddie Mac, encourages us to share the work among multiple people, including those with ordinary privilege. "In organizations, we typically tap the same person to take the lead on these issues," Subha observes. "But, instead, we need to learn from how a flock of birds flies." The lead bird of the V formation literally flies into the headwind, cutting the wind so that the other birds can coast in the jet stream. The key to the flock's success is that the lead bird is not permanent. The lead rotates backward, allowing another bird to step into the role. In her current role leading Working Mother Media, Subha advises organizations to "find other people to step up. Do it for a limited period of time and see what they come up with." Give people the psychological standing to get involved. Do not rely on the same people, especially the people facing the headwinds all the time, to lead the flock all the time. Invite others in to be educated and to use their ordinary privilege. More of us can do more than we realize.

There are tough obstacles to moving from believer to builder. Our minds do not see everything in front of them. What we do see is what we want to see. We have surrounded ourselves with people like us. We know that we will be less likely to see a world in which meritocracy is not assumed, especially if we have a hint of power or money. As we learn what we do not want to know and as the invisible becomes visible, we may want to turn away—even (or especially) as believers. Builders opt for more awareness at these points. As we will see next, it is often a matter of will (and grace).

Part III

Builders Opt for Willful Awareness

One of the simplest paths to deep change is for the less powerful to speak as much as they listen, and for the more powerful to listen as much as they speak.

—GLORIA STEINEM, *MY LIFE ON THE ROAD*

6

Keep Your Eyes Open, Anyway

Kyle and Kevin Ferreira van Leer began dating in college. Kyle grew up in a white family in New Hampshire, one of the nation's three whitest states. Kevin grew up in New Jersey, in a white, multicultural family with Portuguese-Colombian roots. In college, Kyle and Kevin had a favorite Indian restaurant where they had "intense conversations." Laughing, Kyle says, "That's what we called them, instead of fights."

Kevin challenged Kyle's white view of the world. "I had a surface-level idea of racism, which was about one-on-one racist acts. Kevin pushed me to the systemic level. He was relentless," Kyle remembers. "In retrospect, he helped me get past my own bravado around what I knew."

As Kyle and Kevin became more serious (they are now married), Kevin met Kyle's family. They immediately embraced Kevin and his relationship with Kyle. Kyle's parents were believers, whom Kyle describes as "well-meaning white people." His parents' decision to live near Dartmouth College was partially for the diversity the faculty and student body brought to the community, relative to the rest of the state. They supported the homeless and other causes with time and money.

Before Kevin, Kyle does not remember talking about race at

the family dinner table. Kyle says, "Kevin and I pushed them. They had never thought of the systems narrative." When Kyle and Kevin explained how tailwinds benefit well-meaning white people, moral identity reflexes kicked in.

"But I am a good person," Kyle's mom, Jodi, protested. "I'm not a racist." The word "racism" evoked images of torches and robes, far from the beliefs of Kyle's family. Kyle and Kevin were bringing a thorny, socially charged issue to the dinner table.

"I Am a Good Person"

Kyle's mom was not new to thorny, socially charged issues. In fact, Kyle's mom is literally famous for diving headfirst into such thorns. With more than thirty-three million copies of her books in print, Jodi Picoult is a bestselling author. Her books usually debut at the number one spot on the *New York Times* bestseller list. More than a big-name author, she is a publishing megabrand. You cannot walk through an American airport or bookstore (as well as many overseas) without seeing her books on display.

Like many female fiction writers, Jodi is inaccurately stereotyped as a manufacturer of light beach reads. She more accurately describes her work as moral fiction. Current events often inspire her to burrow into thorny terrain, such as assisted dying, school shootings, the Holocaust, mercy killing, stem cell research, gay rights, the death penalty, and suicide. My first Jodi Picoult book was a naive impulse purchase en route to a few days of vacation on the beach. It was like I hit play on the DVD player thinking *Mamma Mia!* was in there, only to realize someone had swapped it for *Schindler's List*. The impulse purchase had a surprising upside. I had no idea what intelligent and thought-provoking storytelling I had been missing.

Still, after writing more than two dozen thematic and timely books, Jodi had yet to write about race. She tried once, years ago, when she read about white police officers who shot their African American undercover colleague four times in the back. She struggled to create a voice and character that felt believable. Despite her trademark one-bestseller-per-year productivity, she abandoned the project.

As her career progressed, the theme of race fell into the background, mirroring the role it had played in her life thus far and in Kyle's dinner-table conversations growing up. Jodi says, "I grew up on Long Island, in a predominantly white town. It wasn't as if I really thought about race. Frankly, I didn't have to think about it."

Now, Jodi wondered if it was time to try again to write about race. When she mentioned the idea to Kyle and Kevin, they hesitated and glanced at each other. After all, they knew Jodi would do her trademark extensive research. "But I worried that she might be trying to tell a person-of-color story. I worried about who she was writing it for and why she was writing it," Kevin says. "And I particularly worried about perpetuating an understanding of racism that is individually based. There's a self-reflection process you need to go through." In private, Kevin and Kyle wondered how to help Jodi navigate this space.

Acts of Will

Kevin had an idea. He suggested that Jodi join him at an anti-racism workshop that he was already planning to attend.* Jodi was

---

* The workshop was "Undoing Racism," led by the People's Institute for Survival and Beyond and the Haymarket People's fund. I also attended this workshop in Brooklyn, New York, in April 2017. More information can be found here: http://www.pisab.org/workshops.

delighted. The workshop seemed like a perfect addition to her standard research plan. She, too, had been wondering, "How am I going to listen to the people who have actually lived this experience [of being black in America], because I haven't, and how do I replicate it as honestly as possible?" She could learn and listen to multiple voices at the workshop.

Kevin and Jodi headed to the three-day immersion workshop. Some attendees were like Kevin, activists already engaged with issues of race and other justice issues. Others were like Jodi, believers who were new to this type of space. Jodi recalls that the majority of attendees were people of color. Kevin recalls a more even distribution between white people and people of color, "or maybe more white people." When I mentioned the discrepancy while fact-checking, Kevin remarked, "That's funny." Jodi and Kevin were at different stages of their bounded awareness and Kevin chuckled at the differences in what they saw in the same room.

Jodi heard from people who did not share her ethnic or racial background. A young Asian American woman cried because she felt unattractive. She had internalized the notion that wide, Western, eyelinered eyes defined beauty. An African American woman said she put on a "mask" each morning to cope with stereotypes pinning her as an angry black woman. Jodi did not expect to feel so wrecked. This was not the racism, and racists, she expected to learn about. She was part of the racist system they were describing, which extended through every system in society. At these pivotal moments, Jodi could shut down or even leave, or she could mentally and physically stay in the room. Staying in the room, still listening, was an act of what I call "willful awareness."

The workshop unpacked systemic racism, as Kyle and Kevin had done at the dinner table. Jodi could not dodge her own role in the system as a white person. She remembers, "I was an absolute mess. I would sob in front of everyone. It was like being slapped across the face ten times. I walked out and realized, 'Whoa, I'm not doing research for a book. I'm doing research for me.'" Here was the self-reflection Kevin had hoped for.

Jodi's eyes were opening to things she did not want to see. She had a choice to look *away* or look *anyway*. She opted to look anyway. She started with herself, noticing things that had not troubled her in the past. Jodi recalled, "My grandmother was an astounding woman who volunteered four days a week into her nineties." Jodi's grandmother interacted with people of color as a nursery-school teacher in an underserved community. Jodi says, "She would never have called herself a racist." Still, her grandmother sometimes used a Yiddish slur to refer to black people. "That is a racist thing to say," Jodi says. "I never said the word, but I also didn't speak Yiddish. And I had never talked to her about it."

Also, she had long felt proud of the diversity of her college relative to her hometown. A group of Jodi's creative-writing classmates—including an African American friend—would grab lunch after class. Jodi felt glib about her claim that she had "a black friend in college," as if that credentialed her in some way. If the black friend had been white, Jodi wondered if she would have referred to her as a friend. Perhaps they were more acquaintances than friends. Despite superficial differences, her supposedly diverse college experience was not too different from her less diverse childhood. "I was ignorant," says Jodi. "I didn't see it." The more aware she became, the less she liked what she saw.

Jodi began to wonder how her career had benefited from the history of systemic racism in America. No doubt her tremendous talent and work ethic fueled her success. But literary agents and editors—the vast majority of whom are white—steer the publishing industry. I asked Jodi if her whiteness had been a tailwind in her success. "One hundred percent," she stated without hesitation.

As Jodi's bounded awareness morphed into willful awareness, she kept looking.

Different Stages of Racial Identity Development

As Jodi's awareness morphed, Kyle and Kevin reminded themselves to honor her learning process. Kyle says, "I am past that white guilt phase. But after the workshop, Mom would talk about how sad she was. And I'm like 'Yeah, but think about the other person in that workshop who is struggling a thousand times worse.' I wanted to validate her but also remind her that she did not deal with this her entire life."

Kevin recalls, "For a while, in any space we were in, Jodi would say, 'Wow, look at how many white people are at this thing.' And I would think, 'Yes! This is how it always is. Did you not know?'" Kevin, Kyle, and Jodi were all moving forward, but each was in a different place in their learning.

In fact, Jodi was moving through the natural stages of white racial identity development.* These stages were defined by psychologist Janet Helms and refined by psychologists Derald Wing Sue and David Sue. Most white people in the United States are in the first stage, which is characterized by a lack of awareness of race, a color-blind/color-mute approach, and a strong belief in meritocracy. Jodi had willed herself out of this first stage. It is common for people entering this awareness to vex people in different white identity stages or with different racial identities. Luckily for Jodi, Kyle and Kevin understood. With this bit of awareness, self-threat was high.

---

* For telling Jodi's story, I am going to rely on models of white racial identity development, as they explain her story best. But other models of identity development also exist (e.g., black, Asian American, gay and lesbian).

Research shows that the more we care about something, the more likely we are to willfully ignore negative relevant information about it. Management researchers Kristine Ehrich and Julie Irwin found that we underseek ethical attribute information about products we consume. Care a lot about child labor and love your sneakers? Then you are especially unlikely to check on the manufacturing practices of the sneaker manufacturer. They also find that we are *more* likely to underseek that information when we care *deeply* about that particular attribute. In other words, the more we care about something, the less we want to know, lest we be burdened with troublesome knowledge.

In these early stages of white racial identity development, what happens next is critical. The natural reflex is to reduce the pain and self-threat. Some individuals do this by doubling down on the meritocracy belief and color-blindness, generating the affirmation needed to reduce the self-threat. They might even blame the victims. They opt back into willful ignorance. Alternatively, people like Jodi stick with willful awareness and move to the next identity stage where they redefine how to be white. They move closer to being the person they mean to be.

For example, Jodi read and loved *Between the World and Me*, the powerful book by African American author Ta-Nehisi Coates. When Jodi loves a book, she often shares her enthusiasm with her large fan base and tweets praise at the author. She was about to do so for Coates's book. She wanted to tell him that the book helped her to understand and feel things in a way that she had not before. Then she saw some tweets from Coates in which he described his ambivalence about the praise and prizes his book was receiving from white audiences. He had not written the book with that audience in mind. Jodi was taken aback.

She reached out to an African American writer friend. "I don't think he wants to hear from me," Jodi told her friend. "And she's like, 'Uh-huh.' And I was like, 'Well, I don't understand. I know if it were me, I would want to hear from someone who was a fan. Why would you isolate yourself from readers who may not be the same race as you?' And she goes, 'Uh-huh.' And then it was like a lightbulb went off and I said, 'Oh my God. I'm making it all about me.' And she goes, 'Bingo.'" Jodi was centering herself and missing the issue that Coates was raising.

Jodi was discovering the power of what educators often refer to as a good mistake. Good mistakes unlock learning because they focus our attention on a key step or insight that may have previously been out of focus. For mistakes to be good, a growth mindset is needed. Research measuring electrical activity in the brain backs this up. Electrical activity indicates how much attention we are giving to whatever we are thinking about. The subjects in one study filled out a survey measuring the degree to which they were more fixed versus growth mindset in their beliefs about intelligence. Then they did a number of intellectual tasks, getting some right and some wrong.

The researchers found that, after a mistake, people in a fixed mindset paid less attention to mistakes than people in a growth mindset, as shown by the electrical activity in their brains. Fixed mindset people were more likely to continue making mistakes, failing to learn from the mistake. On the other hand, growth mindset people who paid extra attention to mistakes showed improved performance. This is the power of a good mistake, if your eyes stay open. In fact, a powerful way to foster a growth mindset in yourself and the people around you is to use language like "that was a good mistake." By normalizing mistakes as part of learning, we can nudge people away from an either/or mindset.

Jodi's willingness to talk about her mistakes reveals the dual power of a good mistake. When she makes her learning visible to others, she helps other people look for their own good mistakes. Again psychological safety grows. When Jodi spoke with her friend and came to realize that she was centering her needs inappropriately, she vocalized what she had learned to her friend. Her friend said "Bingo!" The open discussion of the good mistake normalizes the learning from the mistake. All of us make these mistakes though most of us do not talk about them. What if we did, even with one person in our lives? Who could that be in your life? What if we shared our good mistakes? Imagine how much that person would learn, both from our mistakes and from our willingness to learn.

Will and Grace

I asked Jodi what helped her will her eyes open. "Grace," she proclaimed. I asked her what grace meant, expecting she might have meant it in a religious sense. To my surprise, she described a growth mindset. "We need grace to let in the idea that we may not be as perfect as we thought we were. Grace means everyone is at a different point in this journey. Grace means that we all make mistakes. I'm going to say the wrong thing, do the wrong thing. It's more important to take a risk and talk about racism and know you might screw up than to not talk about it at all. Because then you get to say 'I'm sorry, I didn't know that, I'm learning from that.' We get defensive really easily. We need grace." Grace is the antidote for self-threat.

Jodi also began to experiment with how she was going to continue her pivot to willful awareness. The tailwinds in her life hid the systemic and unconscious issues affecting others. How was she going to keep learning? One could only attend so many workshops. And she still planned to write a book centering on racial issues.

She knew she would need the help of others. At the same time, she wondered how to seek their help with grace. "You can't expect everyone to want to teach you. If you have a question for a person of color and they say 'Go look it up,' you can't get pissy with that person. It's absolutely their right to say that after being isolated and marginalized in white society. And there are some people of color who have a real deep and abiding anger for all white people. No, that is not your fault as an individual white person, but you have to own up to it and say 'Okay, you're right, I get it. Thank you.' And find someone else." Willful awareness requires grace.

Jodi did begin to notice opportunities to deepen superficial friendships. "I still live in a place that is very white," she notes. "But through this process, I met some women [of color] who really are my friends." Jodi seems to have redefined friendship, moving beyond the superficial "going to lunch" to a relationship "where we can talk honestly about race." Still, she noticed that some days required a reboot, like when she allowed herself to be upset about Coates's tweets.

Jodi is not alone. Our default mode is willful ignorance. Our psychology will not naturally lead us to see what is different than what we believe and what is contrary to what we want. Our geography will not naturally lead us to people different than us. Our sociology will not naturally lead us to diverse networks. Still, while our default mode is willful ignorance, we can opt for willful awareness.

Willful Awareness for Everybody!

In Jodi's excellent book *Small Great Things*, a white supremacist couple refuses to let a black nurse, Ruth, treat their newborn baby. The hospital acquiesces to the family's request, ordering Ruth to stay away from the child. As fate would have it, Ruth is the only one present when the baby experiences a medical emergency. This fateful moment sets in motion a legal proceeding in which a liberal white attorney, Kennedy, is representing Ruth. To her dismay, Kennedy realizes she has much to learn about her own unconscious biases and role in systemic bias. Jodi says, "What I tried to do with this book was to get ordinary white people, nice people, people who are not white supremacists, to realize they still play a role in racism."

Though the book was written well before the 2017 events in Charlottesville, Virginia, Jodi's plea to readers is similar to the discussion that emerged after that deadly showing of white supremacy. Kennedy's evolution begins with her belief that racism is flaming torches and white robes, racism of the form that showed up in Charlottesville. She comes to learn that other forms of racism perpetuate a world she does not believe in. She believed that there was a problem but had not believed it was in her mind and in her world. Her experiences with Ruth challenge that belief. It is less white savior narrative and more white learner narrative.

Jodi hopes her white readers will look for themselves in Kennedy. In a special author's note, she described the process of writing her book: "I was exploring my past, my upbringing, my biases, and I was discovering that I was not as blameless and progressive as I imagined. . . . This book will stand out for me because it made me aware of the distance I have yet to go when it comes to racial awareness." She implores her readers to opt for willful awareness, and she is open about her own struggles to do so.

Some readers have declared *Small Great Things* to be the *To Kill a Mockingbird* of the twenty-first century. White readers on Twitter share their lessons. One tweeted that the book had helped her "examine my true feelings on race." Another tweeted that it "has made me rethink everything I ever believed regarding racism."

And another summarized, "I get it now." Kyle and Kevin's "non-fights" during college migrated to the dinner table with Kyle's family and then to the pages of Jodi's book and into the lives of Jodi's readers.

Over time, conversations with Kyle's family have expanded to include a different topic, of gender identity and gender expression. It is a topic on which Kyle and Kevin have less-conventional views than Jodi. "We're definitely the ones bringing that one up," notes Kyle. "That one's in the earlier stages."

Willful awareness greases the way for action. Today, Jodi has moved to a stage in her racial identity development where she still has much to learn. But she feels she can act and she must act. "Once you see it, you can't unsee it," Jodi says.

Remember Jodi's grandmother (and Kyle's great-grandmother)? She has since passed away and her family remembers her with love. When she was still alive, Jodi and Kyle finally spoke to her about the racial slur. To their amazement, she listened with care and openness. She was one hundred and two years old.

How to Keep Your Eyes Open

Opting for willful awareness can come in a variety of forms, including what Jack Welch, the former CEO of General Electric, called "reverse mentoring." Younger folks often reverse mentor their bosses, parents, and grandparents about technology. Young people field many a phone call from Grandpa about the "weefee" (wifi) not working or an email from a boss asking for help printing an attachment.

This generational flip also sometimes applies to social issues. Jodi had natural reverse mentors in Kyle and Kevin on issues related to sexual orientation and race. She saw perspectives in her son and son-in-law's peer group, which were absent in her life. She even saw it when Kyle and his siblings were younger. "My kids began to outstrip me. They really did have black friends. And they really did understand some of the struggles."

Consider the differences in a world experienced by a young person in 2018 versus 1998 versus 1968 versus 1948. We are each a product of the time and place in which we live. Look for the opportunity to ask someone of a different time and place about his or her perspective. Reverse mentoring sounds very formal, but it can be casual. Start a conversation with a young cashier or a young colleague or a young relative.

It can be a one-off conversation or an ongoing dialogue. Ask their views on current events. Ask them about what is considered "normal" in their peer group, who is excluded or included, who is considered cool, and what is considered taboo to say. Ask them to challenge a perspective you have as "old-fashioned" and then really listen to the challenge. Ask multiple people to create a more well-rounded perspective. You do not need to accept their perspective as truth, but you can use it to nudge your time-and-place perspective toward willful awareness.

Many other resources also exist to help us pivot toward willful awareness. For example, black female activists Leslie Mac and Marissa Jenae Johnson created a powerful resource called the Safety Pin Box. They were frustrated by the empty promise of people wearing safety pins to signal their allyship with marginalized groups after the election of Donald Trump, without any thought of how they would act to support those people. What was needed, they argued, was not the show of safety pins but measurable advances in awareness, action, and financial support for people on the front lines of activism.

To this end, they created a paid subscription program delivering specific learning and tasks each month for those interested in "putting your money, and your time, where your mouth is . . . every single month." The subscription fees support social justice activists and work (full disclosure: I was a subscriber, though I was not an active participant). Each monthly task guides learners to educate themselves on topics ranging from reproductive justice to colonialism to law enforcement. Social media, webinars, and workshops create accountability and provide learning support. This is just one of the possible paths out of willful ignorance. We can keep our eyes open in a variety of ways as long as they stay open.

As we strive to keep our eyes open, we want to also be aware of some common psychological pitfalls. Even with our growth mindset activated and our ordinary privilege visible, our good intentions may lead us astray. So the next step in our willful awareness is to be aware of those dangerous modes of being good people. We need to know what to look out for.

7

Look Out for These Four "Good" Intentions

I was steeped in self-threat when I first met Mel Wymore through a speaking engagement in 2011. To my knowledge, I had never met a transgender person (which does not mean I had not). Being nervous and ignorant is not the person I mean to be, but that was the person I was that day. On the plus side, I brought a growth mindset along with my ignorance and nervousness to the meeting. I did not know much, but at least I knew I did not know much.

The resolution to my internal drama was anticlimactic. Meeting Mel was like meeting any other new person through work— that is, if anyone else is warm, easy to talk to, and interested in getting to know you. We made small talk, asked about each other's background, and then got to work. The meeting dissolved my nervousness and chipped away at my ignorance.

In hindsight, I wish I had taken the initiative to do some reading before I showed up for that meeting, as it seemed that Mel did all the work to make me less ignorant, when that should have been my job. Since then, I have started to learn more, particularly from the work of developmental psychologist Kristina Olson, who summarizes her research in an eye-opening *Scientific American* article titled "When Sex and Gender Collide."

Olson did not set out to study transgender children. She had been an expert in how children think about themselves and the world around them when she stumbled into thinking about how children develop an understanding of their gender. Today, Olson is the director of the TransYouth Project, an ambitious research project tracking more than three hundred transgender and gender-nonconforming kids in the United States and Canada over two decades. She is studying how gender develops and how it may or may not be the same as sex in these children. Sex is a biological category while gender refers to the ways in which one identifies with the social and cultural features associated with each sex. A person is described as cisgender (or "cis") when their sex and gender are the same and transgender (or "trans") when their sex and gender are not the same.

Olson uses a variety of measures—both conscious and unconscious—to measure a child's gender identity. She writes that the most surprising thing in her research so far is the "myriad ways in which trans kids' early gender development is remarkably similar to that of their peers." Contrary to misconception, the trans kids are not confused, pretending, or just in a phase. As young as age three, the trans kids can have a gender identity as clear as the cis kids. For example, a biological male who identifies as a girl has a gender identity as a girl no different than a biological female who identifies as a girl. Olson's finding is consistent with early evidence from twin studies conducted by other researchers, which indicate that a transgender identity may have genetic underpinnings.

In general, transgender children and adults have exceptionally high rates of depression, anxiety, and suicide because peer bullying and family rejection is common. Among transgender and gender-nonconforming adults whose families no longer speak to or spend time with them, 57 percent attempt suicide. However, among adolescent transgender children whose families have supported them, the life outcomes appear dramatically different.

Other families have gender-nonconforming children who do not appear to be transgender but also do not conform to a binary (male/female) set of gender options. Olson thinks that studying nonbinary children will be important to our understanding as well. All of this research, of course, is emerging during Mel's adulthood. When Mel was growing up, we knew much less about transgender development.

Mel's Story

Mel was named Melanie at birth. Melanie was raised as a girl and married a man as an adult. They started a family. Still, something felt off. Melanie thought she might be gay and came out to her husband, family, and friends. Eventually, she learned about gender identity and realized the issue was not sexual orientation. Mel says, "My experience of gender is way different than what society tells me it is. It's on a continuum. There's this blurry middle part." After extensive research and family discussions, Mel began a transition. Today, Mel has a wonderful relationship with his two grown children, who call him "Mom."

Mel has experienced the world through a variety of binary categories: as someone gay and as someone straight, as someone cisgender and as someone transgender, as someone presenting as a man and as someone presenting as a woman. Furthermore, he has experienced the world as someone who sees the limitations of binary categories and the missed opportunities of a continuum of identities. More than many of us, Mel has experienced being excluded and treated as the "other."

He does not think he is the only one. "One of the things I have noticed is that everyone has some feeling of exclusion," says Mel. He decided to tackle this issue at his children's school, where he served as PTA president and prioritized diversity and inclusion. Because the school is private, it has the latitude to shape the student body beyond the more racially segregated neighborhoods of many public schools. Over his decade-long tenure, the diversity of the student body increased from 16 percent to 40 percent.* He has experimented with different ways of building connections among people, including discussion forums where seemingly different individuals shared various dimensions of their identities and uncovered surprising similarities and differences between them.

Mel's beliefs about exclusion are the catalyst for his work as a lifelong community organizer and two strong runs for city council. He lives on New York City's Upper West Side, a neighborhood that includes high-income residents in doorman buildings, low-income residents in government-subsidized housing, and small business owners struggling to stay open. His work ranges from starting a meals program for homebound seniors to supporting mom-and-pop shops fighting zoning battles. He often goes from person to person and door to door, where he can look people in the eye and vice versa. Mel says, "To me, the way we overcome the natural tendency to exclude people—to make people 'other'—is to get to know each other."

Mental Launch Sequences

The research says that Mel is right. Our minds can perceive someone as something other than a human being when we otherize

---

* Mel Wymore's campaign materials.

them. We are able to make them less human and less like us than they really are. When we otherize someone in this way, they become more like an object or category and less like a person. We are more likely to assume their experiences differ from ours and less likely to respect that difference.

There are four modes of behavior that prevent believers from humanizing others and prevent them from becoming a builder. In these four modes—savior, sympathy, tolerance, and typecasting—good intentions are counterproductive. By trying to be a hero, by feeling bad, by treating difference as something to be tolerated or ignored, or by typecasting someone to be someone they may not be, we operate in modes that do more harm than good.

To understand just how easy it is to fall into these modes, we need to understand how the brain thinks about people, especially people we do not know as individuals. We start with neurological and visual research about a basic mental launch sequence: how your brain perceives who is human. Then we look at the surprising ways in which our good intentions can create the distance we hope to avoid.

The Varying Degrees of Humanness

The first step in feeling connected to another human is to figure out who is human and what is not. Using fMRI studies, neuroscientist Jason Mitchell and his colleagues have cataloged the effortless processes our brains use to distinguish people versus objects. If the result is "human," then our brains get busy figuring out just how human they are.

Even among human faces, we encode some faces as less human than others, through what psychologist Katrina Fincher and her coauthors call "perceptual dehumanization." It is the difference between seeing the face of your spouse versus the face of a homeless stranger. We perceive both as human, but we may not see the full humanity behind the face of the homeless person. We are less likely to feel their suffering in the same way we would feel it for someone we identify with more closely.

Fincher and her colleagues trace this difference all the way back to our visual perception. They begin with our standard way of viewing someone's face, perhaps in our home or at work. In the typical scenario, we see the face and deploy a megasupply of holistic processing power to interpret that visual data. This process allows us to distinguish thousands of faces from one another, even when they get older or cut their hair. We recognize micromovements in facial muscles and know which ones signal anger versus surprise versus fear. We track people's gazes with the precision that can detect a 1.3-degree shift in focus. We do all this faster than you can read this sentence.

However, we do not deploy this holistic processing prowess for all humans. We are more likely to operate in this way when we think of people as individuals. When we are not thinking of people as individuals or when we are thinking of them as threats, our visual processing works in a different way. Instead of holistic processing, which allows for nuanced perception, we rely on more piecemeal processing of faces. We see the features of the face—the nose and the eyes—as standalone visual stimuli, not as part of a coherent whole. As a result, we do not deploy the same cognitive prowess in detecting the thoughts, emotions, and motives of this three-dimensional human being. We, literally, see the homeless stranger as less human.

Psychologists believe that perceptual dehumanization plays a functional role in situations of scarcity. When we need to compete with someone else for limited food, it is useful to not worry about his or her humanity. It is possible that the utility of perceptual dehumanization **extends beyond** these competitive contexts. For example, we encode people from lower social classes or other races and people we view as outside our group (even from our own race) as less human. We are more likely to punish or judge those faces. When we dehumanize someone, we are more willing to inflict pain on them and less likely to be bothered by it. Psychologically, we can more easily otherize and punish them.

Not only do our minds activate different processes for people versus objects and more human versus less human faces, they also activate different processes for people we think are similar to us versus people we think are not. We can see how this plays out in interpersonal interactions, where we often make assumptions about what another person is thinking. Are they planning to steal our idea, or interested in dating, or genuinely jazzed by our latest startup idea? The way we answer these questions rests on whether we think the person is similar to us or not. If the person is not like us, another launch sequence is activated in a different part of our brains. Here, stereotypes steer thinking.

Otherizing Made Easy

The sophistication and speed with which our minds can otherize is formidable. First, we figure out who is human. Then we figure out how human they are. It happens in an unconscious flash, leaving us to otherize those we may wish to support, particularly those who come from groups often marginalized in society.

According to the research, Mel was right. The more we get to know people as individuals, eye to eye, the greater chance we have of being builders, not just believers. From a distance, we (literally) do not see people as individuals.

My nervous mind must have been whisking through these

otherizing processes when I first met Mel. I saw him as a category, not a person. Perhaps all that small talk at the start of the meeting was more important than I realized. The more I could tip my mind toward seeing the humanity in Mel, the less likely I was to otherize him.

I speculate that otherizing does not only emerge from people who are hostile or exclusionary but can also emerge from well-intended allies. Our good intentions can lead us to view those we wish to help from an otherizing distance. In fact, our good intentions make us especially prone to do so. Let's explore four modes of well-intended behavior that can lead to otherizing.

Savior Mode

When Mel (Melanie, at the time) first moved into his apartment building, he was pregnant. Across the street, there was a low-income public housing building, with one or two people per room and shared common spaces. That day, someone jumped from the fifth floor of the building across the street. Crowds gathered; an ambulance came. Minutes later, everybody returned to their routines.

Shaken up, Mel asked people in his new building what had happened. No one knew anyone in the other building. They urged him to stay away from that building and its residents. Mel ignored this advice and crossed the street to introduce himself to his neighbors, some of whom were elderly. He enjoyed meeting them, but the unmet needs of food and medical treatment affecting some of the residents shocked him.

Mel knew that resources existed to help people in these situations, but the resources were not reaching his neighbors. A tenants' association was needed, as was influence with local authorities. The residents did not know how to navigate local government. As a community organizer, Mel did.

His role, he decided, would be to advocate but not to save, to be a voice but not to be the voice. Mel was striving to center their needs, not his own. The balance was tricky. "I'm sure there were times when I spoke on behalf of the tenants' council where I could've had one of the residents speak. And I think there were probably times when I had someone speak when it might have been more effective for me to speak." On a practical level, the spotlight would shift to him rather than to his neighbors. On a psychological level, it was a path toward otherizing, in which he would not see his neighbors as individuals. They knew their own needs better than he did.

He often reflected on his role, steering away from the temptation to be the person who saves the day at the expense of the humanity of others. Somehow, through his life, Mel came to know that the savior mode was a dangerous one, in which the distance between him and his neighbors would grow too big. Some people realize this when their own needs are crowded out by the desire for someone else to feel heroic. We have a range of motivations for helping others. We volunteer our time and contribute our dollars to people and causes and, in doing so, we feel good when others let us help them. Social scientists call this the "warm-glow effect."

That warm glow is a few favors away from being a serious problem in which we see ourselves as saviors who sweep into causes and communities to perform a rescue mission. In the savior trap, we get hooked on the warm glow. The work becomes more about us than others. We miss opportunities for others to take the lead or gain capabilities because we would lose the opportunity to be a savior. We otherize others. So Mel was smart to reflect often on this balance.

I have been in savior mode more than a few times. For example,

I had a student who I often mentored. For a few days, he was secretly living in the NYU library, as his financial and housing situation had crumbled. When I found out, I was upset that he had not told me. Of course I was worried for him. If I'm truthful, I was also angry because he had taken away my chance to be heroic. I could have found him a place to crash while he sorted things out. This was the kind of problem I knew how to fix, and he had stolen my chance. When I did find out, I did fix it, true savior style. Saviors like problems because we get to solve them. That is a good feeling. But when we are in savior mode, we forget that there are real people behind the problems. When I am in savior mode, I otherize the very people I want to support, prioritizing my needs over theirs.

The way out of savior mode is to redirect your attention to the person or issue you care about. I find when I ask myself, "Who feels an ego boost after I do XYZ, me or the other person?," it is obvious how I am centering my needs over theirs. I can see how much space my feelings and needs are taking up, which is embarrassing. I do not like feeling embarrassed, so once I see what is happening, the adjustment follows quickly.

Sympathy Mode

Mel serves on a board on the Upper West Side whose constituents include mostly black residents of a public housing complex and a group of wealthy white women. The group of women are sympathetic to the residents but have never actually met them, other than perhaps a fund-raiser where one of the public housing residents addresses the audience. The sympathy mode is much like the savior mode, but it is less about solving the problem and more about being the one who does not have the problem. We feel bad for those who do have the problem, but not in a way that connects us. "I call it the charity mindset," Mel explains. "There is no consciousness or empowerment developed on either side. There is no relatedness; it is just about money and hierarchy." The alternative Mel envisions involves relationships and discussions between the two groups to develop a vision of the community values.

Sympathy is different from empathy, as illustrated in the hit animated movie *Inside Out*. The five main "characters" in the movie are five emotions—joy, anger, sadness, fear, and disgust. The Joy character has trouble relating to the Sadness character. Joy feels bad for Sadness but does not "get" her. Joy even draws a circle and suggests Sadness stay inside the circle. Of course, as Hollywood would have it, Joy and Sadness find themselves depending on each other under dangerous and challenging circumstances far from home. It is only when Joy is able to feel what Sadness is feeling that they are able to forge a true partnership and find their way home.

Sympathy is what we are feeling when we are looking at someone in the circle. We feel sorry for them, but we do not try to feel what they are feeling. We view them from a distance, with their feelings otherized from our own. Our well-intended sympathy makes it more about us than about them. Our own feelings are at the center.

Empathy works the other way. We allow ourselves to feel what is happening in the circle. We allow the feelings to spill out of the circle or we are willing to enter the circle. Our attention is centered on what others are feeling, not on what we are feeling. Empathy leads to the behaviors allies strive for.

Sympathy has other costs. When we feel sorry for someone, we inadvertently put ourselves in the high-power position. You may recall from earlier chapters that a feeling of power can emerge easily. For believers, this feeling of power can lead us to unintended perceptions and actions. Research by management scholars Joe Magee, Deborah Gruenfeld, and Adam Galinsky shows that we tune in to our own emotions and needs rather than those of others when we are in the higher-power position. We are less affected by the distress and suffering of others and more likely to attribute blame to the individuals involved. This leads us to be less attuned to their actual needs and to be more attuned to our own emotions. As a result, our emotions can become a burden to the people we are trying to support ("white tears").

Sympathy can also backfire for the target of our sympathy. If the person believes our actions are born of sympathy and not of their merit, their self-esteem and motivation takes a hit. In addition, psychologists Jillian Swencionis, Cydney Dupree, and Susan Fiske explore how our beliefs of the stereotypes others have of us affect our interpersonal interactions. Building on the research about warmth and competence dimensions of stereotypes, they show how people compensate for the warmth or competence dimension they are stereotyped to be lacking in. People stereotyped as being high warmth/low competence—people who often elicit sympathy—will play down their warmth in an effort to play up their competence. In other words, our sympathy can lead the target to be less sympathetic. In sum, sympathy is more costly than helpful to those for whom we feel sympathetic.

Tolerance and Difference-Blindness Mode

Mel takes issue with the word "tolerance." "I don't like that word. It actually doubles down on the otherness factor. When you say you tolerate something, what you're saying is that it's a foreign body. I'm going to tolerate it rather than remove it."

We talk about tolerating gay people, and Muslims, and immigrants, and so on. Mel's challenge is that we consider why it is that we are "tolerating." Author Suzanna Walters explains the problem in her book *The Tolerance Trap*. Tolerance is not an end goal, she says, but a dead end. Activist and comedian Hari Kondabolu echoed this sentiment on the David Letterman show. "What's this tolerance business? What do you tolerate, back pain?" Hari fakes a grimace with a hand on his back. "I've been tolerating back pain . . . and the gay Latino at work.' It's a very low bar for humanity." Tolerance otherizes difference.

Corporate efforts to "manage diversity" are another well-intended but misguided example of the tolerance mode. Business school professor Martin Davidson explains in his book *The End of Diversity as We Know It* that managing diversity suggests there is a problem to be solved. The alternate approach is leveraging difference, where there is an opportunity to be seized. When organizations opt for managing diversity rather than leveraging difference, they engage in different activities and reap different outcomes as a result. The tolerance mode is defensive and narrow.

Color-blindness is another flavor of tolerance and in America it is a popular flavor. Believers are apt to say they "don't see color" or "don't even notice if someone is black or white." Ironically, these statements seem to be said more often when speaking about or to a person of color than about or to a white person, negating the speaker's point. Social psychologists Evan Apfelbaum, Michael Norton, and Sam Sommers ran an experiment demonstrating how deeply ingrained color-blindness has become among white Americans. They used a modified version of the children's game Guess Who. They paired white participants (let's call them Partner As) with either a white or black partner (let's call them the white or black Partner Bs). The goal is for Partner A to guess which one of the thirty-two pictures Partner B is looking at, by asking as few questions as possible. Half of the pictures featured white faces and half featured black faces.

The obvious first question might be "Is the person white?" or "Is the person black?," which would cut the field in half. This strategy, in which racial information is relevant and useful, is not widely pursued by Partner As. Only 57 percent of the Partner As paired with a white Partner B referred to race and only 21 percent of the Partner As paired with a black Partner B referred to race. The Partner As sacrificed their performance in the game in order to be, or appear, color-blind. As a result, they otherized who they were looking at by pretending they did not see them fully. They were motivated by a desire not to be, or appear to be, racist. The effort was for naught. The color-blind Partner As were *more* likely to be viewed as racist than those Partner As who used the relevant dimension of race in their questions.

In the real world, many of us adopt this strategy. Our tolerance and color-blindness began when we were children who asked our parents: "Why does that person have such dark skin/a turban/ only one arm/his arm around that man?" Some of our parents whispered "Shhh" and we inferred that difference was bad.

From there, we carried these ideas of tolerance and color-blindness into adulthood. College admissions expert Karen Crowley is a white woman who still shudders when remembering a conversation with an African American college classmate from more than twenty years ago. In that conversation, Karen proudly declared her color-blindness. "How can you claim to not see my color?" her classmate rebuked. "If you don't see my color, you deny who I am. You deny so much that is wonderful about me. You deny the struggles I've been through. You deny me."

Decades later, Karen still has vivid memories of that conversation. She says it shifted her world view forever. "She was right," Karen reflects. "I really had to sit with that to understand it, but she was right. How could I claim to care about equality if I was blind to the realities of inequality? She was helping me see the difference between not seeing race and not letting race determine how I treat someone." In their book *The Color Bind*, scholars Erica Foldy and Tamara Buckley contrast this kind of color-blindness with "color cognizance," in which race can be openly discussed, even at work.

It is as if our nation collectively misunderstood Reverend Dr. Martin Luther King Jr.'s 1963 "I Have a Dream" speech. When he wished for his children to be judged not "by the color of their skin but by the content of their character," he did not mean that race was never relevant. He meant that we were making it relevant when it was not.

In his book *Racism Without Racists*, sociologist Eduardo Bonilla-Silva explains how color-blindness sets the stage for "color-blind racism," ways of thinking that rely on non-race-related justifications for the vast differences in life outcomes between races. He writes that "at the heart of color-blindness . . . lies a myth: the idea that race has all but disappeared as a factor shaping the life chances of all Americans." Through extensive interviews and survey data, Bonilla-Silva finds that many white people hold an ideology about race in which race is not relevant, which leads to the logical outcome that racial inequities are the fault of the minority group.

Color-blindness is a version of difference-blindness and tolerance that ignores headwinds and tailwinds. When we do this, we unintentionally mask the reality that we are not all walking through life having the same experiences and the same conversations. In America, being black or gay or Muslim affects one's daily reality in ways both positive and negative. When we "don't see difference," we don't see the reality of headwinds and tailwinds. We unintentionally perpetuate a narrative in which that reality does not exist. We negate all that is positive, even glorious, in the experiences of others. Color-blindness assumes everyone has the same experience regardless of their skin color. This is a philosophical statement beyond simply not noticing skin color. When we tolerate or are blind to the real differences between ourselves and others, in order to better "connect" with them, we are doing the exact opposite.

Furthermore, our claim is disingenuous. The research is clear. When we meet someone new, we immediately process and categorize them based on their age, gender, and race/social category. The actual race/social categories may vary by culture. That is, Americans may process race (black, white, etc.) while Indians may process regional origin (North Indian, South Indian, etc.). Regardless of the particular social categories in that culture, the processing occurs automatically. It is rare that we can truly claim that we did not perceive this information. In fact, eye-tracking studies show that the strategy most used to avoid noticing race is to avoid looking at people of color altogether. This is otherizing at the extreme.

The Typecasting Mode

Mel has always been good with kids, the type who would play peekaboo with children of strangers while waiting for the traffic light to change. Now that Melanie is Mel, things are different. When he plays peekaboo with little kids on the street, he is met with distrust by parents. He misses the delight of making a child laugh. He is no longer positively stereotyped, or typecast, as a woman.

The typecasting of women as "wonderful, more nurturing and benevolent than men" is what psychologists call "benevolent sexism." As Melanie, being good with kids was expected. Women are supposed to be nurturing and communal, and thankfully for her, Melanie was. But not all women are good with kids, so if

Melanie had happened to be awkward at peekaboo, she would have been judged harshly. When "women are wonderful," they are penalized for "nonfeminine" behavior, such as competitiveness, ambition, conviction, and career focus. Women are put on a narrow pedestal and the fall is steep.

Those who put women on pedestals rarely see the problem, which lies in the expectation that women *should* behave specifically in this typecast way. When women like Serena Williams are competitive or women like Elizabeth Warren are assertive, we otherize them for not meeting our expectations that women should solely be nurturing and communal. We otherize them for behavior we would not think even once about in men. We also penalize men for behavior we expect from women, as Mel has experienced. There is limited room on the pedestal. Typecasting also emerges from other positive stereotypes, like the "model minority" stereotype of Asian Americans as smart, hardworking, docile, and wealthy. When we assume academic orientation, we miss athletic potential. When we assume financial security, we miss economic need. We see the pedestal, not the person.

Positive stereotypes erode trust. In one study, black participants were shown a video of white participants expressing positive stereotypes about black athletes. They were then asked to evaluate those white participants. The black participants who saw the positive stereotype video evaluated the white speakers as more biased and less likable. The white participants may have been well intentioned, but typecasting otherizes those we mean to compliment. At the core, positive stereotypes are like all stereotypes: they get in the way of seeing people as individuals.*

---

* There are other problems with positive stereotypes beyond their otherizing effects. For example, our positive stereotypes can impose unintended performance pressure, creating the potential for choking under high expectations (Cheryan and Bodenhausen, 2000). Also, our positive biases often have an unspoken negative connotation in a backhanded compliment kind of way (e.g., "she has a pretty face").

De-otherizing

I recently taught a leadership course in a men's prison. Through the New York University Prison Education Program, incarcerated students are enrolled in several courses per semester, earning college credits toward an associate's degree. When I started, I had never met someone incarcerated and I wondered what the students would be like. As a society, we have disproportionately imprisoned black and brown men, and we choose to physically otherize them by removing them from our communities. In my mind, people who were in prison were the ultimate "other." So a lifetime of explicit and implicit biases about incarcerated black and brown men was hard to dodge in my mind as I drove to the prison.

To be clear, I wanted to help. I believe that people who commit crimes deserve punishment and I also want people who commit crimes to be less broken when they return to society, not more broken. Everything I read about mass incarceration told me that the odds were devastatingly in the wrong direction. I wanted to be part of the rehabilitation that is not built into the system.

I went with good intentions to help—and some serious otherizing. I wanted to be the savior professor there to rescue those on wayward paths. I was brimming with sympathy regarding the injustices imposed on innocent or oversentenced men trapped in mass incarceration.

As I would make the long drive to the prison, which sits in a rural area far from where I and most of the men live, I challenged myself to de-otherize my students. It began with learning their names. This was not trivial in prison, where the men were known by numbers, not names. As I learned their names, it made it easier to discover their personalities. I was reminded of Sarah's effort to learn how to say Gita's name and how that led them to de-otherize each other through more open discussion.

As I got to know them, I was startled to realize how "normal" my students were, and I put that word in quotations because I am embarrassed that this is the adjective that kept coming to mind. Some were serious, some were funny. Some were talkative, some were quiet. They were as different from one another as are all of my students. They were a less educated, more intellectually curious version of my MBA students. When I teach my MBA students, I do not expect them all to be the same. I expect that each student will bring a different background and perspective and I seek out those differences. Still, I am always amazed at how I can find some commonality with every student, something that makes us both laugh or that reminds me of myself or that we have both experienced. This was no different with my incarcerated students. The fact that I was surprised reveals how much I had otherized them.

I could see myself in each of them, regardless of who they were or why they were there. One student spoke of how useful it was to learn there was a name for something like "emotional intelligence"—that naming it made it real. I knew that exhilaration of learning. I know that feeling of clarity that comes with learning there is a word for something that I did not know was a "thing." Another student connected the leadership skills in our course to his role as a father. I often lean on (or should lean on) leadership skills as a mother. I definitely related to his struggle. An older student saw himself in the ill-fated protagonist of a case study. So did I. A student cried when he role-played a difficult conversation he needed to have with his ex. I cried, too. To my shock, when I de-otherized, I had as much in common with my incarcerated students as I did with my MBA students.

You Check Your Otherness

Being a savior, feeling bad, being color-blind, typecasting—M
has seen each of these modes in believers with good intentio
He has also seen people with good intentions humanize tho
around him. The difference lies in the connections forged betwe
people, the eye-to-eye, person-to-person humanizing.

Mel remembers what happened after he had made his gend
transition public. Some people questioned his choice or whisper
about his family. Some distanced themselves. Some just did n
know what to say so said nothing (I can imagine myself being
that group). In the eyes of many, he was being otherized.

One person stood out during this time. While Mel did n
know the secretary at his kids' school well, she maintained th
friendly dialogue after Mel's transition was made public. S
sensed his interest in talking and asked him questions. "Eve
day, she would ask me a different question. She was just rea
curious and interested and engaged," Mel says. "We had differe
conversations about what bathroom I am going to use, and ho
the kids are experiencing me, and what did I think about dive
sity in different ways. It was an ongoing wonderful conversatio
It seemed that he felt supported not saved, empathized with n
sympathized for, supported not tolerated, and seen not typecas

Of course, not everyone welcomes questions. Our openne
may vary based on mood, other demands, and who is asking t
questions (and why). Some questions are rude and intrusive. Tir
ing matters and cues should be honored. In Mel's case, the que
tions were welcome, perhaps because they had a focus on him, n
on the secretary. When that happens, psychologist Karen Hua
and her colleagues found that question asking led to more likir
They studied live dyadic conversations and then measured hc

much the speakers liked each other. For example, they found that speed daters who ask more follow-up questions are more likely to get second dates. The follow-up question—one that is responsive to the speaker's previous statement—was particularly good at generating liking. Follow-up questions signal three key intentions on the part of the question asker: understanding of the other person's thoughts, validation of the other person's perspective, and care for the other person. Understanding, validation, and care make us more likable to others, and make them less "other" to us.

Our knowledge of how the brain works suggests that Mel's acquaintance was activating a slew of nonotherizing mental processes in their conversations. Mel was more human and more similar to her as a result of her intentional and responsive efforts to get to know him.

What a difference it makes to be humanized rather than otherized. When otherizing is a threat, Mel explains, the whole point of diversity and inclusion is lost. The identities that lead us to be otherized in the eyes of others are also the identities that should make us valued by believers. Instead, Mel says, "You check your otherness. You learn how to withhold. We're actually acculturating away what makes us special and different, our own diversity within ourselves. And my personal journey has been largely to reclaim all the aspects, all the otherness aspects of myself that I checked and severed and shipped away."

How to Look Out for the "Good" Intentions Without Feeling Overwhelmed

All the dos and don'ts may feel overwhelming. This moment is a good one for remembering how taxing a fixed mindset can be. Yes, there are modes in which we do harm when we mean to do good.

However, we will make things worse if we think of those modes in the either/or mindset. All of us will fall into all of these modes some of the time. If we can approach that reality with a mindset of getting better, rather than of not being bad, we will feel less taxed by the fear of doing something wrong.

If you find yourself thinking "I can't be a savior or that will make me a bad person" or "I will not let myself feel sympathy because people will think I am a racist," you are setting yourself up in an either/or mindset. You are going to try so hard to do the right thing and be so threatened by the possibility of doing the wrong thing that you will probably do the wrong thing or even nothing at all. If we are works-in-progress, we will sometimes do the wrong thing. Try, instead, to think or say "I just slipped into savior mode . . . let me drag myself out by refocusing on you and how you are seeing this situation" or "I'm really caught up in how sad this is making me feel right now. Can I have a moment to regroup so I can focus on your experience instead?" Otherwise, the fixed mindset tax will make it hard for you to do anything. Remember the psychology of good-ish people.

These dangerous modes of good intentions are just that, modes. We can use our growth mindset to pull ourselves out of them. Otherwise, the infinite number of mistakes we can make—some of which we will make—will paralyze us. Ultimately, our goal is to fight bias. At this point, we've done the important internal work to that end: activating a growth mindset, seeing and using our ordinary privilege, and opting for willful awareness. We are ready to start building.

Part IV

Builders Engage

I know you didn't do it, and I didn't do it either, but I am responsible for it because I am a man and a citizen of this country and you are responsible for it, too, for the very same reason. . . .

—JAMES BALDWIN, "WORDS OF A NATIVE SON"

8

Be Inclusive

Max Bazerman is a world-renowned business school professor who is frequently invited to give presentations in high-profile, exclusive forums. Bazerman often accepts, under the condition that the invitation include the PhD student* involved in the work. Some professors do this some of the time, but few as often as he does.

Then Bazerman shares the invitation with the doctoral student. In this example, she happens to be a thirtysomething married mother. Even though she has previously declined similar invitations from Bazerman due to family commitments, he tells her that he does not want to assume her availability one way or the other. The work is hers, so the invitation is hers to accept or decline, not his. She seizes the opportunity and accepts.

In the preparation for the presentation, the student has a different point of view than Bazerman about how the work should be presented. While Bazerman is senior to her, she knows the ins and outs of the project, so he does not assume his viewpoint should take precedence. Bazerman listens to her, without cutting her off, and then they come up with a solution.

As they travel to the event, Bazerman uses the plane time to chat with the student about her other research projects. Looking

---

* PhD students (also called doctoral students) are similar to entry-level hires in many other industries, though some have work experience before starting their PhDs.

at their calendars, they do some work planning and notice they
have different upcoming religious holidays. She and Bazerman
compare notes on holiday plans and traditions, without any jokes
about the holidays or assumptions about which ones are important. Bazerman asks for clarification on the appropriate language
for wishing someone well on her holiday. She asks his advice about
some ideas for her dissertation. He lets the student in on useful
background information about the people she will be meeting the
next day and asks if there is anyone in particular she would like
to be introduced to.

The discussion between Bazerman and the student is warm
and professional without being overly personal. As a straight man,
Bazerman does not say or do anything that he would not say or do
with a male student or in front of his wife. The student never feels
uncomfortable or the need to change the subject. Upon reaching
their destination, Bazerman ensures that the student is safely in
the hotel and then wishes her a good evening.

When the student presents the work the next day, Bazerman
sits on the sidelines and does not interject. Bazerman redirects
questions from the audience to his student, confident that she can
handle the questions, and "reminds" the audience that it was she
who proposed the idea for their latest study. When the accolades
roll in for the work, sometimes when the student is within earshot
and especially when she is not, Bazerman is vocal about her contributions to the work. Afterward, Bazerman includes her in the
wrap-up dinner, providing her access to gatherings that are often
reserved for senior academics, many of whom happen to be white
and male (like Bazerman).

That example is typical of thousands of similar inclusive interactions Bazerman has had over the years. The fortunate student in
that particular example is me. The impact of Bazerman's inclusive
approach over several decades is stunning. For his fiftieth birth-

day, his former students constructed an "academic family tree" to trace where his students—and their students—are now. The tree is a who's who in his field of organizational behavior, all of whom can be traced back to a single mentor. Many of his female mentees have reached very senior levels and broken glass ceilings. Each got to experience what inclusion looks and feels like firsthand.

There are ways we can all be more, or less, inclusive. To understand these opportunities, it is important to distinguish between diversity and inclusion. Some people use these as interchangeable buzzwords. However, building diversity and building inclusion are distinct, as we will see next.

Diversity Is About the Gateways; Inclusion Is About the Pathways

Two of the superstars on Max Bazerman's academic family tree are Columbia Business School professor Modupe Akinola and Wharton professor Katherine Milkman. I was lucky enough to attend graduate school with Modupe and Katy. The three of us are now research collaborators—an all-female, racially diverse (black, white, and brown) research team. Our diversity, collaboration, success, or friendship is not an accident. It is born of the inclusion he fostered.

When we were PhD students, I suspect we each contributed to the diversity statistics tracked by our program. Diversity is often captured in statistics like these. As earlier stories in the book pointed out, it is important and useful to track diversity in sex, gender, race, ethnicity, sexual orientation, religion, and so on. For some organizations and communities, this is the first step. Unfortunately, for many, it is also perceived as the only step. They make the mistake of believing that diversity and inclusion are the same thing.

Inclusion is what happens before and after the official decisio in which people are formally brought into a group. Think of dive sity as the gateways to schools, organizations, and communitie and inclusion as the pathways leading up to and after that gat way. In other words, gateways are the decision points when v track the diversity numbers, such as admissions, hiring, prom tions, and salary decisions. Pathways are the moments that sha those outcomes, but they are not tracked by a formal statistic.

In my example as a PhD student, I had already made it throug the gateway and had been admitted to the program, but my succe would now depend on what happened on the pathway. Bazerma in a slew of small acts in that example, was building inclusion c the pathway. These are the points on the pathways that can tr you up or send you in the right direction. The impact of wh happens on the pathways is harder to track and more informa Modupe, Katy, and I often reflected on how Bazerman's inclusi approach helped to counter headwinds facing women and pe ple of color in our field. He included us in spaces where we d not have natural networks, avoided mansplaining, and redirect credit to us where it was due, even when others tried to give to him. In our world, these small pathway acts have had maj career consequences in the form of greater visibility, enhanced j opportunities, and a persistent sense of belonging.

Soon after we had each completed our PhDs, Katy had an id to translate our real life experience with Bazerman's inclusi approach into a research project. We could study another sma act that was consequential in our world, even before the gatew admissions decision. Many prospective doctoral students wri to the faculty before applying to a doctoral program (as each us did). These emails can lead to meaningful contact, mentorin and networking, which influences admissions decisions when fa ulty members are looking for PhD students with a specific set research interests, skills, and experiences.* Some professors (including us) receive hundreds of these "cold call" emails. In many institutions, this is an informal process that each professor figures out how to handle. Some professors reply to all prospective students; some reply to none; some reply to some. Our central research question was this: Does the responsiveness vary depending on whether a prospective student is or is not a white male?

To find out, we conducted an experiment.† We sent emails to randomly selected professors from 259 American universities. The sender of each email was a (fictional) prospective PhD student from out of town whom the professor did not know. The prospective student expressed interest in the professor's PhD program and sought his or her guidance. The emails were identical and impeccably written, varying only in the name of the student sender, which included Meredith Roberts, Lamar Washington, Juanita Martinez, Raj Singh, and Chang Huang. We tested these names with earlier research participants, who described the names as belonging to either a white, black, Hispanic, Indian, or Chinese student, respectively. We used twenty different names in ten different race-gender categories, some white male and some not.

On a Monday morning, we sent out one email per professor—more than sixty-five hundred in all. Then we waited to see which professors would write back to which students. Of course, some professors would naturally be unavailable or uninterested in mentoring. Since we randomly assigned a student to each professor, these unavailable or uninterested professors would be spread out evenly among all the students. Given that the emails were iden-

---

* Our field, like many academic fields, has a handful of PhD students who work closely as junior research collaborators with faculty members. This feature makes the PhD admission decision more similar in its approach to a hiring decision than a college admission decision.
† Our study was carefully reviewed and approved in advance by two research ethics committees.

tical, the treatment of any particular student (on average) should not differ from that of any other student (on average)—unless professors were deciding (consciously or not) which students to help on the basis of their race and gender.

Let's begin with the fairly good news. Despite the unsolicited nature of the emails, 67 percent of the faculty members responded. More than half of the responders even agreed to meet on the proposed date with a student about whom they knew little and who did not even attend their university. (Importantly, we immediately canceled all meetings, as soon as the professor wrote back.)

The bad news lies in who received those responses. Student identity mattered. Professors were more responsive to white males (in comparison to other students) in almost every discipline and across all types of universities. In a perverse twist of academic fate, bias was most severe at private universities and in disciplines paying higher faculty salaries, with our discipline of business showing the most bias. There, 87 percent of white males received a response compared with just 62 percent of their nonwhite-male counterparts. Even when the student and the faculty member shared a race or gender, we saw the same levels of bias.* Ouch.

This pathway was informal, unmeasured, and fluid. The prospective applicants had not even gotten to the gateway stage of submitting an application, and they were already at risk. The "small stuff" on pathways does not stay small for long. The Matthew Effect still applies, where small disadvantages add up to big things over time.

In your world, there may be different small stuff that matters and different pathways. Some pathways tend to be universal, however: meetings, listening, and credit sharing. These are path-

---

* The one exception was Chinese students writing to Chinese professors. Nonetheless, Chinese students were the most discriminated-against group in our study overall.

ways we travel every day, which gives us many opportunities to make them more inclusive.

Meetings Are a Big Opportunity

Humorist Dave Barry once said, "If you had to identify, in one word, the reason why the human race has not achieved, and never will achieve, its full potential, that word would be: 'meetings.'"

The average employee spends about six hours per week in scheduled meetings with three or more attendees. That number surely goes up if we include meetings with two attendees or virtual meetings. Given how hard it is to synchronize multiple people's presence and attention in a single time and potentially a single space, one might expect meetings to be sources of great value. Instead, employees report a high failure rate that would be unacceptable in most activities; nearly half of their meetings are ineffective. It is as if we filled the most premium real estate on our calendars with shoddy shacks and ramshackle junk.

Tony Prophet, the chief equality officer at Salesforce, thinks this is a missed opportunity. Meetings are filled with "thousands of moments" that reflect the culture of an organization and the culture of more or less inclusion. Tony believes this means meetings offer a prime opportunity for change.

Tony's view of meetings evokes the idea of a "keystone habit" from Charles Duhigg's book *The Power of Habit*. Keystone habits support other habits. For example, for me, going to bed on time is a keystone habit. When I get that one habit right, I cascade into a bunch of other healthy habits (e.g., get up on time, go to the gym, eat a healthy breakfast, be patient with my children, and write early in the morning). Miss my bedtime and I eat Lucky Charms and lose my temper with my kids before 8 a.m.

Meetings can operate as a keystone habit for inclusion. Just
systemic patterns in society will continue unseen and unfelt,
will systemic patterns in meetings. Meetings will replicate t]
headwinds and tailwinds of the organization and society unle
we design them to do otherwise. Run a better meeting, build
more inclusive organization.

Tony likes to ask people to think about the last meeting th
were in. "Who spoke? Who took the majority of the airtime? W]
was checking their messages when a certain person was talkii
and then started paying attention when someone else was talkin
Who threw an idea at the table that wasn't received as a great id
and then, ten minutes later, who else put the same idea on t]
table and all of a sudden it's an incredible idea? Who interrupte
Who was interrupted? Who did you not hear from? Who g
invited to the meeting? Who didn't get invited?" In other word
Tony wants us to notice how inclusive our meetings are.

Start with Noticing

Consultant Max Krasilovsky was attending a training session
work and was assigned to a five-person team to work on a bus
ness case simulation. Max's team included him (a white America
man), two white American women, one man from India livir
in the United States, and one man from Mexico who lived ar
worked in Mexico. By design, all five team members worked f
the same U.S. company and none had worked directly togeth
before. From a gateway perspective, this was a relatively diver
team with different backgrounds and experiences.

As the team began working together, they had a discussic
about roles and responsibilities. The conversation was lively ar

moving fast. The team was varied and interesting. There was a lot of work to do and Max felt they were off to a good start.

However, one of Max's teammates saw things differently. She noticed a pattern in the conversation. Their teammate from Mexico had said very little, though his professional background was relevant to the discussion. She wondered if he was seeing a space for himself in the conversation. "She invited him into the conversation with questions like 'Luis,* you've been within this industry for X number of years; how have you seen trends shift? How do you see things working well and not working well?'" remembers Max.

Luis immediately engaged, going from silent to active participant, suggesting that her theory that the meeting had not been an inclusive one was right. Max realized that he had assumed that assigning clear formal roles and responsibilities would lead to strong performance. Research shows, however, that teams where members contribute more equally to the discussion perform better. Their diverse team was now moving toward inclusiveness.

Max also saw how running more inclusive meetings had benefits for everyone. "It's also about inclusivity of working styles and thought processes, about the uniqueness of every individual," he says. Everyone would be noticed more because "knowing how they're wired and taking that into account in how we reach them" would mean they would tap into the performance benefits of all kinds of diversity. Bottom line, more inclusive meetings were good for the bottom line.

Max's observant colleague tapped these benefits by noticing what was happening. I encourage people to do their own observations of the meetings in their lives, focusing on Tony's questions and more. You may find what researchers find (most of the ex-

* Not his real name.

isting research on this topic has focused on gender). Women are more likely than men to be interrupted (by both men and women). This disparity tends to occur in unstructured activities rather than in situations when people are assigned specific tasks. Power differences have an important role in conversation—for men, that is. When men are in the high-power position in a meeting, they are likely to talk more, whereas women do not talk more when they have more power. Men are also more likely to receive credit for their contributions to collaborative work than women. We can also imagine that further research might reveal parallel patterns on other dimensions like race.

Also, notice how expressions of anger and frustration are treated. Does everyone seem to have the same range of emotions available without judgment from others? Are passion and conviction received the same from everyone? Look at the seating. Who is in a seat where everyone has a good view of him or her? What contributes to, or takes away from, psychological safety in the meeting? Again, the research suggests that you will notice patterns.

Make these observations at multiple meetings and compare. What accounts for the similarities and differences? Ask someone else to do the same and then compare notes about the patterns you noticed. Often, we do not notice whose voices are missing or silent. Arguments in favor of diversity usually hinge on the power of diverse voices. If we do not hear the voices, we lose these benefits. These are the day-to-day behaviors that are creating more, or less, inclusion.

Seating at Meetings

Better meetings make a difference. Research shows that when meetings are satisfying, they actually leave the attendees feeling empowered and, of course, there is the added benefit of the work getting done better. More "deliberative design" of meetings has the potential to redirect headwinds and tailwinds.

The actual design of the meeting depends on its purpose. There is no right or wrong answer to whether meetings should be more or less formal, structured, or facilitated. But the high failure rate of meetings suggests that business as usual is not working. Meetings are neither effective nor inclusive, and chances are that more inclusion will be essential to becoming more effective.

One easy way to redesign meetings is to think about who sits next to whom. When Subha Barry led a wealth management practice at Merrill Lynch, she began thinking about how headwinds and tailwinds were being replicated in the process of how brokers interacted with clients. Certain prospective clients were getting lots of attention and others were not. That was not just bad for inclusion reasons, it was also bad for business. Opportunities were being missed.

At a lunch meeting with a group of clients and brokers, she decided to experiment. One of her "white male, very Midwest brokers would probably be more comfortable sitting with a client who looked like him." Subha sat him next to a doctor with a strong Indian accent. She explains, "If I had not contrived the seating the way I did, they would not have sat next to each other. Sometimes you have to very deliberately create the circumstances and the opportunities where these interactions can occur." Meetings are not only about what is discussed but also about who interacts with whom.

"By the end of the lunch, they had found so many things they had in common. I think they had even made a golf date," she exclaims. Subha used deliberative meeting design to create a more inclusive meeting.

If you are noticing patterns in who sits with whom, and you have influence over the seating, consider assigning seats with a particular purpose in mind, or even randomly. If you do not have influence over the seating (or even if you do), you can also shake things up more informally by sitting next to someone different than usual or in a different part of the room. Get to the room early to do this. If you are worried about offending the people you usually sit near, give them advance warning of what you plan to do and invite them to do the same. You might say, "I've noticed our meetings seem to go the same way each time. I thought it would be good for the group to keep things fresh, so I'm going to switch up where I sit. Are you up for doing the same?"

At the core of an effective meeting is effective listening. Even if we are not in formal, senior positions and even if we do not attend meetings often, listening is still critical to inclusion. How well we do it has great influence over how others experience what communication scholars call the "talk-saturated" moments of our lives. Tony says, "It's just simple things. There are thousands of interactions and nuances."

Listening Better

Few of us are good listeners. Most of us think faster than others speak, creating the potential for significant mind wandering. Immediately after we hear someone speak, we have likely already forgotten about half of what was said, even when we were listening carefully. Communications experts Ralph Nichols and Leonard Stevens shared this finding in a classic *Harvard Business Review* article titled "The Busy Executive Spends 80% of His Time Listening to People—and Still Doesn't Hear Half of What Is Said." This study was done in the 1950s (as evidenced by the male pronoun), before the distractions of technology and the speed of life made listening even harder.

To make things worse, we are not as good at listening to some people versus others. Being a better listener also tunes us in to whose voices are being discounted or muted. This kind of pathway bias is hard to measure and prove to others, so it becomes critical that we bear witness to it when it happens (or listen to those who did bear witness). Then we can amplify those who are muted and include those who are excluded. My dissertation research looked at this issue.

To do this research, I walked up to strangers in the waiting area at a big train station in Boston and recruited them to participate in my study. I gave them the chance to earn some money for getting answers to difficult questions right. My pretests revealed that nobody was good at these questions (e.g., the number of jelly beans in a jar).

But my participants got some help. They got to hear someone else's answer, after which they could use or discount that advice as they saw fit. Unbeknownst to them, I rigged the game so that all the advice they heard was correct. The only variation was the voice behind the advice, which was either male or female and sounded stereotypically "white," "black," or "Hispanic."

The voice mattered. Those participants who were randomly assigned to a female or nonwhite adviser were less likely to take the advice offered. It cost them. Participants with female advisers earned only 69 cents for every dollar earned by the participants with a male adviser. I call this a "stereotype tax" because the game players' stereotypes cost them real money. Without intending to, the game players (both male and female) discounted or essentially muted the female and minority voices. Now imagine how this is playing out in our talk-saturated lives.

Consider Frank Polley, a former Capitol Hill staffer. He remembers a discussion in grad school with his study group. Like his grad school, his group was majority male. At one point, he offered a thought. To his surprise, a female teammate glared at him. "I already said that," she stated flatly. Frank had no idea and did not think it was a big deal. "I sort of brushed it off and apologized at the time. But lying in bed that night, it struck me 'that [it] was a total cliché moment, the kind of moment they have in skits and I just did it.' I think of myself as a progressive, forward-thinking person on this issue, but there I was, guilty of a basic infraction."

Frank says his wife opened his eyes to the big impact of these "small" slights. They entered the workforce at the same time. "She's probably a better worker than I am," Frank admits. Yet he noticed that she was perceived differently than he was. For example, he remembers when she got a performance evaluation saying that she was not "nurturing" enough to her colleagues. "Nobody would ever tell me that, no matter what I did. That's just something I would never have to deal with. She's probably better at bringing people up through the workforce than I would be." It was clear that she was being seen and listened to differently than he was. Research on letters of recommendation and performance evaluations show a similar pattern. Frank suspected that meant that some of what his wife said was not being heard due to the biases through which she was being seen. He could see how similar biases might explain his listening lapse with his female teammate.

Credit Sharing

Frank started thinking about the role listening plays in the sharing of credit. If he was not listening to everyone in the same way, and thus not hearing everyone, then perhaps he was also not giving credit to others for their contributions. Even worse, he might be taking credit for their work.

Credit sharing is complicated. Studies of both collaborators and spouses show that individuals tend to claim excessive credit for their contributions to joint efforts. Ask a husband and wife how much they contribute to the work of a household and the sum adds up to well over 100 percent. We see ourselves as contributing more and we also want to be seen as contributing more. So even good people tend to "round up" in their own favor.

Frank worried that the pattern goes beyond the normal human desire for credit. He remembered an instance where a female colleague did "the lion's share of the work" on a project. However, when the praise came in, Frank was thanked and she was not even acknowledged. "You wake up each day and think, 'What am I going to do to position myself to better my career?' At the time, you take the credit. Looking back on it, I could have done a lot more to redirect the praise to where it was deserved. But I didn't want to give up this moment of praise," he confesses.

Frank's honesty reveals the challenge. Overclaiming credit is something many of us do. Undercrediting people from groups facing bias is also something many of us do. Together, these two patterns are dangerous to inclusion. We do not listen to the contributions from people around us and then we claim their contributions as our own. This makes others less likely to listen to those people. The pattern of exclusion goes on.

The research says that Frank's experience is far from unique. Frank is a believer in a diverse workforce. What makes him a builder of an inclusive workplace is his growing capacity to notice the inclusion failures when, or perhaps after, they happen, and try to do better going forward. He is fighting bias on the pathways.

Gateways are about diversity. Pathways are about inclusion. Gateways are about numbers. Pathways are about behaviors. Gateways are governed by the few. Pathways pertain to us all. Gateways happen occasionally. Pathways happen all the time. Gateways are about who gets let in. Pathways are about who gets listened to.

We have looked at the daily ways in which we can be more inclusive of others on the pathways. The moments when we are more or less included in the presentation, more or less part of the meeting, more or less listened to, more or less credited for our work—these moments shape whether we are given equal chances for success and effectiveness. For those who tend to be more included, confirmation bias will lead us to think everyone is feeling included. We will literally not see or hear the examples of exclusion unless we look for them. Even worse, we will perpetuate it. Now we consider the role we can play in steering conversations to not only be more inclusive in how we have them but also in what we are saying.

9

Steer the Conversation

Before babies can sit up or say a word, they are crafting narratives and telling stories. Psychologists have creative ways of peering into babies' minds, mostly by tracking what they look at, how long they look, and the startle of their eye blinks (which reveals surprise when expectations are violated). When babies watch simple shapes—circles, squares, triangles—move on a computer screen, their eyes reveal that they are constructing a story. They see cause and effect. They form a narrative. They fill in blanks. They are already storytelling to make sense of the world around them.

Humans have been called the "storytelling primate" and "homo narrans." From infancy to the grave, we breathe in and breathe out narratives like Beverly Daniel Tatum's smog. The smog of our culture is everything from the books we read to our babies to the conversations we have with our friends to the explanations we give for current events. We are always forming a narrative of how the world works. These narratives carry our beliefs about headwinds and tailwinds, often in coded and subtle ways that we do not notice.

We can do more than we realize to shape these narratives. Part of what we can do takes place in the microconversations we are (and are not) having when we interact with our friends, family, colleagues, and neighbors. What you say to your children, what you say at work, and what you say in your social circles, these are all microconversations. Part of what we can do takes place in the macroconversations we are (and are not) part of when we consume media and post on social media. What you post on Facebook, who you follow on Twitter, and what movies you see, these are all macroconversations. Each of these conversations carries a narrative as well. We get used to narratives, which hide unconscious and systemic biases in plain sight.

When we steer conversations, we make others aware of the narratives in their minds. These narratives often go unnoticed until we steer the conversation toward making them visible. To illustrate this feature of narratives, we turn to a show that turned Broadway upside down.

What Is True

Hamilton is a smash musical that opened on Broadway in 2015 and went on to win multiple Tony Awards and the Pulitzer Prize. It spawned additional productions in London and Chicago, as well as two national tours, a bestselling book, a chart-topping music album, and the hottest scalper's market in Broadway history. *Hamilton* is a cultural touchstone even for millions of fans who may never see the show. There has never been anything quite like *Hamilton*, the show or the phenomenon.

Lin-Manuel Miranda is the hardworking genius behind *Hamilton*. Much has been written and discussed about how he conceived of, wrote, and starred in the production. Not one bit of it is an exaggeration. He is bilingual in English and Spanish, with parents from Puerto Rico, and an ally to people from many marginalized groups, which is reflected in his work. On top of his creative output, Miranda has a dynamic personality and an accessible social media presence with a huge number of followers.*

Miranda's vision for *Hamilton* was to tell the story of our nation's founding fathers, especially the less famous one, Alexander Hamilton. Both the topic and music of the show were unusual for a Broadway production. Many refer to the show as a "hip-hop musical" (though it is actually a blend of hip-hop, rap, classic show tunes, and Brit pop). It is provocative to some and exhilarating to many to hear music that originated in African American culture used to describe the birth of a country that has systemically enslaved and excluded African Americans. *Hamilton* is, as the show's original marketing tagline said, "the story of America then, told by America now."

Thomas Kail is Miranda's longtime collaborator. While the press has lavished Miranda with the vast majority of the credit for *Hamilton*, Miranda is quick to speak about Thomas, who directed *Hamilton*. Miranda says Thomas is his "creative spouse." As a stage, film, and TV director, Thomas creates narratives for a living. He begins with the vision of a writer and then welds together the work of performers, choreographers, designers, and crew. "My job is to take the blueprint from the writer and serve the writer's vision," he explains. The decisions Thomas made in crafting *Hamilton* made Miranda's vision work, and offer us an example of how visible, and invisible, narratives are in our daily lives.

Coming into the project, Thomas knew all about the founding fathers in a very particular kind of way. "I grew up in northern Virginia, fifteen minutes from Mount Vernon, George Washington's

---

* My husband and I became rabid fans of Miranda years before *Hamilton* opened, when we became obsessed with his first Broadway show, *In the Heights*. We waited for Miranda at stage doors, jogged after him to say hello during a random sighting at LaGuardia Airport, and even framed his autograph. This is the first, and likely only, occasion ever where I have been ahead of a pop culture trend.

home. I went to soccer camp at the University of Virginia, which was founded by Thomas Jefferson. To get there, I would drive by James Madison University. So James Madison, Thomas Jefferson, and George Washington—they seemed one hundred feet tall when I was growing up. They were not real men."

Thomas, a white man with Jewish roots, knew this was not the narrative that Miranda, a New Yorker with Puerto Rican roots, wanted to tell. Something was missing from that narrative. While our history books, monuments, and currency carry the narrative of a country birthed and built by heroic, one-hundred-foot-tall white men, our founding fathers were three-dimensional, human-sized people.

These founding fathers did not birth and build this country alone. The headwinds and tailwinds of the 1700s trapped women in domestic roles and chained Africans kidnapped from their homes to generations of backbreaking labor. Their work was un-paid and the execution of their duties was mandated by either expectation or enslavement. None of this work is represented in the narrative of who founded and built America. Rather, we exalt those who lived in the White House while ignoring the slaves who literally built the White House.

Thomas understood that who we see, and do not see, is a nar-rative in and of itself, even in our leisure-time entertainment. "We know that this country did not come only from the work of white men," Thomas explains. "It would have been a misrepresentation for us to make that case. And so we did the opposite of that. We divided that effort and that work." One result was color-conscious casting in which every *Hamilton* cast features people of color play-ing the founding fathers (George Washington, Thomas Jefferson, James Madison, Alexander Hamilton) as well as Hamilton's wife, in-laws, and most of the soldiers in the Revolutionary War. As director, he steered the conversation about the reality and totality of who built America.

Thomas and his team also did this through design choices, such as Andy Blankenbuehler's choreography and Paul Tazewell's costume design in the show's battle sequences. "The choreography that the men and the women do is often unified. They are wearing [almost] the same clothes, they are moving in the same way. Our women are playing soldiers at a time when women were typically not soldiers." These design choices lead the audience to notice the unnoticed narrative, in which men and women typically dress and dance differently onstage. The result is not only a new narrative about their roles, it is also the realization that many of us had not even noticed what the old narrative was telling us.

"Whatever the facts may say, there's a difference between something that is factual and something that is true. That's the conversation that is happening in our show implicitly and explicitly," Thomas says. Steering the conversation is about helping people focus on what is true.

Thomas has a full portfolio of projects independent of Miranda as well, including the stage production of *Tiny Beautiful Things*, based on the Cheryl Strayed book by the same name. The story focuses on an advice columnist who goes by the pseudonym Sugar and the people who write to her. In the show, each letter writer "appears" in Sugar's kitchen and stays until she replies to his or her letter. While many letter writers appear, the show has only four performers, one playing Sugar and the other three rotating among the various letter writers. When I saw the show, I was taken aback in the first few seconds when a young Latina letter writer appeared onstage and began her letter with "I'm a sixty-four-year-old man." The pattern of the demographics described in the letter not matching the actor onstage repeated throughout the show.

Thomas explains that when a performer walks onstage, with a particular age, gender, and race, we graft things onto who they are. His direction was an attempt to shake up our thinking. "What we're saying is that it can be anybody, that we're all connected, that we have this thing that binds us and bonds us. We wanted to identify our cast as interchangeable and accessible, but specific early in the show." Their stories and identities were unique, but their humanity was universal.

His craft offers a unique opportunity to steer the conversation. He creates art that the rest of us consume and then talk about. With *Tiny Beautiful Things*, he even selected an earlier start time for the show, because he wanted it to end early enough for people to grab dinner and talk about it afterward. He understands that art steers conversations.

"Most of the shows I do concern a group of people who are not listened to or are not heard. I don't claim to understand an experience that is not mine but I still work to understand it," he says. When he was younger, he admits, "I probably came in guns blazing with a lot of things to say. Eventually, I thought, 'You should just shut up and listen a little bit more.'" This growth has allowed him to see narratives and share narratives that would otherwise not be visible to the audience.

The lesson of *Hamilton*, *Tiny Beautiful Things*, and Thomas Kail is not that we all need to become high-profile, Tony Award– and Emmy Award–winning directors in order to steer the conversation. The lesson is that the unnoticed narrative is in our conversations. Some narratives travel through entertainment. Some narratives emerge through our news coverage of who the good guys and bad guys are. Some narratives flow through our talk-saturated lives when we refer to mostly white neighborhoods as good neighborhoods, tall men as presidential, girls with blond hair as all-American, and misbehaving men as boys-will-be-boys. We are always telling and consuming stories about how the world works—through our media, parenting, social circles, social media, and workplace. Let's look at how our consumption of media steers the national conversation and the conversation in our minds.

The Media We Choose

Almost all of us watch movies or TV, listen to music, read books, stream videos, or follow the news. These media narratives are critical to how we view one another and ourselves because media acts as both windows and mirrors. As windows, media offers a look into lives of people very different from us who we might never meet, including those whose stories are undertold. As windows, media has been a powerful force for social change, from *All in the Family* to *Black-ish*, from *Guess Who's Coming to Dinner* to *Brokeback Mountain*.

Psychologist Elizabeth Levy Paluck used a carefully controlled, yearlong field experiment to illustrate how this social change happens through media, using a radio soap opera to study social divides in postgenocide Rwanda. Radio is the most widely consumed form of media in Rwanda, and when Rwanda's Hutu majority killed eight hundred thousand minority Tutsis, the media played an active role in inciting violence. Paluck found a radio soap opera called *Musekeweya* (translation: *New Dawn*) that was trying to quell the violence by featuring an interethnic romance that leads to a peaceful revolution. She ran an experiment. Half of her participants listened to *Musekeweya* for a year while the other half listened to a radio soap opera with a story line about health and HIV. She was interested in how these two programs affected three things: what people believed, what people believed that other people believed, and what people did.

She found that *Musekeweya* did not change what people believed, but it did change their perceptions about other people's beliefs as well as their behavior, as compared to the viewers of the health-themed program. For example, it did not change their beliefs about interethnic marriage, but it did change their perception of how society viewed such a marriage and their willingness to let their own children do so despite their own beliefs. Those who heard *Musekeweya* were more likely to behave differently, with more cooperative problem-solving behaviors, even in ethnically mixed groups. Paluck's work highlights the importance of media as windows that allow us to view social norms, which then affects our behavior and social change.

Media narratives are also mirrors, reflecting back our own humanity. Some of us see ourselves represented positively and accurately in those images. Others rarely do, as we heard about earlier in the "epidemic of invisibility" media studies. Comedian Aziz Ansari satirized this underrepresentation when he recalled being asked if he was excited about *Slumdog Millionaire*, a movie featuring multiple actors of South Asian descent, like Ansari. "And I was like, Yeah! I am! I have no idea why, though, as I had nothing to do with that movie! It's just that some people who kinda look like me are in it, and everyone loved it and it won some Oscars and stuff. And then I was like, whoa whoa whoa—are white people just psyched *all the time*? It's like, *Back to the Future*—that's us! *Godfather*—that's us! *Jaws*—that's us! Every f–ing movie but *Slumdog Millionaire* and *Boyz n the Hood* is us!"

Each time we consume any of these media, we are steering the conversation. The media landscape has changed in dramatic ways in our lifetime, making it easier for us to consume hyper-targeted media and nothing else. Our media can be all mirror, no window.

This problem is exacerbated because certain types of people are overrepresented in mainstream media, as *Project Greenlight's* attempts highlighted. When we exclusively or predominantly consume media that overrepresents some people, it becomes less likely that media with and by underrepresented people will get financed. What we are willing to pay for (via dollars, clicks, eye gazes, views, shares) affects what media creators and distributors will invest in. We consume millions of media narratives in our lifetimes, and each of those is a powerful "grab your wallet" opportunity in which we can be intentional about our media consumption.

We can also multiply the impact our consumption has by being intentional about when we consume the media. Getting a book, album, show, or production financed is very difficult for anyone, and it is especially difficult for less-represented voices. The key insight is this. Early engagement carries the most weight, especially for "not mainstream" projects. Producers and investors view these projects as higher risk and give them less benefit of the doubt when looking at the early numbers. So we can steer the conversation by front-loading our consumption of media about and from marginalized voices through preorders and early engagement. Preorders are often consolidated into week-one sales, which then has a snowball effect on marketing budgets, media coverage, tour dates, store orders, public relations strategies, bestseller lists, and future contracts.

There are easy ways to not only support work you want to see more of but also send a signal to those financing the work to deepen their investment. Buy tickets for those movies in advance and go on opening weekend (or if you are unable to go but have discretionary income, consider buying tickets online for the movie anyway). Preorder those books and albums. Watch those pilots. Follow and share those social media. Be buzzy about all of these media when you interact with people from outside the marginalized group. They are less likely to have heard about it and the project's financial viability may hinge on broader support. (And be on alert for the cookie craving that makes you want to run and tell your black/brown/gay/etc. friends that you saw that great black/brown/gay/etc. movie.)

We can also steer the conversation through more analog media consumption, such as books. If reading fiction is your thing, consider what you read and make it a priority.* Research shows that reading fiction increases empathy, social perception, and emotional intelligence, which we need for becoming the people we mean to be. In addition, fiction has been shown to change beliefs more effectively than nonfiction because reading fiction with social content activates specific parts of the brain. Look at the last three books you read. If the authors all share your identity, you may be missing an opportunity to peek through the window into other perspectives and develop the broader perspective you mean to have.

Finally, a word of warning about a specific form of media: local news. Research has shown that black males are overrepresented as perpetrators and underrepresented as victims on local TV news, as compared to actual arrest reports. News reports are also more likely to portray black males as nameless, and to share information about any prior arrests as opposed to white males. This bias may be unconscious or it may be a deliberate stoking of fear and ratings. Either way, if we are watching the news to know what is true about what is going on in our backyard, we are not getting it. We can steer the conversation by not watching any local news program with this orientation.

---

* Many of us do not "have the time" to read. I am a "born again" reader who discovered in my forties that many of the most impactful and busy people in the world find time to read. For ideas on how to do this, go to www.dollychugh.com

Parenting

While not all of us are parents, parenthood offers another opportunity for noticing narratives. Parents are the Thomas Kails of our children's narratives. Especially when children are young, we write the scripts they hear at home, we choreograph their growth, and we orchestrate their interactions with the world (or at least we try). So one place to begin is to consider what we are and are not discussing with them.

In chapter 7, we debunked the difference-blind, difference-mute approach (e.g., color-blindness and tolerance). This approach is what many of us are consciously or unconsciously teaching our children. For example, researchers found that almost none of the white mothers in their study discussed race with their children (ages 4 to 5) even when sharing books that directly or indirectly dealt with race. Tailwinds make these discussions unnecessary. Meanwhile, children of color do have these conversations with their parents, early and often, because they are necessary to survive the headwinds.

This silence is particularly destructive given what we know about how children build narratives starting in infancy. For example, when psychologists asked children (ages 5 to 10) for an explanation of why the first forty-three presidents were white (this study was conducted in 2006), 26 percent of the children believed it was illegal for a black person to be president. In the absence of a narrative being provided to them or constructed with them, they had created a narrative complete with cause and effect. Another study found that by the age of about 5 or 6, white children show the same implicit biases as their mothers. Our silence creates a loud narrative.

Steering the conversation is not limited to what we talk about.

Research says we are missing opportunities to steer the conversation with our children through positive images of people from different groups, cross-group friendships that they form, and even cross-group friendships that they witness. We can influence what books our kids are reading, what shows they are watching, and what games they are playing. Are your white children reading books with nonwhite protagonists? Are your boys watching TV shows and movies with female leads? Are your straight children meeting your gay friends?

Consider these findings from the Geena Davis Institute on Gender in Media, which focuses on portrayals of women and girls in media directed at children eleven and under. This particular study focused on family films (rated G, PG, or PG-13) and their gender portrayals. The researchers, led by media scholar Stacy Smith (who did the "invisibility" work featured in chapter 1), focused on the speaking characters in 122 films released between 2006 and 2009. Of the 5,554 distinct speaking characters, 29 percent were female and 71 percent were male. Furthermore, 24 percent of the females shown were in sexy, tight, or alluring clothing. These are kids' movies, including animated films. Furthermore, their analyses were virtually unchanged when compared to a similar study of family films done twenty years prior and echo the findings of analyses of movies for grown-ups.

They also found that 7 percent of the directors, 13 percent of the writers, and 20 percent of the producers of these films were female, an even smaller percentage than those in the study from chapter 1, which focused primarily on movies for grown-ups. Their analyses revealed that when one or more women were writers, it led to a 10 percent increase in the speaking roles for women in the movie. What happens behind the camera and what happens on camera are not unrelated.

The movies specifically created for children are feeding them a diet filled with stereotypes and biases. We can steer our children to a more balanced consumption of movies. Other film options do exist, but they may require us to do a bit more research. We can also steer the conversation in our families and in our minds about these movies, which many of our children are going to want to see. We can point out imbalances, ask them to look for patterns, and draw their attention to certain characters (fair warning: my kids sometimes request that we "just watch a movie tonight without Mom commenting," so it is possible to go too far).

As we move from believer to builder, we are also modeling a mindset for our children. I have lost count of how many times my implicit biases have shown up uninvited in comments I have made to my daughters. When they call me on it, it embarrasses me to no end. When they ask, "Mommy, why did you assume the boss was a man, not a woman?," my instinct is to cover up until my growth mindset pokes me, reminding me that I am stumbling upward and that my children are watching how I handle my own mistakes. So, instead, I try to resist the urge to cover up. I laugh at the mistake, activate my growth mindset, and let my kids teach me.

Social Circles

As a leadership coach, Jeana Marinelli helps people rise up to their best selves and thrives on bringing people together into learning communities. As a white Christian woman, she has white friends from her childhood in suburban California; black and Latinx friends from her work in the education and nonprofit sectors; and Christian friends of multiple races and ethnicities from her church and across the country. We have worked together in the past and I am one of those friends.

As Jeana travels through multiple demographics in her personal and professional lives, she notices stark differences in narratives. For example, in 2016, videos of police shootings of unarmed black men kept surfacing, leaving her grieving and heartbroken. She noticed this news cycle was not being processed in the same way across her friends. "Half of the people in my life were grieving, crying, emotionally bleeding," Jeana says. "The other half either knew it was terrible yet weren't sure why it was happening or weren't talking about it at all. Many of my white Christian friends were in the second group." It was this lack of conversation that made her wince and wonder what she could do. "As long as I'm not talking about these issues within my own community, I am part of the problem. It is complicit silence." She felt pulled to start a conversation, particularly with friends who looked like her.

A few months later, on the heels of the 2016 presidential election, Jeana was organizing her annual pre-Thanksgiving gathering of friends. She had started this "feast of gratitude" tradition several years prior, when a close friend died at a young age. She hoped the group would put aside the election for the evening and focus on what they were grateful for. Then, during a conversation with me, an insight hit her. "I realized that people who were more directly affected by the outcome of the election did not have that privilege," she recalls. As a white Christian woman, she was feeling a responsibility and recognizing her ordinary privilege.

Jeana felt she needed to host an additional evening. She invited twenty white Christian female friends, people who shared three aspects of her own identity (race, religion, gender). "I knew we were grieving the outcome of the election, yet we needed to grapple with the fact that the majority of women who share a similar identity voted for the very outcome that we were grieving." She wanted the narrative that had been present in the United States long before the 2016 election to surface.

Jeana felt it was important that people make a clear choice to participate and engage fully, so her invitation spelled out the purpose and commitments of the evening. She wrote that "the primary goal of this conversation is to do that which we don't normally do—talk about the intersection of our faith, our shared beliefs, our privilege, our gender, our race, our responsibility, our failings, and our feelings. We will listen, we will talk, we will pray." She laid out eight commitments she asked each person to make, if they wanted to attend, including doing one hour of pre-reading, being willing to share their thoughts, being willing to listen to others' thoughts, upholding confidentiality, and practicing grace for others. Jeana received interest from sixteen of the twenty invitees and twelve—exactly the number she could fit in her apartment—were available to attend on the Monday after Thanksgiving. She was terrified and wondered if she was the right person to be doing this. Nonetheless, she still moved forward.

Jeana sent those twelve participants the prework. She gave them articles on topics such as white privilege and white silence and asked them to work on reflection questions, centering on the readings as well as their own experiences. She also asked each participant to come with a passage from the Bible that spoke to how they were feeling about the election. "I had participants do the majority of the thinking, writing, and speaking so that they could actively engage and make connections to where they are and how they need to move forward," she says.

Jeana's Christmas tree and many candles lit up the room as the participants arrived. To her shock, they were early (unusual in New York City). Jeana was encouraged, as she had requested that everyone eat beforehand, arrive on time, leave their technology in their bags, and stay until the end. She asked them to sit in a circle facing one another. As she looked around the room, she noticed that the women had a broad range of positions of power and influence, as journalists, artists, finance executives, nonprofit leaders, photographers, parents, spouses, and more.

They began the evening with prayer and then some joy and laughter as Jeana had everyone pair off and tell each other their favorite Christmas song. Then she led the group into a more serious discussion, with prompts such as "Describe your journey to faith" and "What sources of strength do you see in your identity as a white Christian woman?" "At this point," Jeana explains, "we were positively connecting to who we are, what we believe, and our identity."

From there, Jeana brought up the prereadings. She wanted each person to be reflective more than reactive, and for that reason she had questions prepared in advance that each person responded to, with every segment of the agenda timed. Jeana felt that the structure and timing would create a sense of safety for each person to practice sharing and practice listening. The group broke up into trios to discuss what resonated with them in the readings and what challenged them. They closed this segment with the question "What is your role in how we got here?"

The evening ended with a group activity. Together, the group wrote a progressive prayer by writing a line and then passing it to the next person. Each of them took home this new prayer, born of their growth together. While the evening formally ended at 10 p.m. as scheduled, many of them stayed longer. "Even some of the people who had to get home to little kids stayed around. For the most part, no one had ever thought about these issues before," Jeana says. The evening's conversation blew her, and her friends, away. "Wow, I considered myself educated on these issues, and I had no idea how much I wasn't," one friend wrote later.

One year later, Jeana emailed the group to ask about the impact of the conversation. One friend reflected, "Our conversation encouraged me to not just stop [by looking inward], but to continue to educate myself and to advocate for change. This year has been all about both." Another friend, who has a digital platform that reaches more than two hundred thousand women, said the conversation pushed her to become "more aware of the lack of diversity in my own life and relationships and to ask myself 'why.' I noticed that our platform featured almost solely white women—and blond women at that. We've been actively pursuing new partnerships, and building relationships with a more diverse group of women." They were seeing and using their ordinary privilege in new ways. By steering the conversation in her social circle, Jeana steered their conversations in their worlds, as each of them works in a different organization, lives in a different neighborhood, and comes from a different family.

Jeana's confidence was bolstered as well. "The confidence I got was that it is okay to act even if you are scared. It is impossible to do any of this without making a mistake. Not acting when I was scared would be another act of privilege," she says. She went on to initiate conversations with local church leaders, nudging them to lead conversations with their communities. She privately messaged friends after questionable social media posts and asked if they would be willing to talk or consider an alternate perspective. Some were. Jeana says, "I realize that what appear to be big changes are really the result of tiny steps that we might be terrified to take."

Social Media

It has never been easier to trap yourself in an echo chamber and it has never been easier to drop into someone else's echo chamber with social media. We can hear voices far outside our echo chambers. If you are not black but want to learn more about the beauty and burden of being black in America, Twitter is a blessing. The percentage of black Internet users who use Twitter is twice that of white Internet users, and black Twitter users tend to be more active than white Twitter users. This trend has led to a porous virtual community known as Black Twitter.

Not everyone on Black Twitter is black, and everyone black on Twitter is not engaged with Black Twitter. Those who are engaged with Black Twitter go in and out of a 24/7 conversation, fueled by current events and pop culture. Activism, humor, advice, camaraderie—it can all be found there. Of course, there are as many perspectives from black tweeters as there are black tweeters, reminding us of the diversity of the black experience. Ethnographer Meredith Clark had the insight that this virtual community can be studied through scholarly methods, just as physical communities are. Her research belies some narrow media accounts of Black Twitter as a place for "the black perspective." She found that the medium was playing a robust number of roles.

Black Twitter offers all of us an opportunity to learn. Only Internet access is needed to get started. A search for #blacktwitter will lead to the most recent trending hashtags and the most followed tweeters. Additionally, a quick Internet search for "who to follow on Black Twitter" reveals whose voices are most influential at the moment.

It is important to note that these conversations are what Clark describes as "public-private" conversations. Just as one might eavesdrop on a nearby conversation at a coffee shop, one can do the same on Black Twitter. Of course, being able to hear the conversation is not the same as being invited to join. To engage is to listen harder and stay quieter, especially when something makes you mad or uncomfortable. This may be a moment when your privilege is being revealed to you, if your growth mindset will allow it. The headwinds of most spaces make it difficult for the conversations of Black Twitter to happen freely. Do not create a headwind in this space.

You may find the rules that Felicia Fulks created for the private online space we heard about in chapter 4 helpful.

More broadly, social media allows us to wander beyond our personal networks. Black Twitter is just one example. We can follow listservs/blogs/hashtags that are written primarily for and by people with different identities than our own. We can surf news sites that include stories specifically relevant to people outside of our demographic. It is easy and private, and expands the narratives in our minds.

Workplace

It has taken me a long time to decode workplace narratives. I confess that I have said that women are opting out, that there are no qualified African Americans in the pipeline, that a recent hire needed to dress more professionally, and that a first-generation college graduate might not be a good fit for our culture. Of course, people opt out, pipelines need to be filled, professional dress is important, and a person who is a bad cultural fit can be a problem.

Still, sometimes what looks like opting out is a reflection of headwinds; think about Kim Davis at the senior women's event where people looked through her (she did not opt out, but many of us would). Pipelines may not be filled because they were de facto closed pathways in the past; think about Project Greenlight Digital Studios. Professionalism standards are often a reflection of a single culture, body type, hair texture, and beauty standard, as Jodi Picoult heard from attendees at the antiracism workshop. On both sides of the interviewing table, I have spoken with passion about the importance of "fit." I have looked for people who "were a good cultural fit" and pitched myself as a "strong fit for a performance-oriented culture."

Sociologist Lauren Rivera reveals that "fit" can be a code word. In her ethnography of investment banks, law firms, and consulting firms, she studied students from elite universities applying for jobs in elite consulting and investment banking firms (that would be me, earlier in my career). She found that fit is often more about passion-oriented hobbies (e.g., marathon running) and alma maters (e.g., those at which people of color are underrepresented) than work aspirations. I see now that my statements about "fit" revealed a narrative that presumes a workplace—and a world—with no headwinds and tailwinds.

The language of the workplace also carries many narratives. Journalist Jessica Bennett decoded some of the sexist language in her useful (and funny) book *Feminist Fight Club*. To figure out "is that description sexist?" she recommends the "law of reversibility" as follows: "Step 1: Reverse the gender of your subject. Step 2: See if it sounds funny. Step 3: Repeat." Consider when we describe women as emotional, crazy, bossy, or aggressive. Would you use those same terms to describe a man? The law extends to other identity dimensions, such as when we describe African Americans as well-spoken, articulate, clean, or qualified. Would you use those same terms to describe a white person? We can catch ourselves, and gently catch others, based on the law of reversibility.

Our unconscious biases often have easy access to our key decisions and activities because of how the systems and structures are set up. Some readers may have direct influence over the systems and decisions of their workplaces. In those cases, there is a growing body of evidence to guide you on how to redesign those systems for greater equity. For example, behavioral economist Iris Bohnet argues in her excellent book *What Works: Gender Equality by Design* that "behavioral design offers a new solution . . . by debiasing organizations instead of individuals." She guides readers on how to collect and use data within an organization to adopt evidence-based interventions that strip bias out of a decision-making process, before it does damage, by being more intentional about creating role models, crafting groups, shaping norms, and increasing transparency.

"Nudges," first written about by economist Richard Thaler and legal scholar Cass Sunstein, are also useful. Nudges do not dictate people's choices, but they do direct them. Laszlo Bock, who led Google's innovative People Operations group for ten years, describes the value of nudges in *Work Rules!* For example, his team found that providing checklists to managers—which simplified the number of choices and decisions a manager faced when onboarding new hires—improved managerial behavior and onboarding success. Similarly, these kinds of nudges may be powerful in countering bias. Any employee could draft a checklist on how to ensure one is not "hitting the easy button" when putting together a panel or recruiting new employees. Senior leaders can build these kinds of nudges into the systems of the organization.

Most of us have more limited influence. Still, we can make use of what Kevin Ferreira van Leer (Jodi Picoult's son-in-law) calls the "ripple up" effect. He noticed that many workplace narratives are simply never questioned. Like buzzwords, they just become what everyone says and thinks. We can play dumb or we can play tough, but either way, a powerful way to shape the conversation is to ask a question. What do you mean by fit? Would you feel differently about her behavior if she were a man? Have we ever tried interviewing at the state university in addition to the private colleges on our recruiting list? How can we encourage more people of color to apply? How might we be inadvertently discouraging LGBTQ+ employees from joining informal social events? Why are only people of color joining the diversity initiative? We can ask our colleagues, our bosses, our human resources team, our vendors. When we ask polite questions, we gently force people to make the case for the narrative or to adjust it.

As we steer conversations, we will also encounter biased behavior and statements in others. Many of us find these moments stressful. We wonder what to do and whether our actions even matter. As builders, we want to engage, but we do not know how. Now we dig into how to handle those moments—what to say, who to say it to, when and where to say it, and why and whether to bother.

10

Educate and Occasionally Confront Others

We had reached the final event of our multiple-event Indian wedding. That was where I lost my cool with a guest and regretted my outburst for years. It had been a lovely and laid-back backyard brunch. Then a guest cracked a "joke." "It's too bad," he said, "that your wedding announcement was ruined when they put those two women next to you in the newspaper." His homophobia got a laugh. I wanted to vomit. I do not remember what I said, but I do remember that I lashed out in an indignant bluster.

He looked befuddled. The uncles and aunties within earshot sank into silence and the rest of the event was awkward. Psychological safety was nowhere to be found. I felt regret and shame for ruining the celebratory mood. I was convinced that I should have kept my mouth shut, not because I was wrong but because I knew I had not put a dent in his homophobia.

For every instance like that one, there are a dozen others where I was a bystander. The bystander effect is the perverse reality that we are less likely to help a person in need when others are present, which means that if you are going to have a medical emergency on a sidewalk, you are better off if there is only one person walking by versus if there are fifty people walking by. The same concept applies to situations where people say or do something biased. In fact, the bystander effect is even more pronounced in these situations. Non-target-group members tend to not feel it is their responsibility to respond if target-group members are present. These are the moments when allies are needed the most and are hardest to find. I have sometimes been more bystander than ally. I did not know what was worse—saying something that did not matter or not saying anything at all.

Saying Something (Usually) Does Matter

The research says that I was wrong to think about it in that way. Saying something *does* matter. While these moments often feel like negative and unsatisfying confrontations, studies show that they nonetheless can reduce bias in subsequent behavior and attitudes. Even people who react defensively when confronted about biased behavior go on to show less biased behavior in the future. When I learned this, I remembered Lin-Manuel Miranda's *Hamilton* lyric about "planting seeds in a garden you never get to see." The research on the impact of confronting individuals after their biased behavior is encouraging.

The research on social norms is also encouraging. Social norms are the unspoken rules dictating what will earn us the approval, or disapproval, of others.* For example, in some places, it is customary to make eye contact and say hello when passing a stranger on the street. Out-of-town visitors will notice the norm and adapt to it. Most of the time, most of us follow social

---

* Social norms are either what we think everyone is doing (descriptive norms) or what we think everyone should be doing (prescriptive norms). For our purposes, both are relevant.

norms. When others donate to charity, vote, conserve energy, reuse hotel-room towels, cheat, and binge-drink, we are more likely to do the same.

Recall the work by psychologist Elizabeth Levy Paluck that shows how media affects people's perceptions of norms and behavior, even when it does not affect their beliefs. Additional research shows that the degree to which people act in prejudiced ways is highly correlated to the degree to which they think it is okay—in the eyes of others—to act in prejudiced ways. If they think it is the norm to laugh at certain jokes or say certain things, they will. If they think it is not okay, they will not. The implication of this tight correlation is that a change in norms could lead to a change in behavior. If we signal that it is not okay to say or do biased things, that may be enough to change some behaviors.

Just one person violating a social norm can loosen its hold. Few want to be the first one on the dance floor, but plenty are willing to join in once the norm of being too cool to dance is broken. If one person expresses antiracist views, others are less willing to tolerate racism. When multiple people appear to violate a social norm, that is even more powerful. Paluck stressed that attitude change is not necessary for behavioral change. In one study in a high school, she found that changes in norms—specifically, encouraging a small group of "in" students to change their stance on bullying—reduced bullying by 30 percent, a far better intervention than the usual, broad-based efforts aimed at changing everyone's attitudes about bullying.

The takeaway is that changing people one at a time is not the only path we have for educating and confronting people. We can also change, or at least violate, norms. In fact, doing so may be more efficient than changing people one at a time.

Heat of the Moment

Based on the research, I became convinced that it was right to say something at my wedding brunch, but I could have been savvier about how I did it. Again, research can guide us on what does and does not work. Psychologist Aneeta Rattan says that her research with Carol Dweck demonstrates that "your belief system about others [and their capacity for growth] can either be a barrier or a staircase where you can take that first step." They find that our mindset about the malleability of others' personalities (fixed—people won't change; growth—people can change) determines whether we confront prejudice. Here, we are not referring to our own growth versus fixed mindset, but to our mindset about others.

These beliefs are useful guides for making the flash decisions needed for incidents that catch us by surprise. We have little time to plan our response to such incidents and ample time afterward to second-guess it. Thus, it is useful to have an easy framework to guide those heat-of-the-moment decisions. This framework will help you make quick decisions about

WHOM to engage with (and, more important, whom not to);

WHY you are engaging them (to change behavior or to change norms);

HOW you engage (making your growth mindset visible to others);

WHERE AND WHEN to engage (on the spot versus later, in public or in private); and

WHAT you say (humanize or factualize).

Global change consultant Susan Lucia Annunzio leads the Center for High Performance. Long ago, we worked together and she taught me the 20/60/20 rule she uses to help companies through massive culture change initiatives. She challenged the prevailing view that change efforts needed to convert every employee. Her insight was that there are three types of individuals in organizations facing change. One group of 20 percent is on board with the change and ready to go. Another 20 percent will resist or even sabotage your efforts; they will drain your energy. The leverage rests with the "movable middle" 60 percent; they are reading the room and can be influenced by either 20 percent group.* Educating and occasionally confronting others is taxing work and we cannot possibly act on every opportunity or be effective in influencing everyone. We are wise to prioritize. The 20/60/20 rule offers guidance on which of those opportunities to act on and which to pass on.

While Annunzio developed the 20/60/20 rule in a different context, we can adapt it to the psychology of educating and occasionally confronting others. For example, psychologists Ashby Plant and Patricia Devine studied what motivates people to become less biased or to "control their prejudice." They found that people hold internal and/or external motivations. An internal motivation comes from their own values, their own pull toward being the person they mean to be. An external motivation is tied to how they are viewed by others. People can be high in both, or high in one and low in the other, or low in both. Plant and Devine found that people who have high internal motivation and high external motivation are the most receptive to growth. In the 20/60/20 framework, this group is the 20 percent who are ready to go. I call them the "easy 20."

---

* The numbers are more symbolic than mathematical. The key is that there are three groups and the middle group is the biggest.

Another group lacks both internal and external motivation to control prejudice. I call this group the "stuck 20." They are not believers and are not showing signs of being open to growth. They may be loud and opinionated or quiet and resistant. Either way, they will suck the life and sustainability out of you if you try to educate or confront them. A good test for whether you are dealing with a stuck-20 person is to respond to their claim of "It seems to me that XYZ is overreacting" or their "joke" about a marginalized community by saying "I see it differently. Are you open to listening to my perspective?" Ask this question calmly and respectfully as early in the conversation as you can. Give them the opportunity to activate their growth mindset. If they resist or hedge, you are probably talking to a stuck-20 person.

You may have argued with this person at Thanksgiving or on Facebook. If your goal was to change them, this was time wasted. Their ability to hurt others needs to be neutralized. Focus your energies on the people who are being hurt. This is not an issue of education or confrontation.

When they are family or close friends, you have a choice to distance yourself from the relationship or not. If you choose to stay connected, as many of us do, the challenge is to state your stance calmly and then disengage, sometimes repeatedly. The key is not to remain silent and not to escalate. Escalation goes nowhere with this group and will drain you. Note the difference between stating "I and many others see things differently, Uncle" versus trying to convince Uncle that he is wrong. State your dissent and then focus on others who may be listening, which brings us to the "middle 60."

The middle 60 percent is best characterized by passivity and silence, the people we are least likely to notice. This is the group most susceptible to influence, from either of the 20 percent groups. They are the high-external/low-internal-motivation-to-control-prejudice group. This group is influenced by social norms. We often forget about this group. This is where our attention is most effectively—and least likely to be—spent.

Revisiting the Wedding Brunch

The 20/60/20 rule highlights the mistakes I made at my wedding brunch. First, I did not consider whether this was the right person to engage. I didn't even really know him (traditional Indian weddings are sprawling affairs with many guests who do not have direct ties to the people getting married). I was ill equipped to determine if he was a middle 60 or a stuck 20. Just the fact that he told the joke suggested he might be a stuck 20. I could have tested this by saying "I feel different about that wedding announcement. In fact, a good friend of mine and his husband just got married. Would you like to hear about their wedding?"

Had he shown interest, our conversation could have begun. Had he dismissed my remark, I could have disengaged with him and turned my attention to the middle 60. That is, once the "who" was clear, I could see the "why" more clearly; I needed to engage with the observers to change the norms, not the offender to change the individual. I could have chatted with people in smaller groups about the issue, with less tension and more intimacy. As a bride, I had a captive audience.

This brings us to the "how." The "how" is important with everyone, but especially with the middle 60. Remember, most of us have a highly central moral identity. We value feeling like and being seen as good people, so we are unlikely to gain anyone's trust by accusing them of being bad people. Does this mean we are conceding to white fragility and its counterparts for straight people, etc., in order to create psychological safety? Somewhat.

This is another way to use your ordinary privilege. Engaging with the fragility of others is excruciating for those who are the target of their bias. As a straight bride, I was not the target of the offender, so I could carry the weight of accommodating the fragility of others. In other words, I could take responsibility for creating psychological safety so that those being targeted did not have to.

This brings us to one important component of the "what." Especially with the middle 60, make your own growth visible in order to build psychological safety. In my case, I lashed out with moral certainty, as if I had never been on the wrong side of history. Yes, of course my gay friends are no less human than me and deserve no fewer legal rights, wedding events, and silly newspaper announcements. Still, I have plenty to learn and I could show that to others by saying things like "I confess that I look twice when I see two women holding hands, but . . ." or "I did not grow up talking about these issues, but I am trying to learn more and here is what I have learned so far."

To further put others at ease, I also could have used humor. Despite what my children tell me, I have a decent, self-deprecating sense of humor. I could have used it to build psychological safety especially since this was a public setting, not a private conversation. "Oh, Uncle, you're kidding, right? You look too young to be that old-fashioned!" or "I agree, Uncle, they looked so pretty, they made me look shabby in my wedding announcement!"

When it comes to "what" to say, you may wonder whether you should lean more on facts or stories during your attempts to persuade. The research on persuasion is helpful here. With the easy 20, either facts or stories are useful. With the stuck 20, neither facts nor stories are useful. With the middle 60, all other things being equal, stories are the way to go. Persuasion researchers find that attitude change happens through dual processes, both central and peripheral processes. The central process relies on careful consideration of facts and logic while the peripheral process is based more on stories and emotion. Research reveals that the less invested someone is in an issue, the more effective the peripheral process is. The middle 60 tends to be less invested. Stories generate quick bursts of emotion and humanity. Facts are obviously important, and are useful for rebutting falsehoods, so know and remember as many as you can. When in doubt, however, stories are more likely to persuade the middle 60.

In terms of "when" and "where," consider whether embarrassment of the other person works in your favor. It might, if they are a stuck 20 and you can shift norms of the middle 60. It might also shame them, which we know is not good. They will be less likely to listen, and if it looks like we are attacking them, that may invoke the support of the movable middle 60. Never forget, especially with the stuck 20, that you are playing to the crowd listening in. They are the ones you are trying to educate. At the brunch, it would have been easy to wait a few minutes and then pull the gentleman aside privately.

These rules also work on social media. In fact, I do sometimes "argue" with people online, but I am intentional in framing my arguments toward the middle-60 people I know are reading, not the person with whom I appear to be engaging. This makes me willing to "lose" arguments (in the eyes of the person with whom I appear to be arguing) by disengaging early or ignoring bait. According to my goal to speak to the middle 60, I win, because I have countered the norm of that space. They are listening, even if they are not commenting. Winning the argument is not what breaks the norm. Breaking the norm breaks the norm.

If the target of the bias is present, we may be less inclined to get involved, because we feel it is not our place or we do not want to speak over or for someone. Yet a big part of allyship is speaking up and not leaving people on their own when they are targeted. This balance between not being a bystander but not speaking over or for someone is tricky. One approach is to turn to the target and simply ask for their guidance on whether they would like you to intervene. We can say "Would it be okay if I jumped in here?" or "I know you can handle this, but I'm here as backup" or "I'm happy to take this one" or "Say the word if I can help." When in doubt, say more, not less.

Do not speak for people, but speak for what you have learned without centering yourself in the conversation. Be attuned to signals that you have made a misstep (everyone does, at times) and step back when asked, without defensiveness or explanation. Use your ordinary privilege for others until you are directly or indirectly told to stop, and then stop and learn from that moment. We have a natural instinct to seek affirmation from the target for our efforts. Crush that instinct. Do not let the moment become about you.

The 20/60/20 rule illustrates a variety of light-based ways for educating or confronting others. We often assume heat and darkness are our only options, and this is not true. Given that I have no objection to heat but am not particularly skilled at using it, light-based options give me more opportunities to move from believer to builder.

Practice is a big part of applying the 20/60/20 rule in educating and occasionally confronting others. Stories from three individuals who have been practicing and learning over time bring these lessons to life. In each story, we will hear of a different context and approach. First, David will tell us about his strategy to keep the conversation going with his boss. Then Bassey will describe her strategy of hooking into the other person's personal experience. Finally, Jessie will tell us about her strategy of leaning on the relationship with a friend. Each is a case study in how to do better.

Keeping the Conversation Going

Consultant David Johnson* let down his female teammate. A pro bono client had told David and several of David's colleagues how women were best suited for lower-level jobs in the client organization. David, who is a straight white male, disagreed strongly but said nothing in defense of his one female colleague's equal role on the consulting team. No doubt it was a tricky situation fraught with power issues (not wanting to offend the client) and cultural considerations (the incident took place outside the United States).

Still, he disappointed a valued friend and professional contact with whom he would interact time and again. "The thing that bothered me the most was that this is a friend who is exceptionally capable and doesn't fit into the description he's putting out there, and I didn't do anything in that moment." In the cab afterward, he apologized to her, but the damage was done.

She helped him realize that he could have said something like "Oh, that's interesting. Our team is set up differently. For example, both Jessica and I have the same roles on this team. She and I will both be handling your project." At the time, he could not think of what to say and the risks of saying anything seemed great. But it was not even a paid consulting assignment. Their team was part of a student consulting organization doing pro bono work overseas. In the heat of the moment, the risks may have seemed higher than they actually were.

Several years later, that moment is still with him as he advances in his consulting career. The consulting firm where David currently works is similar to many organizations in its gender balance. There are similar numbers of men and women in the ju-

* At his request, his name and others in his story have been changed.

nior ranks, and far more men than women in the senior ranks. Diversity, in general, is actively talked about. "But I have never heard the managers talk about the difference between diversity and inclusion," he notes. The focus is on the numbers and David fears that they do not see the headwinds and tailwinds behind those numbers.

In particular, David works closely with a "very senior" manager based in Chicago doing work requiring significant travel and long hours. His manager "comes from a school of thought that some of these women are going up for partner or making partner even though their merit does not justify it on a numbers [revenue generation] basis." David says the gender conversation comes up frequently. "Just in the past two days, it has happened twice, once at a work dinner and once after a meeting, when the female members of the team had left the room."

David has made a conscious choice to encourage and engage in this conversation, by trying to educate his manager on headwinds, tailwinds, and missed opportunities. "I've tried to engage him in thinking about implicit biases and the inherent challenges of rising within a male-dominated consulting firm and the perceptions of people trying to balance family life," he says. "There are a ton of barriers out there that she is facing and overcoming that you—as a confident, good-looking white male—do not have to face."

David seems more like a tempered radical than a radical, as an organizational insider who does not present as a rebel and is a good performer. He is very ambitious and committed to career advancement. So I wondered about his boldness and calculation of career risk. "Nothing I say is ever about him, never about saying his points might be wrong. It's more like I am adding onto the conversation, giving him additional things to consider. I don't think going at him directly will work." David also uses humor to ease the tension. In other words, David keeps an eye on the self-threat his manager might be feeling so that the self-threat does not shut down the conversation. His goal is to keep the conversation going. David has already been thinking about the next issue he hopes to add to his manager's thought process: the impact of female partner representation on the performance and motivation of junior female employees. "I don't think he's thinking about that," says David. He knows there will be more conversation on the topic and he wants to be ready to engage.

David admits that he is not always sure of how much impact he has been having. "He is definitely listening," David says, "but he is also very stubborn. I don't think I'm going to shift his overall perspective, but I might get him to consider other factors before he reaches a conclusion." Ongoing conversations like the one David is creating with his manager may be the only meaningful conversation the manager is having on these topics. If David's manager tunes him out, it is not clear that he will be thinking about these topics at all.

If David's ongoing conversation with his manager was a video game, it would be the kind of game where you cannot win the game at any particular point, but you can always lose by getting killed off or quitting. His goal is to stay in the game.

Hooking into the Other Person's Personal Experience

Bassey Ikpi is a mental health advocate and author. As a straight, cisgender, African American woman, she often advocates for gay rights. "I talk to people in my family, in my community when they're being homophobic, transphobic, whatever. I have that conversation with them, not as somebody who's speaking for, as someone who's able to relay that information."

Bassey uses her own learning experience to fuel that of others. Until a few years ago, she used a derogatory t-word for transgender people. "I heard RuPaul use the word and I didn't know it was a slur," she confesses. It was through Twitter that she learned more about the experiences of transgender people and corrected herself. "I had to learn about the LGB community, and then I had to learn about the T community. Then I had to learn about the Q community."

For Bassey, things clicked when someone connected her work in mental health to the struggles in the transgender community. "As somebody who deals with depression, as someone who's had suicidal ideation, when you say that to me, I got it." Other people met her where she was and that opened her up to listening to them. They hooked into her personal experience.

She tries to do the same when educating others. "It's not my job to teach other people basic humanity. It's not. It is never the marginalized group's job to have to teach the privileged group anything. Never, ever, ever, ever." Still, she does engage in this work, and explains why. "If you have an opportunity to correct somebody or to show them another perspective, I think that it is important, because people just don't know. I didn't wake up knowing. Nobody is born woke."

Bassey says, "At the very root of the biases is usually the inability to see yourself in the other party. There's something foreign or alien. [They say] 'I don't know any gay people or black people.' I'm a mental health advocate and they say 'I don't know any crazy people.'" Her goal is to connect what seems alien to who the person is.

People with antigay views sometimes ask her how she would feel if her son were gay. She replies, "I wouldn't feel anything. How would you feel if your daughter married a closeted gay man?" She was making the issue personally relevant. She makes it clear that she is not questioning those who stay in the closet. She is questioning those with antigay views who make it difficult for people to come out of the closet.

Bassey finds that she is continually surprised by what people do not think about as relevant to their lives. She often worries about how the police will treat her young African American son and her six-foot-plus African American brothers. Her son's volunteer soccer coach is a white police officer, an acquaintance with whom she had a cordial relationship but would never share her fears. One day, she found herself pulled into that unwanted, unplanned conversation by a third party at the end-of-the-season picnic.

Bassey's brothers would cheer for their nephew from the sidelines, and she knew the coach liked them. She brought them up. "They are two good guys," said the coach. She asked him, "Imagine these guys getting pulled over, and because of how they look and how they are big guys, one of your buddies gets fidgety and one of my brothers gets shot and killed. How do you know they are good guys? Because you see them every Saturday and Sunday, because they joke around with your kid. You don't know anything about the guy that you pulled over. They could be the same guy."

The coach was taken aback. He said it had never occurred to him that her brothers would be the people who got pulled over. Bassey says, "It was weird to me because he had never considered that. If you rewrite the narrative and show them why there shouldn't be a fear, that can only help."

I asked Bassey about the impact of her work educating and confronting others. "Well, there is no scorecard. You don't know what happens when somebody walks away from you. The conversation, the communication, has to be where it starts," Bassey says. Hook into their experience. Then she emphasizes, "Talk to the people [like you] who will listen to you, because they're not listening to us. Talk to your people."

Leaning on the Personal Relationship

Business school student Jessie Spellman is a white person who grew up in a mostly white community. "I was three years old and we were in a pizza shop. A black man wearing a do-rag walked in. I looked at my mom and I said 'Mommy, is he gonna rob us?'" Jessie's progressive mom was shocked and reminded her of this story when she grew older. She was breathing in societal smog as a child, shaping the unconscious views she would take into adulthood.

Over time, the headwinds created by views like these gradually became more visible to her. In college, she read research by sociologist Devah Pager showing that a black man with no criminal record was less likely to get called in for a job interview than a white man with a criminal record. Jessie remembers being stunned. "What?! I thought that Martin Luther King fixed this. I didn't know this was still a problem." Motivated in part by this realization, she joined Teach for America after college and taught middle school in West Philadelphia. Most of her students and colleagues were nonwhite. Through many interactions and friendships, she felt herself grow. She started noticing opportunities to use her ordinary privilege in educating others, especially people with whom she had close personal relationships.

Jessie was chatting with two good friends—one white and one black. Her white friend had grown up in a very liberal part of the United States, "the type of person who would be at the Women's March and who white supremacists would hate," explains Jessie. So she was stunned when the white friend referred to a white celebrity using a slang derivative of the n-word, substituting *w* for *n*. Neither Jessie nor her black friend said anything in the moment.

After the white friend left, Jessie and her black friend turned to each other to confirm that they had heard the same thing. They were both shocked to hear the word come from this particular friend, "a lovely person" who marched and hashtagged. Of course, we know that believers are also highly prone to feel self-threat if confronted about a diversity issue, which made this a tricky personal situation.

Nonetheless, Jessie ran after her. She opened with "I'm saying this because I love you."

The friend appeared confused. "I want you to know that what you just said is not okay. It's not who you are. I know you didn't mean anything by it, but that is not a word you should ever use," Jessie said. "You're basically saying that if you dress in a stereotypically black way, then you are that word, but as a white person. That word 'is' the n-word."

Jessie remembers that her friend seemed "shocked, taken aback." She told Jessie she had not realized the meaning of the word. "We never talked about it again, but it didn't change our relationship at all. And I haven't heard her use that word since," Jessie reflects.

Jessie literally opened her remarks with a reminder of the love she had for her friend, affirming her. She then created room for her friend to learn by leaning on the relationship. While Jessie used some central processing persuasion tactics—the factual etymology of the word—she also relied on peripheral processing by paying lots of attention to how she delivered the message.

Jessie is not naive about the interpersonal risks she is taking when she speaks up. "I am willing to risk somebody being mad at me or telling me to shut up. If somebody wants me to shut up, then I don't want to be friends. I don't want to be affiliated with that person." She pauses. "But I still care a lot about what people think. I still want people to like me." She notes, however, that if the person knows her and likes her, that actually gives her more latitude—not less—to say something "as long as I do it in a way that is respectful."

Jessie also has people in her life who she suspects are in the stuck 20. She takes a specific approach with those individuals, including a family member whom she used to debate with about food stamps and his view that people should feel public shame if they need government support. Once she realized he was not open to a new perspective, she decided to use the holiday family gatherings to listen more and respond less. She still makes her views known, but then she stops talking. She listens to unpack where his point of view stems from. She also tries to assume good intentions. "This is hard," she confesses, "but it helps." By listening with good intentions to the stuck 20, she accomplishes something important with the middle 60, who are inevitably listening in on the holiday conversation. She exposes the bias and challenges the norms, knowing they are listening. Those relationships are also the ones she wants to be able to lean on.

Getting Better

Thanks to the stories of people who do this well and the science that says what works, I have made progress since my wedding brunch. My biggest gains are in shifting my attention to the middle 60. For example, a few years ago, my young daughter attended a summer camp where they did a CSI-type of learning simulation and the kids investigated (fake) crimes. It was a clever, experiential way to get the kids to learn about chemistry, biology, and anatomy. I was thrilled at how engaged she was. Then I saw the pictures on my daughter's phone of their "investigation." To my shock, based on the guidance of their white instructor, they had "arrested" one of very few black employees at the camp, complete with "handcuffs."

I suspected the talented, caring, and dedicated teacher was not intentionally racist. She had done a wonderful job with my daughter throughout the camp. I feared she would be offended if I said something or would minimize my concerns. For a few days, I wimped out and said nothing while dropping off and picking up my daughter multiple times.

During that time, I thought about what builders like Bassey, Jessie, and David would do. I concluded that they would say something. Since my wedding, I had practiced more with light, and it had gotten easier with practice. Using the 20/60/20 rule, I guessed that the instructor was in the middle 60 on race issues, which gave me the information I needed to put a plan together. I decided to focus on educating her, not addressing norms, and to make it a private conversation. I would begin by affirming her, during what I anticipated would be a high-self-threat conversation. "I was not sure about whether to speak with you about a concern I have, but you are so open to learning and dedicated to teaching, I realized you would probably want me to share a concern with you. Would that be okay with you?"

I laid out my issue. She told me that she had invited several colleagues to "play a part" in the simulated investigation. Her black colleague could have declined. I asked her to consider the awkward position of her colleague (who may or may not have been uncomfortable; I have never spoken with her). I confessed my own implicit biases and how they sometimes slip into my teaching. I asked her if she was familiar with the evidence that black people are oversearched, overstopped, overinvestigated, overcharged, and oversentenced for crimes (she seemed to be somewhat aware of this). I asked her to think about the implicit biases this exercise reinforced in the children. She was polite and stoic. We said good-bye and I doubted that I would ever hear from her again. To my surprise, the teacher emailed me weeks later asking for more resources that she could use and share with other teachers in her school. She had been listening.

The more I realized that my willingness to be a work-in-progress would help others be a work-in-progress, the easier it became. Opportunities to educate, particularly among the middle 60, became more obvious to me. These are the people we are most likely to overlook and the people we are most likely to influence. These are potential believers and builders. They—like us—were not born knowing and we can engage them.

The 20/60/20 rule is a quick go-to when educating and occasionally confronting others. If we are dealing with an easy-20 person, then the objective is to educate that person. He or she is open to it. If we are dealing with a middle-60 person, then the objective can be to either educate the person or educate the (quiet) observers. The key is to remember that there are two audiences. If we are dealing with a stuck-20 person, then the objective is to educate the observers (and not get distracted by the stuck-20 person). The stuck-20 person is not open to change but is likely to tangle us in a useless argument. Engage with them only to the extent that you feel the observers may still be listening and play to that audience.

We have seen how being more inclusive, steering the conversation, and educating others are ways to engage. Now we consider how showing support can be meaningful, especially to those who take the heat and to those who bring the heat.

11

Show Meaningful Support

Rabbi Eric Solomon welcomed his guests to the Beth Meyer Synagogue in Raleigh, North Carolina. As the new rabbi, his installation ceremony marked the beginning of his service in 2005. Many members of the synagogue, local community leaders, and leaders of nearby churches were arriving to participate in this long-standing tradition.

And something was different from tradition. When Rabbi Solomon first arrived, he had reached out to his counterpart in the Muslim community, Imam Mohammed Baianonie. They spent some time getting to know each other over tea and biscuits. Rabbi Solomon invited the imam to the installation ceremony and he came, bringing members of his congregation and his blessings.

Some people were surprised to see them walk in. Surprise quickly melted into hospitality. For the first time that anyone could recall, a Jewish community leader had reached out to a Muslim community leader. "My congregation received our honored guests as if they were entering the Tent of Abraham. It was one of the proudest moments of my career," Rabbi Solomon later wrote.

Over the following decade, the relationship between the rabbi and the imam grew. They talked about religion. They ate together. They brought their congregants together to do volunteer work in the community. They built a relationship between themselves and their communities.

Rabbi Solomon also built relationships with other marginalized communities, such as the LGBTQ+ community, and with migrant workers. For him, the "intersection of Judaism and social justice [was] a cornerstone" of his leadership and that began with knowing "people's stories, practices, and faith."

Rabbi Solomon's approach is backed up by research, which shows that intergroup contact—interactions with people from a different group than ours—can reduce our prejudice. The more we can do to break out of our bubbles and echo chambers, the better. That said, intergroup contact can be awkward or anxious, even when we have good intentions. We worry about appearing prejudiced, which makes us anxious, which makes us avoid the interactions, which makes us seem prejudiced. Studies show that white participants perform more poorly on cognitive tasks requiring attention and focus after an interracial interaction than after a same-race interaction. Not seeming prejudiced is mentally exhausting, especially when we are worried about not seeming prejudiced (remember the fixed mindset tax?).

This reality may make it hard to be like Rabbi Solomon and reach out to people different than us. Fortunately, research shows that this side effect can be countered. Psychologists Sophie Trawalter and Jennifer Richeson used a very simple statement to shift the motivation with which white participants approached an interracial interaction. One-third of the participants were not given any specific instructions on how to approach this interaction; this was the control condition. One-third read instructions that told them to avoid appearing prejudiced; let's call this the "don't be prejudiced" condition, which mirrors a common approach people take. One-third read instructions that told them to view the interaction as an opportunity to have an enjoyable intercultural dialogue; this was the "enjoy the opportunity" condition.

The researchers were interested in how white participants

erformed on cognitive tasks after the interracial interactions, eflecting how mentally exhausted they were. The "enjoy the op- ortunity" participants performed best on the cognitive tasks. Meanwhile, the control condition participants performed at the ame level as those in the "don't be prejudiced" condition, sug- esting that our default mode is "don't be prejudiced." So while re wear ourselves out trying not to be prejudiced, we could actu- lly be making things worse for everyone.

During his first ten years at the Beth Meyer Synagogue, Rabbi olomon made a point to reach out to many communities and emographics outside of his own. Then a grisly triple murder be- ame national news in 2015. Three immigrant Muslim graduate tudents were shot in the head in nearby Chapel Hill. Conflict ver a visitor's parking spot in their apartment complex had pre- umably escalated. Amid growing Islamophobia, the Muslim ommunity felt terrorized.

The funeral services were held on a soccer field to accommo- late more than five thousand attendees. From across the world, eople and religious organizations reached out to express their ondolences. The mosque was overwhelmed by the outpouring nd needed help coordinating with all those reaching out. Be- ause of the trusting relationship they had built with Rabbi Sol- mon, the leaders of the Muslim community chose him to play his delicate role.

Even Rabbis

Through this and other relationships, Rabbi Solomon has learned few lessons about how to offer support. First, Rabbi Solomon xplains, open your heart to what the other party needs, if any- hing. "It is very humbling to sit and say 'Let me let you lead. Let me ask questions and be curious and listen deeply. Let me listen to what you need.'" As builders, we can hear the growth mindset in Rabbi Solomon's approach. Wise as he and we are, his emphasis is not on the counsel he can offer or the wisdom he can deliver. He is listening to what others already know and experience. Showing support does not begin with having a solution. They know more than he does.

Second, he acknowledges that he sometimes experiences inner conflict while listening to people. For example, if he is speaking to a Jew from another part of the world or a Palestinian, it can be a challenge to be both "curious and openhearted" when they describe a perspective or experience that differs from his. "Sometimes, I know they are speaking sincerely from their heart about what they believe, but I wonder if the narrative is objectively true. What is a fair, legitimate way to ask questions or for details about how they are viewing the situation?" Rabbi Solomon says.

Many of us struggle with this dilemma. Someone tells us about an ambiguous incident of bias and we try to help by saying "Maybe they just meant . . ." or "So-and-so would never do anything like that . . ." or "I know exactly how that feels because . . ." Sometimes, we counter their story with one of our own, which activists call "oppression Olympics" and psychologists call "competitive victimhood." The person we intend to support recoils, withdraws, and we are now the enemy rather than the provider of support.

Our support is needed. Hundreds of studies show that bias has significant health effects. Researchers tracked black and Latinx study participants' blood pressure and also had them keep track of their moods and perceived racism. They found that when the participants perceived racism, their blood pressure did not dip at night, the way blood pressure is supposed to. When blood pressure stays elevated, our arteries harden and our life spans shrink.

Ambiguous forms of bias are particularly stressful, as they leave the target unsure of how to interpret the event or unable to convince others that it happened.

It is not that we can never ask questions or prompt an alternate framing, but to do so, we need to also consider the impact our questions have on the other person and the true intentions of our questions. If the intent of our question is to challenge their perspective, then they are unlikely to perceive us as showing support. Questions with this intention to challenge sound like "Have you considered the possibility that . . . ?" and "What would she have to gain if . . . ?" and "Do you think you might be overreacting?" These questions are not likely to show support.

However, questions that are intended to understand the other person's experience and perspective better do actually increase liking between people, as we mentioned in chapter 7 with Mel's story. Some examples are "Were you expecting her to respond that way?" or "How often do you get treated that way?" or "How did you know what to do in that situation?" The beauty of the follow-up question is that it offers the other person the sense of being listened and responded to, while offering you, as the listener, the chance to genuinely learn more. Both of these benefits address Rabbi Solomon's inner conflict between not seeing the world the same way as the person he is listening to and wanting to show support for that person.

Third, Rabbi Solomon explains, be prepared to be uncomfortable. "Sometimes, when I am proximate to someone's problems, I begin to realize how much privilege I have as a male, as someone with light skin, and so on," he confesses. "It can be very discombobulating internally. Even though I'm trying to be helpful, they are angry at me. And they have the right to be angry. But it can be socially, psychologically dangerous to feel attacked. It's very hard work."

Rabbi Solomon's description—hard work—perfectly explains how it feels to cope with self-threat. We will not always get the affirmation we crave. Craving the affirmation does not make us bad people as long as we work to see the craving for what it is and prevent it from being a burden to others. As writer and thought leader Roxane Gay writes, we "ask the marginalized to participate in the caretaking of [our] emotions . . . to do the emotional labor of helping [us] face the world as it truly is." We know, from the stories and science throughout this book, that this is a predictable craving and a predictable moment. Even rabbis have these moments.

When I Needed It Most

Remember Rachel Hurnyak from the beginning of the book? When she needed support after the Orlando nightclub shooting, she felt pressure to care for the emotions of others. I asked Rachel if she had people in her life who did the hard work of showing support without asking for affirmation. She told me about Ben Schwartzbach.

When I reached out to Ben, he was surprised. A few years prior, he had attended business school with Rachel. They were a year apart and did not know each other well. Ben knew she was president of the LGBTQ+ student organization OutClass because he had attended some of their events to learn how to be a better straight ally. Ben also heard Rachel speak to an audience of four hundred classmates, where she shared a painful experience in which a straight male classmate had forcibly kissed her against her will at a school event.

After graduation, Rachel and Ben had "sort of" met in person only once. They connected on social media and via some networking-type career conversations. Then audio surfaced of Donald Trump speaking about making unwanted sexual advances and sexually assaulting women, followed by his election as president. Ben remembered Rachel's remarks from business school and her courage in trying to open the eyes of people like him. He hoped she knew she was not alone and that she was supported, especially at a time when some Americans were treating such experiences lightly.

Ben sent Rachel an email. He began, "I know we haven't really met (I feel like I know you well from going to OutClass events though) but I wanted to check in and see how you're doing since you've been on my mind recently. Your story about being assaulted at beer blast has stuck with me since I was definitely guilty of thinking that a group of adults at a prestigious, extremely liberal university were better than that, and that because I didn't see it, it wasn't happening." He thanked her and ended the note, "Please don't feel the need to respond if you have too much going on in your life, just know that your courage that day has had an impact. I hope you don't find this email inappropriate given we don't know each other well, if you do, I apologize and please don't hesitate to let me know." Ben remembers hesitating before hitting the send button. "It was a tough email to send because I didn't know how it would be received."

Rachel felt a flood of support when she read Ben's email and wrote back an appreciative note. Ben says, "It's nice to get a response, but I don't think it's necessary. I'd like to think that even if she hadn't responded that I still would have sent messages of support [to other people] in the future."

Some time later, Ben saw an emotional Snapchat Rachel posted about her fears that a potential rollback of LGBTQ rights might mean she could not adopt children. It was difficult to see, but Ben opted for willful awareness about her pain. He wrote her, "There's nothing I can say to make it better, but you're not alone in this. Even though this isn't directly affecting me, I and others will fight for and support you." Again, Ben showed meaningful support.

Sitting with the Pain

One of the hardest parts of showing support is sitting with someone else's pain, especially when there is nothing we can do to make it better. I have long believed that hell is not a place where we ourselves suffer. Hell is where you watch people you care about suffer and can do nothing about it. When we sit with pain, we feel helpless, which makes many of us want to turn away.

I often don't know what to say in sad times, and thus sometimes say nothing. People who have experienced grief, like Facebook COO Sheryl Sandberg, say this is the wrong choice. In her book *Option B*, written with management scholar Adam Grant, she writes of the pain she felt when people said nothing or small-talked after the passing of her husband. Journalist Bruce Feiler set out to investigate what people need during times of grief, exploring the "art of condolence." The conclusion Feiler drew from his investigation was also that the say-nothing approach was not the way to go. Feiler, Sandberg, and Grant offer advice on what we should say, and their advice adapts well to the builder work of showing meaningful support.

Here are some tips on what to say when you do not know what to say. Let's say that a hate crime occurs in your town and you are wondering whether to say something to a local acquaintance who belongs to the targeted group. First, it is okay to be tongue-tied. Barring saying something callous, having the perfect words is not as important to the recipient as it feels to you in the moment. Second, it is not about you. Do not unload about how sad it makes you, how often you cry, and how much you are consumed with rage. Your intention should not be to convince her that you are hurting, but to acknowledge that she might be hurting. Third, let go of your need for affirmation. The acquaintance may express gratitude for your words or appreciation for your wokeness. Or she may be unmoved. That is okay. Move on without judgment. Be sure that your intention is not to steer the interaction into a thank-you. Fourth, do not dodge. Be real about what is happening without trying to diminish it. If she unloads on you about the bad in the world, do not try to convince her that there are good people in the world. Finally, if it's relevant in the situation, offer specific help rather than say a more vague "Let me know if there is anything I can do." Offer to speak to someone on her behalf, attend a meeting with her, or do research on a relevant topic.

Of course, situations vary, and these tips will not apply in all situations. The key, though, is recognizing that silence is often heard as a lack of support. Words are less important than intentions, and if your intention is to be supportive, silence is rarely the way to go.

What Ben Did

When I asked Rachel what made Ben's notes so helpful, she described what he said and the outrage with which he said it ("there was a lot of ALL CAPS and swearwords," she remembered). What I heard underneath her remarks went beyond the words and fonts. She trusted the words and fonts because Ben had spent time educating himself on the issues on his own time. He was growing. He saw his ordinary privilege and was willing to use it on her behalf. He did not look away when it was hard to watch. And he engaged.

Plus, when Ben approached Rachel as both a believer and a builder, he shed the four dangerous modes of good intentions. He had taken the risk of reaching out when he had no solace or solution to offer—he could not be a savior. He had not put his own experience and emotions at the center—he put empathy ahead of sympathy. He acknowledged that he and she were not living the same reality—he was not difference-blind. He did not lean on positive stereotypes to make his point—no one needed to be on a pedestal to be treated like a human.

Those who know Rachel personally may be surprised that the story about her in this book is about her being the recipient of support. It is ironic because Rachel has a long history of being an activist and ally. She is quick to show support to others, not just in words but in actions. She is the person who goes to human resources on behalf of others or petitions leadership to make policy changes that will not affect her. Since having her as a student, I have learned a great deal from her about creating both light and heat, as when she challenged the sexism in a reading I had assigned for class (she was right and I was wrong; I have dropped the reading). The question, however, is what happens to people on the front lines like Rachel—and people without her deep resilience—when people like us do not show our support.

Respect the Heat

As we talk about the value of showing support, we may have a blind spot for a group of people fighting for the same change a us. Ironically, those of us drawn to creating light may undermine those creating heat. We say they are "too angry" or "too radical" or "too disruptive." I confess that a younger version of myself other erized protesters as a different breed of person, underestimating how much we had in common and how much we needed each other. The Toys "R" Us protest I described in the preface helped me to rethink this view, as did a man named Joe McNeil.

Civil and human rights giant Joseph McNeil is one of the four black college students who led the Woolworth's lunch counter sit-ins during the civil rights movement. In 1960, over winter break, Joe had experienced his umpteenth humiliation in the Jim Crow South, a daily occurrence, and had finally said, "No more talking. It is time to do something." With three friends, he led the planning for several weeks in their freshman dorm at Agricultural and Technical College of North Carolina (now known as North Carolina A&T State University), which is now officially an HBCU (historically black college and university).

The four students wanted a national target for their protest. Woolworth's was a prominent nationwide chain with a highly respected brand, something like Panera or Friendly's today, and the lunch counter was a busy spot in Greensboro. There, as in many Southern establishments in 1960, black people were not permitted in white spaces. This was not pathway bias. This was a full-on, legalized gateway discrimination.

On February 1, Joseph McNeil, Franklin McCain, David Richmond, and Ezell Blair Jr. sat down at the Woolworth's lunch counter and politely waited for service. The Greensboro Four, as they would later become known, dressed in suits. When approached by a lunch-counter employee, they asked to be served. When they were refused, as was both custom and law, they remained seated.

They were often surrounded. A circle of white customers taunted them with racist slurs. Some poured coffee on them. Some pushed cigarette butts into their clothes. Others stayed back and watched. The lunch-counter manager and a police officer watched as the four teenagers were verbally taunted and physically provoked by adults. Still, these four young men resisted every natural reflex to strike back. "I was brought up to defend myself. It was difficult to not fight back," says Joe. They stuck to their plan. They were not served that day.

Only one person, an elderly white woman, approached them with open support, a moment that Joe remembers vividly to this day. He often speaks of her. It would be surprising if that woman had any idea how meaningful her support was.

After the lunch counter closed, Joe and the others returned to their dorm and recruited a few friends to join them the next day. While historical accounts later made it clear that Joe and Franklin co-led the Greensboro Four, they deliberately shared credit with others and downplayed their names. The protest was not about individual affirmation or recognition.

Joe also called his parents with the surprising news of what he had done. He told them he would be going back to the lunch counter every day until he was served, jailed, or killed. A studious and levelheaded son who read philosophy for fun in high school, he was an only child whose parents did not see as a radical or firebrand. No one would have voted him "most likely to be an activist" in high school. He told his parents he felt the need to do something, however "small." While his parents were surprised, they showed their support.

Each day, the sit-in grew from what the Greensboro Four started on February 1, 1960. Not everyone joined in. Joe has a vivid memory of one particular day. As he walked to the protest, ready to lay down his life, he passed a fellow student. "He was a football player, lounging under a tree with his girlfriend, while I walked to the protest," Joe says. "His lack of support made me angry."

Still, over the next several months, tens of thousands of other people would join the lunch counter sit-in movement across the country. Finally, later that year, Woolworth's bowed to the pressure and announced that they were desegregating their lunch counters nationwide.

The impact of the Greensboro Four spread across time and country. Iconic activists such as Nelson Mandela, Martin Luther King Jr., and the Tiananmen Square protesters all cited the Greensboro Four as an inspiration. The Smithsonian Institution's National Museum of American History devotes a major permanent exhibit, with living-history actors, to the lunch counter sit-ins. When Franklin McCain passed away, Reverend Jesse Jackson spoke at his funeral.

The International Civil Rights Center & Museum now stands at the site of the former Woolworth's in Greensboro, North Carolina, with statues and portraits of Joe and the other members of the Greensboro Four, which are literally the size of giants. Even pop culture reveals their impact, as many hit movies set in the 1960s, such as *Lee Daniels' The Butler* and *Hidden Figures*, include references to the sit-ins. Still, Joe says, "Seldom do you know of the impact of things that you do and how they impact others."

While the lunch counter sit-ins tend to be evangelized today for their nonviolence, they were still confrontational and disruptive. This was heat more than light. Most of the country was not in favor of what was happening. Remember the polling data from the 1960s showing how little support Reverend Dr. Martin Luther King Jr. had among white Americans? The same polls revealed little support for the lunch counter sit-ins. Only 28 percent of Americans felt they would help. The majority did not favor the sit-ins, nor did they think it would work, similar to today's controversy about Colin Kaepernick and others kneeling. It is easy for us to show our support for the Greensboro Four now, but statistically, few of us would have done so back then.

Furthermore, the historical narrative we have adopted suggests that "good protests" are single, spontaneous acts, says historian

Glenda Elizabeth Gilmore. We falsely view the Greensboro Four and Rosa Parks as disconnected from organized, heat-based efforts. This distortion of history is costly to our goals as builders. Gilmore writes, "White Americans' deep investment in the myth that the civil rights movement quickly succeeded based on spontaneous individual protests has left the impression that organizations such as Black Lives Matter are counterproductive, even sinister." Many were not on the right side of history then and are distorting history now. As a result, we are misinterpreting the present and missing the opportunity to show our support for everyone doing the work, including those bringing the heat.

"The Stuff of Being a Good Person Is Hard"

Joe showed more courage on one day in 1960 than I will show in my entire life. When I first reached out to invite him to be a guest speaker at NYU, I expected him to be some sort of superhuman superprotester. I typecast him. I was wrong. Joe not only accepted my invitation, but he also became a friend over the years. We live just a few miles apart. My husband and I look forward to our semiannual double date with Joe and his wife, Ina McNeil, who is an activist and descendant of Chief Sitting Bull. We talk about religion and politics, as well as travel plans, doctor's appointments, and our kids. Through this friendship and the multiple interviews Joe has granted me, I have learned that giants like him are not so different from the rest of us and that the rest of us have meaningful support we can offer giants like him. We do people like him a disservice by thinking otherwise.

What makes Joe a giant among giants is less about his courage and more about his growth mindset. This extraordinary man of extraordinary impact is not done learning. During Joe's first visit as a guest speaker to NYU, a student asked him to share his views on gay rights. At the time, Joe was probably in his seventies. I remember his face, as he visibly tried to think about the issue in front of hundreds of twenty- and thirtysomethings. He looked at the student and confessed, "This is an area where I am learning." Joe asked the student to share what he saw as the key issues.

I later asked Joe about that moment. "We grew up in cultures where gay persons got the heck beat out of them," he explains. "Well, we grow and learn, hopefully. I've had to grow a lot. Like many people." I noticed that in subsequent visits to NYU, Joe proactively brought up the topic of gay rights, each time sounding more fluent on the issues. Clearly, he had been listening and thinking since his initial visit. "It didn't just happen. I say to myself, 'McNeil, now grow up. You want to treat everybody right,'" Joe says. He pauses, before adding, "The stuff of being a good person is hard."

If the stuff of being a good person is hard for giants like Joe McNeil, for whom museums are built, I wonder if there is hope for the rest of us. But Joe is insistent about hope. He reminds me that finding the right entry point into this work is hard, even for him. "It's a lot to take on sometimes. You're damned if you do and damned if you don't. What's acceptable—incremental change or sweeping change? It's an individual choice."

Joe speaks from his own experience. After graduating from college in 1963, he joined the military. In a career of more than thirty years in the air force, Joe rose to the rank of major general and had more than five thousand people in his command. In some ways, the military was an obvious choice. In the early 1960s, there were significant headwinds for educated African American men seeking employment in the private labor market. The military offered Joe the opportunity to build a career with his degree in engineering physics.

In other ways, the military was a surprising choice. The Greensboro Four had been adamant about building a nonviolent activist movement. Joining the military was a step away from nonviolence and also away from direct activism. As a member of the military, Joe's participation in political protests was severely constrained. He did not attend the March on Washington several months after his graduation, where Reverend Dr. Martin Luther King Jr. delivered his "I Have a Dream" speech. We call it a march, but we sometimes forget that it was a big, disruptive, heat-based protest. "If I had protested, I had to be prepared to give up my military career," he explained.

I asked if that bothered him. "There's nothing that says I have got to protest all my life. I'm entitled to a life, to raise a family, to work, to pursue a career in the military and National Guard. If not me, then who? If I had done something precipitous early in my military career, I probably would never have been a navigator or a commander of five thousand people. I was probably one of, at the time, eighteen or twenty black navigators. There just weren't people knocking down the door. And I felt that if I've got the talents, and the time and motivation, why shouldn't I?"

We Needed Them

Joe understood the role of ordinary privilege and the V-formation of how birds rotate from front to back to front again. He could not lead all the time. Others who had ordinary privilege could have an impact in ways he could not. The rest of us could show support. The sit-in movement included many white allies. Those with ordinary privilege had a role to play so that Joe did not have to play that role every day of his life.

Through his successful career in the military and later at the

Federal Aviation Administration, and in his family and community, Joe engaged in a different way of being a builder. He was inclusive of Native Americans. He steered the conversation about the ability of black leaders to command white soldiers. He educated and occasionally confronted local officials. He showed support to his female military colleagues. Just like the rest of us, he wrestled with when and how to act. But he was a builder, day after day, putting aside affirmation for growth and opting for small actions rather than no action.

Sometimes he was a radical. Sometimes he was a tempered radical. Joe explains, "You're the person who has to live it, so you might as well figure out how to do it. A little bit from Dr. King, a little bit from somebody else, a little bit from the guy that we've never heard of before, our parents, our role models. We're learning. Again, there is no right way."

If there is no right way, then each of us can find our own way to be builders and to support builders. The only wrong way is to settle for only being believers. Joe, the giant, says, "It's important for me to stand tall." When he says that, I also hear him saying that you and I can stand tall next to him. I hear him saying that none of us are sitting in every day (not even him) and some of us will never sit in.

Still, all of us can have the growth mindset of a giant. All of us can see and use our ordinary privilege so that Joe doesn't have to sit at the lunch counter for his whole life. All of us can opt for willful awareness rather than willful ignorance. All of us can engage. We need not all be Joe, but we can all show support for people like him. We can follow their work, ideally firsthand accounts, and when possible, help fund their work. We can dispel myths about protesters being destructive thugs or lazy people without jobs. We can tweet support to people who take brave public stances confronting people in power.

The work of being a builder is exhausting. If you are not exhausted, at least some of the time, chances are you are still a believer only. Joe figured out how to make the work of being a builder sustainable, how to keep himself going. The rest of us can make that easier for people like him. Even if we do not want to be the heat, we do not need to rely on only heat to do all of the work. We can try to understand their work and support it. And we can do our share by creating light.

Sitting at my kitchen table, I asked Joe if there is anything he would do differently with the sit-in movement. "Oh, boy, I think we did it right," he says at first. Then he takes a sip of coffee and looks up. "Except," he says, "I would have been more verbal with the silent observers. I would try harder to explain to them why we needed them. You could always make a very good case for not doing anything. I would have given them the opportunity to be better human beings, too."

Acknowledgments

Writing this book was a process filled with learning. Writing is solitary work but it was an unexpected delight to realize that it is also communal work through which I formed new friendships and deepened old ones. So many people made this book better and I am honored by their efforts. Where there are mistakes, they are mine and no one else's, and let us hope I have a growth mindset when they are pointed out to me. Speaking of mistakes, I am mortified by the possibility that I am failing to thank someone I would want to acknowledge. If that person is you, I pray you forgive me and I owe you dinner!

My training and platform as an academic give me a voice that I am striving to add to those who have been speaking out and fighting for much longer than I have. Many of the ideas and suggestions in this book have been out in the world for a long time, often originating with people from marginalized groups. My goal is not to take credit for those ideas, and I have tried hard to make accurate attributions wherever possible. My goal is to support and amplify those voices with stories and science. I have also tried to connect ideas that may have not been seen as related in the past.

Some, but not all, of the interviews I conducted appear in the book. Nonetheless, each one shaped my thinking. Thank you to all who shared their stories with such candor and their time with such generosity: Shalini Agrawal, Subha Barry, Perrin Chiles, Karen Crowley, Kimberly Davis, Allie Esslinger, Kevin Ferreira van Leer, Kyle Ferreira van Leer, Brian Fitzpatrick, Felicia Fulks, Rachel Hurnyak, Bassey Ikpi, Thomas Kail, Zach Kaplan, Rick Klau, Max Krasilovsky, Joe Lentine, Dave Levin, Jeana Marinelli, Joe McNeil, Kevin Newman, Christopher Owens, Lorri

Perkins, Jodi Picoult, Frank Polley, Tony Prophet, Todd Rogers, Ben Schwartzbach, Rabbi Eric Solomon, Jessie Spellman, Brittany Turner, Gita Varadarajan, Sarah Weeks, and Mel Wymore. Interviews have been lightly edited for clarity. For those whose names were changed or whose stories were made into composites ("Colleen," "David Johnson," and "Fiona Rodriguez"), you know who you are and I thank you.

All of my own research mentioned in this book was co-authored with other outstanding scholars. I have been incredibly lucky to work with Modupe Akinola, Mahzarin Banaji, Max Bazerman, Arthur Brief, Edward Chang, Sreedhari Desai, Molly Kern, Sujin Lee, Katy Milkman, and Zhu Zhu on the projects described in this book. I hope I did our work justice in this general-audience format.

Mahzarin Banaji reshaped how I think and is a role model in every way. Max Bazerman taught me that character and decency are essential to success. The Bazerman Non-Lab and Banaji Lab have been communities of learning, love, and laughter.

I leaned heavily on friends and colleagues to read early pages and drafts. The richness and generosity of their thoughts overwhelmed me. Thank you to: Modupe Akinola, Eliza Armstrong, Leilani Brown, Lisa Carnoy, Edward Chang, Christine Cook, Priya Desai, Allie Esslinger, Joseph Garcia, Robert Greene, Christina Josling, Jeana Marinelli, Dave Nussbaum, Kristina Olson, Taylor Phillips, Charnjit Singh, Nanda Sugandhi, and Jeff Wilser. The book is much improved by your suggestions.

A few people extended themselves in ways that awed me. Thank you to Adam Grant for the advice, introductions, and confidence. Thank you to Laszlo Bock for writing the foreword and being so generous with advice and encouragement. Thank you to Adam Alter for the coffees, introductions, and friendship. Thank you to Allie Esslinger for standing up in front of four hundred classmates to propose that we work together and later suggesting interviewees, resources, and ideas. Thank you to Dave Nussbaum for his zeal in bringing psychology—and this book—to general audiences. And thank you to Jeff Wilser for the guidance, pep talks, spreadsheets, drinks, and the many laughs.

I am blessed to be part of a collegial and brilliant group of colleagues at the New York University Stern School of Business, especially within the Management and Organizations Department. Special thanks to Steve Blader, Joe Magee, Taylor Phillips, and Jamie Tobias for their ongoing encouragement. I am grateful to Anastasia Crosswhite, Peter Henry, Elizabeth Morrison, Susanna Stein, and Batia Wiesenfeld for their enthusiasm and support of my sabbatical in the 2016–2017 academic year, during which most of the book was written. And I thank the Stern public relations team of Janine Savarese, Carolyn Ritter, and their colleagues for their support and guidance.

I am blessed with extraordinary friends, many of whom asked about my progress and offered support. Some were actively involved in the day-to-day flow of this project and they made the challenges of book writing much lighter. I am particularly grateful for the friendship, check-ins, and cheerleading of Modupe Akinola, Cami Anderson, Eliza Armstrong, Max Bazerman, Lisa Carnoy, Joseph Garcia, Wanda Holland Greene, Barbara Juhel, Molly Kern, Jeana Marinelli, Katy Milkman, Lorri Perkins, and Todd Rogers. My love for the "no club" and "WELD" is bottomless.

Many acquaintances and friends shared experiences, contacts, opportunities, and/or advice with me. Many thanks to Max Bazerman, Iris Bohnet, Margo Fleming, Noah Goldstein, Conor Grennan, Corey Hajim, Emily Koh, Lisa King Nouri, Deepak Malhotra, Victory Matsui, Luz Miranda-Crespo, Don Moore, Sendhil Mullainathan, Dave Nussbaum, Adam Schefter, Eric

Schwartz, Maurice Schweitzer, Wendy Smith, Scott Sonenshein, and Seth Stephens-Davidowitz.

My coach, Rena Seltzer, changed the way I approach work and writing. While writing my book, I relied heavily on what I learned from our six years (so far) of coaching sessions as well as from her invaluable book *The Coach's Guide for Women Professors*. I am also grateful for the excellent legal support of Zick Rubin and the smart line editing of Keith Meatto. Several research assistants worked on the book at various points. Thank you to Joseph Garcia, Whitney Graham, and Julia Turrett for digging in with such intelligence and selflessness.

I am grateful to The Yard: Herald Square for the positive energy and productive coworking space. I am also grateful for the virtual assistant services of Fancyhands.com, the transcription services of speechpad.com, and the peaceful writing cave provided by the Hyatt Place hotel.

I am honored to be a client of publicist Angela Baggetta, willing to give her heart and soul to find the audience open to the ideas in this book. I now understand that writing a book is only the first half of getting a message out, and I have Angela to thank for that.

I worked with a terrific team at HarperBusiness. My editor, Stephanie Hitchcock, was the book's greatest champion from the start. Stephanie taught me so much about how to write, structure a narrative, and meet the readers where they are. I am so grateful to have learned from and worked with her. Hollis Heimbouch believed in this book early on and held my hand all the way to the finish line. Sarah Ried jumped in with a gusto that I will strive to copy. She is going places so remember her name.

One thing I have loved learning about is the publishing industry and process, and that has led me to realize how many people and hours go into every book behind the scenes. I have loved working with Brian Perrin and Rachel Elinsky directly. To everyone at HarperCollins—in marketing, publicity, production editorial, cover design, interior design, special sales, the speaker's bureau, and other departments—who worked on this book, thank you for your efforts. Books are gold.

Leila Campoli, of Stonesong, is a dream agent. Her knowledge of the industry and advocacy of her clients are unbounded. She got the book in our first conversation and then stayed by my side at every stage of the process. I am so grateful to be represented by her and to have her as a friend.

My in-laws are special people. I am grateful to Harbhajan, Naginder, and Sarbjit Singh for their constant love and support. Their character and values make the world a much better place.

I have no words to capture my love and gratitude for my parents. They have always encouraged me to write. I have never met anyone who grows and learns as much, year to year, as my mother, Sudesh Chugh. Decades before I had the epiphany at the age of thirty-three to start a psychology PhD and become a professor, she got me a subscription to *Psychology Today* and told me I should be teaching. (Why is she always right?) She has sacrificed more for me than I deserve and inspires me every day. My father, Suresh Chugh, is endlessly supportive. His "dadication" to everything I do is boundless. All he has ever asked of me is that I try my best and not worry about the outcome. This book is my attempt to follow his guidance. Everything I have ever done is a product of his love and sacrifice.

I feel really fortunate to have a sister like Mamta Chugh. I am so grateful for her encouragement, help with the kids, and thoughtful gifts. She is one of those people who give love and inspire others, and probably has little idea of how much good she is doing. It is a lot of good.

My husband, CJ, is the best thing that ever happened to me. His love shows up in ways big and small, day after day. We are a good team, largely because he is a good sport. He seems to think I can do anything and talks me up to anyone who will listen or he can corner. Except for his misconception that he is funnier than me, he is always filled with wisdom. I am so glad we changed "if" to "when."

Finally, I come to my two children. Throughout this project, my older daughter, Maya, would ask me how my writing went that day, and when I grumbled in response, she was quick to offer enthusiastic, even boisterous, encouragement. My younger daughter, Asha, came up with the clever idea for us to write side by side, doing word-count races, and she cheered me on regardless of who won the race (she usually did). Thank you to my cutie-pies for the love, hugs, and celebration dinners. I will keep trying to be the mother I mean to be.

Lastly, thank you to those who read this book. We're in this together. Let's keep trying to be the people we mean to be.

Notes

Foreword

ix   "Are We as Ethical as We Think We Are?": Dolly Chugh, "Are We as Ethical as We Think We Are?," presented at re:Work, 2016, https://www.youtube.com/watch?v=BDX8OeMZSQ8.

xiv "I am not going to stand up": Steve Wyche, "Colin Kaepernick Explains Why He Sat During National Anthem," NFL, August 28, 2016, http://www.nfl.com/news/story/0ap3000000691077/article/colin-kaepernick-explains-protest-of-national-anthem.

xv   "This is because I'm seeing things happen": This is a transcript from Kaepernick's media session, Sunday, August 28, 2016, http://ninerswire.usatoday.com/2016/08/28/transcript-colin-kaepernick-addresses-sitting-during-national-anthem/.

xv   A CBS News/YouGov poll: Kathryn Casteel, "How Do Americans Feel About the NFL Protests? It Depends on How You Ask," FiveThirtyEight, October 9, 2017, https://fivethirtyeight.com/features/how-do-americans-feel-about-the-nfl-protests-it-depends-on-how-you-ask/.

Preface

xvii unlike many negative media portrayals: Jelani Cobb, "The Matter of Black Lives," *New Yorker*: March 14, 2016, https://www.newyorker.com/magazine/2016/03/14/where-is-black-lives-matter-headed (accessed September 24, 2017); Patrisse Khan-Cullors and asha bandele, *When They Call You a Terrorist: A Black Lives Matter Memoir* (New York: St. Martin's Press, 2018).

xx   As an example, let: Michael I. Norton and Samuel R. Sommers, "Whites See Racism as a Zero-Sum Game That They Are Now Losing," *Perspectives on Psychological Science* 6, no. 3 (2011): 215–18.

xx   The average white respondent: Reuters poll, "Agree or Disagree: Minorities Are Treated Fairly in the United States," February 10, 2017–March 10, 2017, http://polling.reuters.com/#!poll/PV15_2 (accessed September 24, 2017).

xx   In another study, participants overestimated: Michael W. Kraus, Julian M. Rucker, and Jennifer A. Richeson, "Americans Misperceive Racial Economic Equality," *Proceedings of the National Academy of Sciences* 114, no. 39 (2017): 10324–31.

xx   According to the Roper Center for: Elahe Izadi, "Black Lives Matter and America's Long History of Resisting Civil Rights Protesters,"

Washington Post, April 19, 2016, https://www.washingtonpost.com /news/the-fix/wp/2016/04/19/black-lives-matters-and-americas-long -history-of-resisting-civil-rights-protesters/?utm_term=.a359a9192e27 (accessed September 25, 2017).

xxi Ali refused to go to war: Krishnadev Calamur, "Muhammad Ali and Vietnam," *Atlantic*, June 4, 2016, https://www.theatlantic.com/news /archive/2016/06/muhammad-ali-vietnam/485717/.

xxi Conservative columnists Matt Lewis and: Jonathan Chait, "It Is Not 1968," *New York*, July 8, 2016, http://nymag.com/daily/intelligencer /2016/07/is-not-1968.html.

xxii The relatively new use of the word: Amanda Hess, "Earning the 'Woke' Badge," *New York Times*, April 19, 2016, https://www.nytimes.com/2016 /04/24/magazine/earning-the-woke-badge.html?mcubz=3 (accessed September 24, 2017).

xxii According to a CBS poll: CBS News poll, "Views of Gays and Lesbians," May 20–24, 2010, http://www.cbsnews.com/htdocs/pdf/poll_gays _lesbians_060910.pdf (accessed September 24, 2017).

xxiv (Research shows the majority of): Brian A. Nosek, Mahzarin R. Banaji, and Anthony G. Greenwald, "Harvesting Implicit Group Attitudes and Beliefs from a Demonstration Web Site," *Group Dynamics: Theory, Research, and Practice* 6, no. 1 (2002): 101–15.

xxiv Similarly, I have published: Brian A. Nosek, Frederick L. Smyth, Jeffrey J. Hansen, Thierry Devos, Nicole M. Lindner, Kate A. Ranganath, Colin Tucker Smith et al., "Pervasiveness and Correlates of Implicit Attitudes and Stereotypes," *European Review of Social Psychology* 18, no. 1 (2007): 36–88.

xxvi Meyerson writes, "Tempered radicals": Debra Meyerson, *The Tempered Radicals: How People Use Difference to Inspire Change at Work* (Boston: Harvard Business School Press, 2001).

xxvi Social movement scholar Jo Freeman: Jo Freeman, *The Politics of Women's Liberation: A Case Study of an Emerging Social Movement and Its Relation to the Policy Process* (Addison-Wesley Longman Limited, 1975).

xxvi Herbert Haines extended this work: Herbert H. Haines, *Black Radicals and the Civil Rights Mainstream, 1954–1970* (Knoxville: University of Tennessee Press, 1995).

Introduction: Good-ish People

1 It was not the good kind: Jeffery A. LePine, Nathan P. Podsakoff, and Marcie A. LePine, "A Meta-Analytic Test of the Challenge Stressor–Hindrance Stressor Framework: An Explanation for Inconsistent Relationships Among Stressors and Performance," *Academy of Management Journal* 48, no. 5 (2005): 764–75.

1 The Grief Index study captures: John W. James and Russell Friedman, *Grief Index: The "Hidden" Annual Costs of Grief in America's Workplace* (Sherman Oaks, CA: Grief Recovery Institute Educational Foundation, Inc., 2003).

2   "The second community grieves": Rachel Hurnyak, "Actionable Ways to Be an Ally to Your LGBTQ and/or Muslim Colleagues After the Orlando Tragedy," LinkedIn, June 13, 2016, https://www.linkedin.com/pulse/actionable-ways-ally-your-lgbtq-andor-muslim-after-orlando-hurnyak.

3   In speech and action, we express: Caroline A. Bartel and Jane Dutton, "Ambiguous Organizational Memberships: Constructing Organizational Identities in Interactions with Others," in *Social Identity Processes in Organizational Contexts*, eds. Michael A. Hogg and Deborah J. Terry (Philadelphia: Psychology Press, 2001), 115–30.

4   Psychologist William Swann has studied how: William B. Swann Jr., "Self-Verification: Bringing Social Reality into Harmony with the Self," *Psychological Perspectives on the Self* 2, eds. Jerry Suls and Anthony Greenwald (Hillsdale, NJ: Lawrence Erlbaum, 1983), 33–66.

4   Psychologists call this a moment of: Mark Alicke and Constantine Sedikides. "Self-Enhancement and Self-Protection: What They Are and What They Do," *European Review of Social Psychology* 20 (2009): 1–48.

4   Along with organizational scholars Mary Kern: Dolly Chugh, Mary C. Kern, Zhu Zhu, and Sujin Lee, "Withstanding Moral Disengagement: Attachment Security as an Ethical Intervention," *Journal of Experimental Social Psychology* 51 (2014): 88–93.

4   Our prediction was that people: Albert Bandura, "Moral Disengagement in the Perpetration of Inhumanities," *Personality and Social Psychology Review* 3, no. 3 (1999): 193–209.

5   Threat, especially self-threat: Sally S. Dickerson, Tara L. Gruenewald, and Margaret E. Kemeny, "When the Social Self Is Threatened: Shame, Physiology, and Health," *Journal of Personality* 72, no. 6 (2004): 1191–216.

5   Threat-motivated stress can lead: Jeffery A. LePine, Nathan P. Podsakoff, and Marcie A. LePine, "A Meta-Analytic Test of the Challenge Stressor–Hindrance Stressor Framework: An Explanation for Inconsistent Relationships Among Stressors and Performance," *Academy of Management Journal* 48, no. 5 (2005): 764–75.

5   One study found that we: Brad Bushman, Scott J. Moeller, and Jennifer Crocker, "Sweets, Sex, or Self-Esteem? Comparing the Value of Self-Esteem Boosts with Other Pleasant Rewards," *Journal of Personality* 79, no. 5 (2011): 993–1012.

7   Most of us have: Karl Aquino and Americus Reed II, "The Self-Importance of Moral Identity," *Journal of Personality and Social Psychology* 83, no. 6 (2002): 1423.

7   A recent *Washington Post* story: Eli Saslow, "The White Flight of Derek Black," *Washington Post*, October 15, 2016, https://www.washingtonpost.com/national/the-white-flight-of-derek-black/2016/10/15/ed5f906a-8f3b-11e6-a6a3-d50061aa9fae_story.html (accessed September 24, 2017).

8 As a result, good people are: Dolly Chugh, Max H. Bazerman, and Mahzarin R. Banaji, "Bounded Ethicality as a Psychological Barrier to Recognizing Conflicts of Interest," in *Conflicts of Interest: Challenges and Solutions in Business, Law, Medicine, and Public Policy*, eds. Don A. Moore, Daylian M. Cain, George Loewenstein, and Max H. Bazerman (New York: Cambridge University Press, 2005), 74–95.

8 Mary Kern and I expanded on: Dolly Chugh and Mary C. Kern, "A Dynamic and Cyclical Model of Bounded Ethicality," *Research in Organizational Behavior* 36 (2016): 85–100.

8 and have developed a model: Dolly Chugh and Mary C. Kern, "Ethical Learning: Releasing the Moral Unicorn," in *Organizational Wrongdoing: Key Perspectives and New Directions*, eds. Donald Palmer, Royston Greenwood, and Kristin Smith-Crowe (Cambridge, U.K.: Cambridge University Press, 2016), 474–503.

17 Instead, I encourage you to consider: June Price Tangney and Ronda L. Dearing, *Shame and Guilt* (New York: The Guilford Press, 2003).

17 As shame researcher, author, and popular: Brené Brown, *I Thought It Was Just Me* (New York: Avery, 2007).

Chapter 1: Stumbling Upward

23 Mindset refers to our belief: Carol S. Dweck, *Mindset: The New Psychology of Success* (New York: Random House, 2006).

26 If an alien were to stumble upon: Stacy L. Smith, Marc Choueiti, Katherine Pieper, Traci Gillig, Carmen Lee, and Dylan DeLuca, "Inequality in 700 Popular Films: Examining Portrayals of Gender, Race, & LGBT Status from 2007 to 2014," USC Annenberg School for Communication and Journalism, http://annenberg.usc.edu/sites/default/files/MDSCI_Inequality_in-700_Popular.pdf (accessed September 24, 2017).

26 These statistics have not: Stacy L. Smith, "The Data Behind Hollywood's Sexism," presented at TED Talk, October 2016, https://www.ted.com/talks/stacy_smith_the_data_behind_hollywood_s_sexism (accessed September 24, 2017).

26 In film, women are even: Stacy L. Smith, Katherine Pieper, and Marc Choueiti, "Inclusion in the Director's Chair?," USC Annenberg School for Communication and Journalism, February 2017, http://annenberg.usc.edu/pages/~/media/MDSCI/Inclusion%20in%20the%20Directors%20Chair%202117%20Final.ashx (accessed September 24, 2017).

26 Media scholar Stacy Smith: Stacy Smith, "The Data Behind Hollywood's Sexism," presented at TED Talk, October 2016, https://www.ted.com/talks/stacy_smith_the_data_behind_hollywood_s_sexism/footnotes?language=en (accessed September 24, 2017).

27 Black and Hispanic job applicants: Derek R. Avery, Morela Hernandez, and Michelle R. Hebl, "Who's Watching the Race? Racial Salience in

Recruitment Advertising," *Journal of Applied Social Psychology* 34, no. 1 (2004): 146–61.

28 In one study, black undergraduates: Derek R. Avery, "Reactions to Diversity in Recruitment Advertising—Are Differences Black and White?," *Journal of Applied Psychology* 88, no. 4 (2003): 672.

28 "By the time we arrived to": Robert Ito, "Matt Damon: You Could Call Him Down to Earth," *New York Times*, December 29, 2015, https://www.nytimes.com/2016/01/03/movies/matt-damon-you-could-call-him-down-to-earth.html?mcubz=3.

30 The beliefs she had about: Amy Edmondson, "Psychological Safety and Learning Behavior in Work Teams," *Administrative Science Quarterly* 44, no. 2 (1999): 350–83.

31 They tested participants on: Jennifer A. Mangels, Brady Butterfield, Justin Lamb, Catherine Good, and Carol S. Dweck, "Why Do Beliefs About Intelligence Influence Learning Success? A Social Cognitive Neuroscience Model," *Social Cognitive and Affective Neuroscience* 1, no. 2 (2006): 75–86.

32 This defensive dismissal: Tom R. Tyler and Steven L. Blader, *Cooperation in Groups: Procedural Justice, Social Identity, and Behavioral Engagement* (Philadelphia: Psychology Press, 2000).

32 A funny example lies: Frans de Waal, "Moral Behaviors in Animals," presented at TED Talk, April 10, 2012, https://www.youtube.com/watch?v=GcJxRqTs5nk.

35 Research shows that we are more: Heidi Grant Halvorson, Christine Cox, and David Rock, "Organizational Growth Mindset," *NeuroLeadership Journal*, https://neuroleadership.com/portfolio-items/organizational-growth-mindset-2016/ (accessed December 12, 2017).

35 We are more likely to apologize: Karina Schumann and Carol S. Dweck, "Who Accepts Responsibility for Their Transgressions?," *Personality and Social Psychology Bulletin* 40, no. 12 (2014): 1598–610.

35 and we offer better, more: Karina Schumann, "An Affirmed Self and a Better Apology: The Effect of Self-Affirmation on Transgressors' Responses to Victims," *Journal of Experimental Social Psychology* 54 (2014): 89–96.

36 In this segment, McGhee: Heather McGhee, "'I'm Prejudiced,' He Said. Then We Kept Talking," *New York Times*, December 10, 2016, https://www.nytimes.com/2016/12/10/opinion/sunday/im-prejudiced-he-said-then-we-kept-talking.html?mcubz=0.

38 my coauthors—Edward Chang: Edward Chang, Katherine Milkman, Modupe A. Akinola, and Dolly Chugh, "Diversity Thresholds: How Social Norms, Visibility, and Scrutiny Relate to Group Composition," *Academy of Management Journal* 61 (in press).

39 Organizational scholar Miguel Unzueta: Miguel M. Unzueta, Eric D. Knowles, and Geoffrey C. Ho, "Diversity Is What You Want It to Be:

How Social Dominance Motives Affect Diversity Construals," *Psychological Science* 23 (2012): 303–9.

39   They will perceive a group as more: Miguel M. Unzueta and Kevin R. Binning, "Diversity Is in the Eye of the Beholder: How Concern for the In-Group Affects Perceptions of Racial Diversity," *Personality and Social Psychology Bulletin* 38, no. 1 (2012): 26–38.

39   Members of minority groups: Christopher W. Bauman, Sophie Trawalter, and Miguel M. Unzueta, "Diverse According to Whom? Racial Group Membership and Concerns About Discrimination Shape Diversity Judgments," *Personality and Social Psychology Bulletin* 40, no. 10 (2014): 1353–72.

40   For example, in 2014: More information about Section II can be found at http://sectionii.com/learn-about-sectionii-lesbian-films-and-series.

Chapter 2: One of the "Good Guys"

45   Of those, we only consciously: Manfred Zimmermann, "Neurophysiology of Sensory Systems," in *Fundamentals of Sensory Physiology*, ed. Robert F. Schmidt (Berlin: Springer Berlin Heidelberg, 1986), 68–116.

48   Among white Americans: Brian A. Nosek et al., "Pervasiveness and Correlates of Implicit Attitudes and Stereotypes," *European Review of Social Psychology* 18 (2007): 36–88; Mahzarin R. Banaji and Anthony G. Greenwald, *Blindspot: Hidden Biases of Good People* (New York: Penguin, 2013).

48   In this comprehensive paper: John T. Jost, Laurie A. Rudman, Irene V. Blair, Dana R. Carney, Nilanjana Dasgupta, Jack Glaser, and Curtis D. Hardin, "The Existence of Implicit Bias Is Beyond Reasonable Doubt: A Refutation of Ideological and Methodological Objections and Executive Summary of Ten Studies That No Manager Should Ignore," *Research in Organizational Behavior* 29 (2009): 39–69.

52   In my research with management: Sreedhari D. Desai, Dolly Chugh, and Arthur P. Brief, "The Implications of Marriage Structure for Men's Workplace Attitudes, Beliefs, and Behaviors Toward Women," *Administrative Science Quarterly* 59, no. 2 (2014): 330–65.

54   In 1998, she and organizational: Katherine Y. Williams and Charles A. O'Reilly III, "Demography and Diversity in Organizations: A Review of 40 Years of Research," *Organizational Behavior* 20 (1998): 77–140.

55   But organizations and individuals: Katherine W. Phillips, "How Diversity Makes Us Smarter," *Scientific American*, last modified October 1, 2014, https://www.scientificamerican.com/article/how-diversity-makes-us -smarter.

55   Women-run organizations have been: Marcus Noland, Tyler Moran, and Barbara Kotschwar, "Is Gender Diversity Profitable?," Peterson Institute for International Economics, February 2016, https://piie.com /publications/working-papers/gender-diversity-profitable-evidence-global -survey (accessed December 12, 2017).

55   racially diverse teams have been: Cedric Herring, "Does Diversity Pay?: Race, Gender, and the Business Case for Diversity," *American Sociological Review* 74, no. 2 (2009): 208–24.

55   The list is long: Caroline Turner, "The Business Case for Gender Diversity: Update 2017," *Huffington Post*, April 30, 2017, http://www .huffingtonpost.com/entry/the-business-case-for-gender-diversity-update -2017_us_590658cbe4b05279d4edbd4b; Katherine W. Phillips, "How Diversity Makes Us Smarter," *Scientific American*, last modified October 1, 2014, https://www.scientificamerican.com/article/how-diversity -makes-us-smarter; Scott E. Page, *The Difference: How the Power of Diversity Creates Better Groups, Firms, Schools, and Societies* (Princeton, NJ: Princeton University Press, 2008).

55   he is likely to work harder: Denise Lewin Loyd, Cynthia S. Wang, Katherine W. Phillips, and Robert B. Lount Jr., "Social Category Diversity Promotes Premeeting Elaboration: The Role of Relationship Focus," *Organization Science* 24, no. 3 (2013): 757–72.

55   he will share unique information: Katherine W. Phillips, Gregory B. Northcraft, and Margaret A. Neale, "Surface-Level Diversity and Decision-Making in Groups: When Does Deep-Level Similarity Help?," *Group Processes & Intergroup Relations* 9, no. 4 (2006): 467–82.

55   he will generate more nuanced: Anthony Lising Antonio, Mitchell J. Chang, Kenji Hakuta, David A. Kenny, Shana Levin, and Jeffrey F. Milem, "Effects of Racial Diversity on Complex Thinking in College Students," *Psychological Science* 15, no. 8 (2004): 507–10.

Chapter 3: If You Are Not Part of the Problem, You Cannot Be Part of the Solution

59   Psychologists Taylor Phillips: L. Taylor Phillips and Brian S. Lowery, "The Hard-Knock Life? Whites Claim Hardships in Response to Racial Inequity," *Journal of Experimental Social Psychology* 61 (2015): 12–18.

60   This natural psychology emerges: L. Taylor Phillips and Brian Lowery, "Herd Invisibility: The Psychology of Racial Privilege," *Current Directions in Psychological Science* 27, no. 3 (2018): 156–62.

60   Researchers find that we actually: Shai Davidai and Thomas Gilovich, "The Headwinds/Tailwinds Asymmetry: An Availability Bias in Assessments of Barriers and Blessings," *Journal of Personality and Social Psychology* 111, no. 6 (2016): 835.

61   Other researchers have found that: Brian S. Lowery, Eric D. Knowles, and Miguel M. Unzueta, "Framing Inequity Safely: Whites' Motivated Perceptions of Racial Privilege," *Personality and Social Psychology Bulletin* 33, no. 9 (2007): 1237–50.

62   The contest sparked so much: Daniel Victor, "'White Privilege' Essay Contest Stirs Up a Connecticut Town," *New York Times*, February 3, 2017,

https://www.nytimes.com/2017/02/03/nyregion/white-privilege-essay
-contest-westport-connecticut.html?_r=0 (accessed September 24, 2017).

63   In her well-known article: Peggy McIntosh, "White Privilege: Unpacking
the Invisible Knapsack," *Peace and Freedom* (July/August 1989): 10–12.

64   One stark example: Jennifer L. Eberhardt, Paul G. Davies, Valerie J.
Purdie-Vaughns, and Sheri Lynn Johnson, "Looking Deathworthy: Per-
ceived Stereotypicality of Black Defendants Predicts Capital-Sentencing
Outcomes," *Psychological Science* 17, no. 5 (2006): 383–86.

64   Antiracist educator and author: Debby Irving, *Waking Up White, and
Finding Myself in the Story of Race* (Cambridge, MA: Elephant Room
Press, 2014).

65   Psychologist Susan Fiske and: Susan T. Fiske, Amy J. C. Cuddy, Peter
Glick, and Jun Xu, "A Model of (Often Mixed) Stereotype Content: Competence and Warmth Respectively Follow from Perceived Status and Competition," *Journal of Personality and Social Psychology* 82, no. 6 (2002): 878.

70   In his excellent book: Ira Katznelson, *When Affirmative Action Was White:
An Untold History of Racial Inequality in Twentieth-Century America* (New
York: W. W. Norton & Company, 2005).

73   These views were found in: Bruce Lambert, "At 50, Levittown Contends
with Its Legacy of Bias," *New York Times*, December 28, 1997, http://
www.nytimes.com/1997/12/28/nyregion/at-50-levittown-contends
-with-its-legacy-of-bias.html (accessed December 12, 2017).

76   In research led by psychologist: Christopher J. Bryan, Carol S. Dweck,
Lee Ross, Aaron C. Kay, and Natalia O. Mislavsky, "Political Mindset:
Effects of Schema Priming on Liberal–Conservative Political Positions,"
Journal of Experimental Social Psychology 45, no. 4 (2009): 890–95.

76   He says that "we know": Tania Lombrozo, "How Small Inequities Lead
to Big Inequities," NPR, July 24, 2017, http://www.npr.org/sections
/13.7/2017/07/24/539010535/how-small-inequities-lead-to-big-inequalities.

76   Sociologist Robert Merton calls: Robert King Merton, *Social Theory and
Social Structure* (New York: Simon & Schuster, 1968); Thomas A. DiPrete
and Gregory M. Eirich, "Cumulative Advantage as a Mechanism for Inequality: A Review of Theoretical and Empirical Developments," *Annual
Review of Sociology* 32 (2006): 271–97.

77   Computer simulations illustrate how: Google, "Tool: Give Your Own
Unbiasing Workshop," https://rework.withgoogle.com/guides/unbiasing
-raise-awareness/steps/give-your-own-unbiasing-workshop; Richard F.
Martell, David M. Lane, and Cynthia Emrich, "Male–Female Differences:
A Computer Simulation," *American Psychologist* 51, no. 2 (1996): 157–58.

78   In fact, studies have found that: Alison Ledgerwood, Anesu N. Mandisodza,
John T. Jost, and Michelle J. Pohl, "Working for the System: Motivated Defense of Meritocratic Beliefs," *Social Cognition* 29, no. 3 (2011): 322–40.

78   Reminding people of the bootstrap: Brenda Major, Cheryl R. Kaiser,

Laurie T. O'Brien, and Shannon K. McCoy, "Perceived Discrimination as Worldview Threat or Worldview Confirmation: Implications for Self-Esteem," *Journal of Personality and Social Psychology* 92, no. 6 (2007): 1068.

78   In "The Asset Value of Whiteness": Amy Traud, Laura Sullivan, Tatjana Meschede, and Tom Shapiro, "The Asset Value of Whiteness: Understanding the Racial Wealth Gap," Demos, February 6, 2017, http://www.demos.org/publication/asset-value-whiteness-understanding-racial-wealth-gap (accessed September 24, 2017).

78   Another research study: Chuck Collins, Dedrick Asante-Muhammed, Emanuel Nieves, and Josh Hoxie, "Ever-Growing Gap: Without Change, African-American and Latino Families Won't Match White Wealth for Centuries," Institute for Policy Studies, August 8, 2016, https://www.ips-dc.org/report-ever-growing-gap/ (accessed September 24, 2017).

79   "This is part of a pattern in our textbooks": James W. Loewen, *Lies My Teacher Told Me: Everything Your American History Textbook Got Wrong* (New York: The New Press, 2008), 146.

81   As journalist Greg Howard wrote: Greg Howard, "The Easiest Way to Get Rid of Racism? Just Redefine It," *New York Times*, August 16, 2016, https://www.nytimes.com/2016/08/21/magazine/the-easiest-way-to-get-rid-of-racism-just-redefine-it.html?mcubz=3&_r=0 (accessed September 24, 2017).

82   The levels are intertwined: Shauna M. Cooper, Vonnie C. McLoyd, Dana Wood, and Cecily R. Hardaway, "Racial Discrimination and the Mental Health of African American Adolescents," in *Handbook of Race, Racism, and the Developing Child*, eds. Stephen M. Quintana and Clark McKown (Hoboken, NJ: John Wiley & Sons, Inc., 2007), 278–312.

82   Or they may work toward: Eric D. Knowles, Brian S. Lowery, Rosalind M. Chow, and Miguel M. Unzueta, "Deny, Distance, or Dismantle? How White Americans Manage a Privileged Identity," *Perspectives on Psychological Science* 9, no. 6 (2014): 594–609.

83   In fact, scholars Miguel Unzueta: Miguel M. Unzueta and Brian S. Lowery, "Defining Racism Safely: The Role of Self-Image Maintenance on White Americans' Conceptions of Racism," *Journal of Experimental Social Psychology* 44, no. 6 (2008): 1491–97.

83   As diversity educator Vernā Myers: Vernā Myers, "How to Overcome Our Biases? Walk Boldly Toward Them," presented at TEDxBeaconStreet, November 2014, https://www.ted.com/talks/verna_myers_how_to_overcome_our_biases_walk_boldly_toward_them/transcript (accessed September 24, 2017).

Chapter 4: Knowing It When You Don't See It

88   According to the Detroit Area Study: Eduardo Bonilla-Silva, *Racism Without Racists: Color-Blind Racism and the Persistence of Racial Inequality in America* (Lanham, MD: Rowman & Littlefield, 2017).

90   According to organizational scholars: Ashleigh Shelby Rosette and Leigh
      Plunkett Tost, "Perceiving Social Inequity: When Subordinate-Group
      Positioning on One Dimension of Social Hierarchy Enhances Privilege
      Recognition on Another," *Psychological Science* 24, no. 8 (2013): 1420–27.

95   These videos and the related: Daniel J. Simons and Christopher F. Chab-
      ris, "Gorillas in Our Midst: Sustained Inattentional Blindness for Dy-
      namic Events," *Perception* 28, no. 9 (1999): 1059–74.

95   Visual attention researcher Jeremy Wolfe: Jeremy M. Wolfe, David N.
      Brunelli, Joshua Rubinstein, and Todd S. Horowitz, "Prevalence Effects
      in Newly Trained Airport Checkpoint Screeners: Trained Observers
      Miss Rare Targets, Too," *Journal of Vision* 13, no. 3 (2013): 1–9.

95   These studies are examples of: Dolly Chugh and Max H. Bazerman,
      "Bounded Awareness: What You Fail to See Can Hurt You," *Mind & So-
      ciety* 6, no. 1 (2007): 1–18.

96   Nobel Prize winner Daniel Kahneman: Daniel Kahneman, *Thinking, Fast
      and Slow* (New York: Farrar, Straus & Giroux, 2011).

96   To see a simple version of how: Peter C. Wason, "On the Failure to Elim-
      inate Hypotheses in a Conceptual Task," *Quarterly Journal of Experimen-
      tal Psychology* 12, no. 3 (1960): 129–40.

97   Studies show that we are more: Susan T. Fiske, "Stereotyping, Prejudice,
      and Discrimination at the Seam Between the Centuries: Evolution, Cul-
      ture, Mind, and Brain," *European Journal of Social Psychology* 30, no. 3
      (2000): 299–322.

97   He says that we like to think: Anthony G. Greenwald, "The Totalitarian
      Ego: Fabrication and Revision of Personal History," *American Psychologist*
      35, no. 7 (1980): 603.

98   Psychologist Alison Ledgerwood: Alison Ledgerwood, Anesu N. Mandi-
      sodza, John T. Jost, and Michelle J. Pohl, "Working for the System: Motivated
      Defense of Meritocratic Beliefs," *Social Cognition* 29, no. 3 (2011): 322–40.

98   Behavioral scientists Michael Norton: Michael I. Norton and Dan Ariely,
      "Building a Better America—One Wealth Quintile at a Time," *Perspec-
      tives on Psychological Science* 6, no. 1 (2011): 9–12.

99   A vast research literature shows: Adam D. Galinsky, Joe C. Magee,
      Deborah H. Gruenfeld, Jennifer A. Whitson, and Katie A. Liljenquist,
      "Power Reduces the Press of the Situation: Implications for Creativity,
      Conformity, and Dissonance," *Journal of Personality and Social Psychology*
      95, no. 6 (2008): 1450.

99   Some research suggests that money: Susan T. Fiske and Hazel Rose
      Markus, eds., *Facing Social Class: How Societal Rank Influences Interaction*
      (New York: Russell Sage Foundation, 2012).

99   Sociologists Emilio Castilla and Stephen: Emilio J. Castilla and Stephen
      Benard, "The Paradox of Meritocracy in Organizations," *Administrative
      Science Quarterly* 55, no. 4 (2010): 543–676.

00 He was perplexed to see that: Emilio J. Castilla, "Gender, Race, and Meritocracy in Organizational Careers," *American Journal of Sociology* 113, no. 6 (2008): 1479–1526.

00 Psychologists Colin Wayne Leach: Colin W. Leach, Nastia Snider, and Aarti Iyer, "'Poisoning the Consciences of the Fortunate': The Experience of Relative Advantage and Support for Social Equality," in *Relative Deprivation: Specification, Development and Integration*, eds. I. Walker and H. Smith (Cambridge, U.K.: Cambridge University Press, 2002), 136–63.

01 A PRRI (Public Religion Research Institute) American Values Survey: Daniel Cox, Juhem Navarro-Rivera, and Robert P. Jones, "Race, Religion, and Political Affiliation of Americans' Core Social Networks," PRRI, https://www.prri.org/research/poll-race-religion-politics-americans -social-networks/ (accessed September 24, 2017).

02 Research by psychologist Drew Jacoby-Senghor: Drew S. Jacoby-Senghor, Stacey Sinclair, and Colin Tucker Smith, "When Bias Binds: Effect of Implicit Outgroup Bias on Ingroup Affiliation," *Journal of Personality and Social Psychology* 109, no. 3 (2015): 415.

03 Studies show that black people: Monica Anderson and Paul Hitlin, "Social Media Conversations About Race: How Social Media Users See, Share and Discuss Race and the Rise of Hashtags like #BlackLivesMatter," Pew Research Center, August 15, 2016, http://www.pewinternet.org/2016/08/15 /social-media-conversations-about-race/ (accessed September 24, 2017).

05 Race and law scholar Kimberlé Crenshaw: Kimberlé Crenshaw, "Demarginalizing the Intersection of Race and Sex: A Black Feminist Critique of Antidiscrimination Doctrine, Feminist Theory and Antiracist Politics," *University of Chicago Legal Forum* (1989): 139–67.

05 Women are often said to earn: Nikki Graf, Anna Brown, and Eileen Patten, "The Narrowing, but Persistent, Gender Gap in Pay," Pew Research Center, April 3, 2017, http://www.pewresearch.org/fact-tank /2017/04/03/gender-pay-gap-facts/ (accessed September 24, 2017).

Chapter 5: The Power of Ordinary Privilege

13 For example, David Hekman: David R. Hekman, Stefanie K. Johnson, Maw-Der Foo, and Wei Yang, "Does Diversity-Valuing Behavior Result in Diminished Performance Ratings for Non-White and Female Leaders?," *Academy of Management Journal* 60, no. 2 (2017): 771–97.

14 Psychologists Alexander Czopp: Alexander M. Czopp and Margo J. Monteith, "Confronting Prejudice (Literally): Reactions to Confrontations of Racial and Gender Bias," *Personality and Social Psychology Bulletin* 29, no. 4 (2003): 532–44.

14 They showed participants: Heather M. Rasinski and Alexander M. Czopp, "The Effect of Target Status on Witnesses' Reactions to Confrontations of Bias," *Basic and Applied Social Psychology* 32, no. 1 (2010): 8–16.

115 In this study, participants: Jill E. Gulker, Aimee Y. Mark, and Margo Monteith, "Confronting Prejudice: The Who, What, and Why of Confrontation Effectiveness," *Social Influence* 8, no. 4 (2013): 280–93.

115 Political scientist Kevin Munger: Kevin Munger, "This Researcher Programmed Bots to Fight Racism on Twitter. It Worked," *Washington Post*, November 17, 2016, https://www.washingtonpost.com/news/monkey-cage /wp/2016/11/17/this-researcher-programmed-bots-to-fight-racism-o -twitter-it-worked/?utm_term=.6df2914e2e94 (accessed September 24 2017).

118 That year, 118 people: Computed using data at https://ordcamp.com/pa -camps/camp-2010/who-came. Names were used to infer gender.

118 Men tend to have networks: Herminia Ibarra, "Homophily and Differential Returns: Sex Differences in Network Structure and Access in an Advertising Firm," *Administrative Science Quarterly* (1992): 422–47.

118 White men tend to receive more: Gail M. McGuire, "Gender, Race, and the Shadow Structure: A Study of Informal Networks and Inequality in Work Organization," *Gender & Society* 16, no. 3 (2002): 303–22.

118 People of color are labeled: "Connections That Count: The Informal Networks of Women of Color in the United States," Catalyst, 2006, http:/. www.catalyst.org/system/files/Connections_that_Count_The_Inform _Networks_of_Women_of_Color_in_the_United_States.pdf.

118 Typically, the more a group is: Ajay Mehra, Martin Kilduff, and Daniel Brass, "At the Margins: A Distinctiveness Approach to the Social Identity and Social Networks of Underrepresented Groups," *Academy of Management Journal* 41, no. 4 (1998): 441–52.

119 Sociologist Nancy DiTomaso's book: Nancy DiTomaso, *The American Non-Dilemma: Racial Inequality Without Racism* (New York: Russell Sage Foundation, 2013).

120 The White Men's Leadership Study: "The Study on White Men Leading Through Diversity & Inclusion," Greatheart Leader Labs, January 2013 http://www.whitemensleadershipstudy.com/pdf/WMLS%20Exec tive%20Summary.pdf (accessed September 24, 2017).

123 Most of us do not get involved: Dale T. Miller, Daniel A. Effron, and Sonya Zak, "From Moral Outrage to Social Protest," *The Psychology of Justice and Legitimacy* (2011): 103.

124 Organizational behavior researcher: Elad N. Sherf, Subrahmaniam Tangirala, and Katy Connealy Weber, "It Is Not My Place! Psychological Standing and Men's Voice and Participation in Gender-Parity Initiatives," *Organization Science* 28, no. 2 (2017): 193–210.

124 These research findings are: "The Study on White Men Leading Through Diversity & Inclusion," Greatheart Leader Labs, January 2013, http:/ www.whitemensleadershipstudy.com/pdf/WMLS%20Executive%20 Summary.pdf (accessed September 24, 2017).

Chapter 6: Keep Your Eyes Open, Anyway

130 Like many female fiction writers: Lynn Neary, "Jodi Picoult Turns Tough Topics into Bestsellers," NPR, March 13, 2012, http://www.npr.org/2012/03/13/148231356/jodi-picoult-turns-tough-topics-into-best sellers (accessed August 12, 2017).

134 These stages were defined: Janet E. Helms, *Black and White Racial Identity: Theory, Research, and Practice* (Westport, CT: Greenwood Press, 1990).

134 refined by psychologists Derald: Derald Wing Sue and David Sue, *Counseling the Culturally Diverse: Theory and Practice* (Hoboken, NJ: John Wiley & Sons, 2008).

135 Management researchers Kristine: Kristine R. Ehrich and Julie R. Irwin, "Willful Ignorance in the Request for Product Attribute Information," *Journal of Marketing Research* 42, no. 3 (2005): 266–77.

136 Electrical activity indicates how: Jason S. Moser, Hans S. Schroder, Carrie Heeter, Tim P. Moran, and Yu-Hao Lee, "Mind Your Errors: Evidence for a Neural Mechanism Linking Growth Mind-Set to Adaptive Post-Error Adjustments," *Psychological Science* 22, no. 12 (2011): 1484–89.

Chapter 7: Look Out for These Four "Good" Intentions

143 Since then, I have started: Kristina Olson, "When Sex and Gender Collide," *Scientific American*, September 2017, https://www.scientificamerican.com/article/when-sex-and-gender-collide/ (accessed December 12, 2017).

144 Sex is a biological category: "Sex & Gender," National Institute of Health, https://orwh.od.nih.gov/research/sex-gender/ (accessed February 12, 2018).

144 Among transgender and gender-nonconforming adults: Ann Haas, Philip Rodgers, and Jody Herman, "Suicide Attempts Among Transgender and Gender Non-Conforming Adults," American Foundation for Suicide Prevention and the Williams Institute, https://williamsinstitute.law.ucla.edu/wp-content/uploads/AFSP-Williams-Suicide-Report-Final.pdf (accessed February 12, 2018).

145 among adolescent transgender children: Lisa Simons, Sheree M. Schrager, Leslie F. Clark, Marvin Belzer, and Johanna Olson, "Parental Support and Mental Health Among Transgender Adolescents," *Journal of Adolescent Health* 53, no. 6 (2013): 791–93; Augustus Klein and Sarit A. Golub, "Family Rejection as a Predictor of Suicide Attempts and Substance Misuse Among Transgender and Gender Nonconforming Adults," *LGBT Health* 3, no. 3 (2016): 193–99.

147 Using fMRI studies, neuroscientist: Jason P. Mitchell, C. Neil Macrae, and Mahzarin R. Banaji, "Forming Impressions of People Versus Inanimate Objects: Social-Cognitive Processing in the Medial Prefrontal Cortex," *Neuroimage* 26, no. 1 (2005): 251–57; Jason P. Mitchell, Todd

F. Heatherton, and C. Neil Macrae, "Distinct Neural Systems Subserve Person and Object Knowledge," *Proceedings of the National Academy of Sciences* 99, no. 23 (2002): 15238–43; Jason P. Mitchell, C. Neil Macrae, and Mahzarin R. Banaji, "Encoding-Specific Effects of Social Cognition on the Neural Correlates of Subsequent Memory," *Journal of Neuroscience* 24, no. 21 (2004): 4912–17.

147 Even among human faces: Katrina M. Fincher, Philip E. Tetlock, and Michael W. Morris, "Interfacing with Faces: Perceptual Humanization and Dehumanization," *Current Directions in Psychological Science* 26, no. 3 (2017): 288–93.

149 We are more likely to: Edwin R. Shriver, Steven G. Young, Kurt Hugenberg, Michael J. Bernstein, and Jason R. Lanter, "Class, Race, and the Face: Social Context Modulates the Cross-Race Effect in Face Recognition," *Personality and Social Psychology Bulletin* 34, no. 2 (2008): 260–74; Caroline Michel, Bruno Rossion, Jaehyun Han, Chan-Sup Chung, and Roberto Caldara, "Holistic Processing Is Finely Tuned for Faces of One's Own Race," *Psychological Science* 17, no. 7 (2006): 608–15.

149 Not only do our minds activate: Jason P. Mitchell, "Contributions of Functional Neuroimaging to the Study of Social Cognition," *Current Directions in Psychological Science* 17, no. 2 (2008): 142–46; Felipe De Brigard, R. Nathan Spreng, Jason P. Mitchell, and Daniel L. Schacter, "Neural Activity Associated with Self, Other, and Object-Based Counterfactual Thinking," *Neuroimage* 109 (2015): 12–26.

151 Social scientists call this: James Andreoni, "Impure Altruism and Donations to Public Goods: A Theory of Warm-Glow Giving," *The Economic Journal* 100, no. 401 (1990): 464–77.

153 Empathy leads to: Nancy Eisenberg and Paul A. Miller, "The Relation of Empathy to Prosocial and Related Behaviors," *Psychological Bulletin* 101, no. 1 (1987): 91–119.

153 Research by management scholars: Adam D. Galinsky, Deborah H. Gruenfeld, and Joe C. Magee, "From Power to Action," *Journal of Personality and Social Psychology* 85, no. 3 (2003): 453–66.

154 If the person believes our: Bruce Blaine, Jennifer Crocker, and Brenda Major, "The Unintended Negative Consequences of Sympathy for the Stigmatized," *Journal of Applied Social Psychology* 25, no. 10 (1995): 889–905.

154 In addition, psychologists: Jillian K. Swencionis, Cydney H. Dupree, and Susan T. Fiske, "Warmth-Competence Tradeoffs in Impression Management Across Race and Social-Class Divides," *Journal of Social Issues* 73, no. 1 (2017): 175–91.

155 Hari fakes a grimace: *The Late Show with David Letterman*, Season 21, Episode 124, CBS, March 26, 2014, https://www.youtube.com/watch?v=T7OahatWVk0 (accessed September 24, 2017).

155 Business school professor Martin: Martin N. Davidson, *The End of Diversity as We Know It: Why Diversity Efforts Fail and How Leveraging Difference Can Succeed* (San Francisco: Berrett-Koehler Publishers, 2011).

155 Color-blindness is another flavor: Eduardo Bonilla-Silva, *Racism Without Racists: Color-Blind Racism and the Persistence of Racial Inequality in America* (Lanham, MD: Rowman & Littlefield, 2017).

155 Social psychologists Evan: Evan P. Apfelbaum, Samuel R. Sommers, and Michael I. Norton, "Seeing Race and Seeming Racist? Evaluating Strategic Colorblindness in Social Interaction," *Journal of Personality and Social Psychology* 95, no. 4 (2008): 918.

157 In their book *The Color Bind*: Erica Gabrielle Foldy and Tamara R. Buckley, *The Color Bind: Talking (and Not Talking) About Race at Work* (New York: Russell Sage Foundation, 2014).

157 In his book, *Racism Without*: Bonilla-Silva, *Racism Without Racists*.

157 This is a philosophical statement: Eric D. Knowles, Brian S. Lowery, Caitlin M. Hogan, and Rosalind M. Chow, "On the Malleability of Ideology: Motivated Construals of Color Blindness," *Journal of Personality and Social Psychology* 96, no. 4 (2009): 857–69.

158 When we meet someone new: Gillian Rhodes, Emma Jaquet, Linda Jeffery, Emma Evangelista, Jill Keane, and Andrew J. Calder, "Sex-Specific Norms Code Face Identity," *Journal of Vision* 11, no. 1 (2011): 1–11.

158 In fact, eye-tracking studies: Meghan G. Bean, Daniel G. Slaten, William S. Horton, Mary C. Murphy, Andrew R. Todd, and Jennifer A. Richeson, "Prejudice Concerns and Race-Based Attentional Bias: New Evidence from Eyetracking," *Social Psychological and Personality Science* 3, no. 6 (2012): 722–29.

158 The typecasting of women: Peter Glick and Susan T. Fiske, "The Ambivalent Sexism Inventory: Differentiating Hostile and Benevolent Sexism," *Journal of Personality and Social Psychology* 70, no. 3 (1996): 491–512.

159 When "women are wonderful": Madeline E. Heilman, "Description and Prescription: How Gender Stereotypes Prevent Women's Ascent up the Organizational Ladder," *Journal of Social Issues* 57, no. 4 (2001): 657–74.

159 Those who put women on pedestals: Peter Glick and Susan T. Fiske, "The Ambivalent Sexism Inventory: Differentiating Hostile and Benevolent Sexism," *Journal of Personality and Social Psychology* 70, no. 3 (1996): 491–512.

159 When women like Serena Williams: Laurie A. Rudman and Peter Glick, "Feminized Management and Backlash Toward Agentic Women: The Hidden Costs to Women of a Kinder, Gentler Image of Middle Managers," *Journal of Personality and Social Psychology* 77, no. 5 (1999): 1004–10; Alice Hendrickson Eagly and Linda Lorene Carli, *Through the Labyrinth: The Truth About How Women Become Leaders* (Cambridge, MA: Harvard Business School Press, 2007).

159 In one study, black participants: Alexander M. Czopp, "When Is a Compliment Not a Compliment? Evaluating Expressions of Positive Stereotypes," *Journal of Experimental Social Psychology* 44, no. 2 (2008): 413–20.

159 At the core: Sapna Cheryan and Galen V. Bodenhausen, "When Positive Stereotypes Threaten Intellectual Performance: The Psychological Hazards of 'Model Minority' Status," *Psychological Science* 11, no. 5 (2000): 399–402.

162 When that happens, psychologist: Karen Huang, Michael Yeomans, Alison Wood Brooks, Julia Minson, and Francesca Gino, "It Doesn't Hurt to Ask: Question-Asking Increases Liking," *Journal of Personality and Social Psychology* 113, no. 3 (2017): 430–52.

Chapter 8: Be Inclusive

173 The average employee spends: Steven G. Rogelberg, Desmond J. Leach, Peter B. Warr, and Jennifer L. Burnfield, "'Not Another Meeting!' Are Meeting Time Demands Related to Employee Well-Being?," *Journal of Applied Psychology* 91, no. 1 (2006): 86–96.

173 Instead, employees report a high: Joseph A. Allen, Nale Lehmann-Willenbrock, and Stephanie J. Sands, "Meetings as a Positive Boost? How and When Meeting Satisfaction Impacts Employee Empowerment," *Journal of Business Research* 69, no. 10 (2016): 4340–47.

175 Research shows, however: Anita Williams Woolley, Christopher F. Chabris, Alex Pentland, Nada Hashmi, and Thomas W. Malone, "Evidence for a Collective Intelligence Factor in the Performance of Human Groups," *Science* 330, no. 6004 (2010): 686–88.

176 Women are more likely than: Tonja Jacobi and Dylan Schweers, "Female Supreme Court Justices Are Interrupted More by Male Justices and Advocates," *Harvard Business Review*, April 11, 2017, https://hbr.org/2017/04/female-supreme-court-justices-are-interrupted-more-by-male-justices-and-advocates (accessed September 22, 2017).

176 This disparity tends to occur: Kristin J. Anderson and Campbell Leaper, "Meta-Analyses of Gender Effects on Conversational Interruption: Who, What, When, Where, and How," *Sex Roles* 39, no. 3 (1998): 225–52.

176 When men are in the: Victoria L. Brescoll, "Who Takes the Floor and Why: Gender, Power, and Volubility in Organizations," *Administrative Science Quarterly* 56, no. 4 (2011): 622–41.

176 Men are also more likely: Heather Sarsons, "Recognition for Group Work: Gender Differences in Academia," *American Economic Review* 107, no. 5 (2017): 141–45.

177 More "deliberative design": Christopher F. Karpowitz, Tali Mendelberg, and Lee Shaker, "Gender Inequality in Deliberative Participation," *American Political Science Review* 106, no. 3 (2012): 533–47.

178 Immediately after we hear someone: Ralph G. Nichols and Leonard A. Stevens, "The Busy Executive Spends 80% of His Time Listening to People—and Still Doesn't Hear Half of What Is Said," *Harvard Business Review* 35, no. 5 (1957): 85–92.

179 My dissertation research: Dolly Chugh, "Whose Advice Is It Anyway? An Exploration of Bias and Implicit Social Cognition in the Use of Advice," PhD diss., Harvard University, 2006.

180 Research on letters of recommendation: Juan M. Madera, Michelle R. Hebl, and Randi C. Martin, "Gender and Letters of Recommendation for Academia: Agentic and Communal Differences," *Journal of Applied Psychology* 94, no. 6 (2009): 1591–99.

180 and performance evaluations: Karen S. Lyness and Madeline E. Heilman, "When Fit Is Fundamental: Performance Evaluations and Promotions of Upper-Level Female and Male Managers," *Journal of Applied Psychology* 91, no. 4 (2006): 777–85.

180 Studies of both collaborators: Michael Ross and Fiore Sicoly, "Egocentric Biases in Availability and Attribution," *American Psychology Association* 37 (1979): 322–36.

181 and spouses: Nicholas Epley, Eugene M. Caruso, and Max H. Bazerman, "When Perspective Taking Increases Taking: Reactive Egoism in Social Interaction," *Journal of Personality and Social Psychology* 91, no. 5 (2006): 872–79.

Chapter 9: Steer the Conversation

183 They are already storytelling: David M. Sobel and Natasha Z. Kirkham, "Blickets and Babies: The Development of Causal Reasoning in Toddlers and Infants," *Developmental Psychology* 42, no. 6 (2006): 1103; Brian J. Scholl and Patrice D. Tremoulet, "Perceptual Causality and Animacy," *Trends in Cognitive Sciences* 4, no. 8 (2000): 299–309.

189 Psychologist Elizabeth Levy Paluck used: Elizabeth Levy Paluck, "Reducing Intergroup Prejudice and Conflict Using the Media: A Field Experiment in Rwanda," *Journal of Personality and Social Psychology* 96, no. 3 (2009): 574–87.

190 Comedian Aziz Ansari satirized this: Aziz Ansari, "Are White People Psyched All the Time?," from *Intimate Moments for a Sensual Evening*, Comedy Central Records, January 18, 2010, https://www.amazon.com /White-People-Psyched-Time-Explicit/dp/B003378BO4.

190 "And I was like, Yeah": Hadley Freeman, "Aziz Ansari: Mouth of the South," *Guardian*, February 16, 2011, https://www.theguardian.com/stage /2011/feb/16/aziz-ansari (accessed December 12, 2017).

192 Research shows that reading: David Comer Kidd and Emanuele Castano, "Reading Literary Fiction Improves Theory of Mind," *Science* 342, no. 6156 (2013): 377–80.

192 In addition, fiction has been: Melanie C. Green and Timothy C. Brock, "The Role of Transportation in the Persuasiveness of Public Narratives," *Journal of Personality and Social Psychology* 79, no. 5 (2000): 701–21.

192 because reading fiction with: Maya Tamir, "Why Do People Regulate Their Emotions? A Taxonomy of Motives in Emotion Regulation," *Personality and Social Psychology Review* 20, no. 3 (2016): 199–222.

192 Research has shown that black males: Travis Lemar Dixon and Daniel Linz, "Overrepresentation and Underrepresentation of African Americans and Latinos as Lawbreakers on Television News," *Journal of Communication* 50, no. 2 (2000): 131–54.

192 News reports are also more: Robert M. Entman, "Blacks in the News: Television, Modern Racism and Cultural Change," *Journalism Quarterly* 69, no. 2 (1992): 341–61.

192 and to share information about: Travis L. Dixon and Daniel Linz, "Television News, Prejudicial Pretrial Publicity, and the Depiction of Race," *Journal of Broadcasting & Electronic Media* 46, no. 1 (2002): 112–36.

193 For example, researchers found: Kristina Olson, "Are Kids Racist?," *Psychology Today*, April 2, 2013, https://www.psychologytoday.com/blog/developing-minds/201304/are-kids-racist (accessed September 22, 2017).

193 For example, when psychologists: Rebecca S. Bigler, Andrea E. Arthur, Julie Milligan Hughes, and Meagan M. Patterson, "The Politics of Race and Gender: Children's Perceptions of Discrimination and the US Presidency," *Analyses of Social Issues and Public Policy* 8, no. 1 (2008): 83–112.

193 Another study found: Luigi Castelli, Cristina Zogmaister, and Silvia Tomelleri, "The Transmission of Racial Attitudes Within the Family," *Developmental Psychology* 45, no. 2 (2009): 586–91.

194 Research says we are missing: Jill Suttie, "Five Ways to Reduce Racial Bias in Your Children," *Greater Good Magazine*, March 23, 2017, https://greatergood.berkeley.edu/article/item/five_ways_to_reduce_racial_bias_in_your_children (accessed September 24, 2017).

194 This particular study focused: Stacy Smith and Marc Choueiti. "Gender Disparity On-Screen and Behind the Camera in Family Films," Geena Davis Institute on Gender in Media, https://seejane.org/wp-content/uploads/key-findings-gender-disparity-family-films-2013.pdf (accessed December 12, 2017).

199 The percentage of black: Feminista Jones, "Is Twitter the Underground Railroad of Activism?," *Salon*, July 17, 2013, http://www.salon.com/2013/07/17/how_twitter_fuels_black_activism/ (accessed September 24, 2017); Maeve Duggan and Joanna Brenner, "The Demographics of Social Media Users," Pew Research Center, February 14, 2013, http://www.pewinternet.org/files/old-media//Files/Reports/2013/PIP_SocialMedia Users.pdf (accessed September 24, 2017); Roger Yu, "There's a Racial Divide on Twitter and Instagram," *USA Today*, February 15, 2013,

http://www.businessinsider.com/theres-a-racial-divide-on-twitter-and -instagram-2013-2 (accessed September 24, 2017).

200 Her research belies some: Meredith D. Clark, "To Tweet Our Own Cause: A Mixed-Methods Study of the Online Phenomenon 'Black Twitter,'" PhD diss., University of North Carolina at Chapel Hill, 2014.

202 In her ethnography of investment: Lauren A. Rivera, *Pedigree: How Elite Students Get Elite Jobs* (Princeton, NJ: Princeton University Press, 2016).

202 For example, behavioral economist: Iris Bohnet, *What Works: Gender Equality by Design* (Cambridge, MA: Harvard University Press, 2016).

203 "Nudges," first written about: Richard Thaler and Cass Sunstein, *Nudge: Improving Decisions About Health, Wealth, and Happiness* (New York: Penguin Press, 2009).

Chapter 10: Educate and Occasionally Confront Others

205 The bystander effect is: Bibb Latané and John M. Darley, *The Unresponsive Bystander: Why Doesn't He Help?* (New York: Appleton-Century-Crofts, 1970).

206 Non-target-group members: Jennifer Randall Crosby, Benoît Monin, and Daniel Richardson, "Where Do We Look During Potentially Offensive Behavior?," *Psychological Science* 19, no. 3 (2008): 226–28.

206 Even people who react: Alexander M. Czopp, Margo J. Monteith, and Aimee Y. Mark, "Standing Up for a Change: Reducing Bias Through Interpersonal Confrontation," *Journal of Personality and Social Psychology* 90, no. 5 (2006): 784; Alexander M. Czopp and Margo J. Monteith, "Confronting Prejudice (Literally): Reactions to Confrontations of Racial and Gender Bias," *Personality and Social Psychology Bulletin* 29, no. 4 (2003): 532–44.

207 When others donate to charity: Erik C. Nook, Desmond C. Ong, Sylvia A. Morelli, Jason P. Mitchell, and Jamil Zaki, "Prosocial Conformity: Prosocial Norms Generalize Across Behavior and Empathy," *Personality and Social Psychology Bulletin* 42, no. 8 (2016): 1045–62.

207 vote: Alan S. Gerber and Todd Rogers, "Descriptive Social Norms and Motivation to Vote: Everybody's Voting and So Should You," *Journal of Politics* 71, no. 1 (2009): 178–91.

207 conserve energy: Hunt Allcott and Todd Rogers, "The Short-Run and Long-Run Effects of Behavioral Interventions: Experimental Evidence from Energy Conservation," *The American Economic Review* 104, no. 10 (2014): 3003–37.

207 reuse hotel-room towels: Noah J. Goldstein, Robert B. Cialdini, and Vladas Griskevicius, "A Room with a Viewpoint: Using Social Norms to Motivate Environmental Conservation in Hotels," *Journal of Consumer Research* 35, no. 3 (2008): 472–82.

207 cheat, and binge-drink: P. Wesley Schultz, Jessica M. Nolan, Robert B. Cialdini, Noah J. Goldstein, and Vladas Griskevicius, "The Construc-

tive, Destructive, and Reconstructive Power of Social Norms," *Psychological Science* 18, no. 5 (2007): 429–34.

207 Additional research shows: Christian S. Crandall, Amy Eshleman, and Laurie O'Brien, "Social Norms and the Expression and Suppression of Prejudice: The Struggle for Internalization," *Journal of Personality and Social Psychology* 82, no. 3 (2002): 359–78.

207 If one person expresses: Fletcher A. Blanchard, Christian S. Crandall, John C. Brigham, and Leigh Ann Vaughn, "Condemning and Condoning Racism: A Social Context Approach to Interracial Settings," *Journal of Applied Psychology* 79, no. 6 (1994): 993–97.

207 When multiple people appear: Charles Tangor, Gretchen B. Sechrist, and John T. Jost, "Changing Racial Beliefs by Providing Consensus Information," *Personality and Social Psychology Bulletin* 27, no. 4 (2001): 486–96.

207 In one study in a high school: Elizabeth Levy Paluck, Hana Shepherd, and Peter M. Aronow, "Changing Climates of Conflict: A Social Network Experiment in 56 Schools," *Proceedings of the National Academy of Sciences* 113, no. 3 (2016): 566–71.

208 Psychologist Aneeta Rattan: Aneeta Rattan and Carol S. Dweck, "Who Confronts Prejudice? The Role of Implicit Theories in the Motivation to Confront Prejudice," *Psychological Science* 21, no. 7 (2010): 952–59.

209 Long ago, we worked: Susan Annunzio, *eLeadership: Proven Techniques for Creating an Environment of Speed and Flexibility in the Digital Economy* (New York: Simon & Schuster, 2001).

209 For example, psychologists Ashby: E. Ashby Plant and Patricia G. Devine, "Internal and External Motivation to Respond Without Prejudice," *Journal of Personality and Social Psychology* 75, no. 3 (1998): 811–32.

211 This is where our attention: P. Wesley Schultz, Jessica M. Nolan, Robert B. Cialdini, Noah J. Goldstein, and Vladas Griskevicius, "The Constructive, Destructive, and Reconstructive Power of Social Norms," *Psychological Science* 18, no. 5 (2007): 429–34.

212 Persuasion researchers find: Richard E. Petty and John T. Cacioppo, "The Elaboration Likelihood Model of Persuasion," *Advances in Experimental Social Psychology* 19 (1986): 123–205.

220 In college, she read research: Devah Pager, *Marked: Race, Crime, and Finding Work in an Era of Mass Incarceration* (Chicago: University of Chicago Press, 2008).

Chapter 11: Show Meaningful Support

225 "It was one of the": Eric Solomon, "One Rabbi's Response to the Chapel Hill Shootings," *Huffington Post*, May 24, 2015, http://www.huffington post.com/entry/one-rabbis-response-to-th_b_6932618.html (accessed September 24, 2017).

226 For him, the "intersection": Eric Solomon, "Leadership Humility," Clergy Leadership Incubator, May 1, 2017, http://www.cliforum.org/2017/05 /leadership-humility/ (accessed September 24, 2017).

226 Rabbi Solomon's approach is backed: Thomas F. Pettigrew and Linda R. Tropp, "Does Intergroup Contact Reduce Prejudice? Recent Meta-Analytic Findings," in *Reducing Prejudice and Discrimination: Social Psychological Perspectives*, ed. S. Oskamp (Mahwah, NJ: Erlbaum, 2000), 93–114.

226 Studies show that white participants: Jennifer A. Richeson and J. Nicole Shelton, "When Prejudice Does Not Pay: Effects of Interracial Contact on Executive Function," *Psychological Science* 14, no. 3 (2003): 287–90.

226 Psychologists Sophie Trawalter and: Sophie Trawalter and Jennifer A. Richeson, "Regulatory Focus and Executive Function After Interracial Interactions," *Journal of Experimental Social Psychology* 42, no. 3 (2006): 406–12.

228 Sometimes, we counter their story: Isaac F. Young and Daniel Sullivan, "Competitive Victimhood: A Review of the Theoretical and Empirical Literature," *Current Opinion in Psychology* 11 (2016): 30–34.

228 They found that when: Elizabeth Brondolo, Daniel J. Libby, Ellen-Ge Denton, Shola Thompson, Danielle L. Beatty, Joseph Schwartz, Monica Sweeney et al., "Racism and Ambulatory Blood Pressure in a Community Sample," *Psychosomatic Medicine* 70, no. 1 (2008): 49–56.

229 Ambiguous forms of bias: Modupe Akinola, "Measuring the Pulse of an Organization: Integrating Physiological Measures into the Organizational Scholar's Toolbox," *Research in Organizational Behavior* 30 (2010): 203–23.

230 As writer and thought leader: Roxane Gay, "Of Lions and Men: Mourning Samuel DuBose and Cecil the Lion," *New York Times*, August 1, 2016, https://www.nytimes.com/2015/08/01/opinion/of-lions-and-men -mourning-samuel-dubose-and-cecil-the-lion.html (accessed September 24, 2017).

232 Journalist Bruce Feiler set out: Bruce Feiler, "The Art of Condolence," *New York Times*, October 2, 2016, https://www.nytimes.com/2016/10/02 /style/how-to-express-sympathy.html?_r=0 (accessed September 24, 2017).

238 Gilmore writes, "White Americans' deep": Glenda Elizabeth Gilmore, "Colin Kaepernick and the Myth of the 'Good' Protest," *New York Times*, November 20, 2017, https://www.nytimes.com/2017/11/20/opinion /kaepernick-protest-kneel-nfl.html?_r=0.

Index

About the Author

DOLLY CHUGH is a Harvard-educated social psychologist and award-winning professor at the New York University Stern School of Business, where she is an expert in the unconscious biases and unethical behavior of ordinary, good people. In her real life, she is trying just as hard as everyone else to be the person she means to be.